Sri Sathya Sai Baba
And
The Golden Age

Sri Sathya Sai Baba
And
The Golden Age

The Fourth Dimension that
Will Change the World

AMALA CHAUDHURI M.D.

New Age Books

ISBN: 978-81-7822-334-6

First Indian Edition: Delhi, 2008

© Author

Photographs: Kindness of Sri C. Sreenivas,
son of the late Dr. C. Rajeshwari, Whitefield

Published by
NEW AGE BOOKS
A-44, Naraina Industrial Area, Phase-I
New Delhi 110 028
INDIA
Email: nab@vsnl.in
Website: www.newagebooksindia.com

Printed in India
at Shri Jainendra Press
A-45, Naraina Industrial Area, Phase-I,
New Delhi-110 028 (INDIA)

Dedication

To Sri Sathya Sai Baba,
the great Cosmic Avatar, this humble offering,
but for whose divine guidance, bestowal of
grace and well-being, would not have
materialized, at this advanced age of 84 years

Preface

The beginning of this book goes back about three years ago when Skye Farris, the Canadian Reiki guru of my foster son, Vinod, visited us in our home in the Blue Mountains, The Nilgiris, in the state of Tamil Nadu, South India.

When Skye handed a book to my son and told him to read it, she had, as it seemed to me, an inscrutable look on her face which arrested my attention. Needless to say, I took possession of the book at the first opportunity and quickly perused the contents, which I found to be of a somewhat startling nature. The name of the book is "Awakening to Zero Point—The Collective Initiation" by Gregg Braden.

After reading the entire book, I was much affected by its contents, emotionally, intellectually, and conceptually. However, before being able to accept without question the mind-boggling information presented, I felt the need for some sort of confirmation or second opinion which I failed to find anywhere. Even the Internet at that time did not seem to be very helpful.

It was a few years later that Vinod came across, 'by chance' in a bookstore the very last copy of a book entitled "A Letter to Earth" by Elia Wise. He mentioned to me that she had referred to Gregg Braden's book—the first reference that had come to my notice in years. Wise's book made a further profound impact on my mind as it also dealt with the same subject matter as Braden's—the dawn of a New Age—I immediately decided that a detailed comparison between Sri Sathya Sai Baba's pronouncements on the Golden Age or New Age and the material presented by these two authors was called for.

Being a multidimensional being herself and having been at first somewhat hesitant to reveal publicly her extraordinary experiences and ideas through the means of a book, Elia Wise explains herself thus: "The understanding shared in this book comes from traveling through and beyond control and fear, into realms of energetic and spiritual reality that brought me to reunion with my soul and the nature of the Universe. The insight and vantage point I share may seem extraordinary, but they are not. I am only an early arrival at this convergence of Self and Soul—an advance scout. As such I am charged with the challenge and the opportunity of conveying the view and informing you of the nature of things.... And so I write to you from my Universal identity, from the wisdom I have gained in claiming my soul and my multidimensional origins." Concluding her letter to the 'People of Earth' she writes, "I invite you to join me on a journey into the Universe ... and the heart of the matter. It is the ultimate in adventure travel."[3]

Initially, I had planned to make the comparison and to keep the material in my personal file for future reference when events warranted it. But Vinod suggested that I should publish the findings in book form. At first, I resisted the idea, but as I went deeper and deeper into the material presented by Sai Baba and those two authors, I relented and changed my approach. The publication in your hands is the result.

AMALA CHAUDHURI

260, Brooklands,
Coonoor-643101
The Nilgiris, India

Note: Numbers appearing within brackets throughout the text refer to the books listed, in the references.

Acknowledgements

First and foremost, I must confess that had it not been for my foster son, Vinod, the book would never have seen the light of day. It was only due to his insistence that I publish the material, that I relented. The books he placed in my hands from time to time, and other materials during the preparation of the manuscript, turned out to be a mine of relevant information. It is his addiction for bookstores wherever he happens to be that some of these surfaced, sometimes miraculously. I am, indeed, deeply grateful to him for all the time and energy spent in assisting me in this manner. Also for surfing the web and fishing out choice tit-bits on the recent Earth Changes which brought me up to date on this subject and for valuable assistance in preparing the Index.

I am greatly indebted to the late Lucas Ralli whose books "Sai Messages for You and Me" Volumes I, II, III, IV and V supplied most of the material on Sai Baba's pronouncements on the Golden Age. I am grateful to his widow, Mrs. Jean Ralli, for kindly granting me permission to quote freely from all the five volumes. I also thank Geesje Lunshof for permission to quote from her book "Inner Dialogue with Sai Baba" which also contained much new and useful information on Sai Baba's views on various subjects. I thank The Sri Sathya Sai Books and Publications Trust for their permission to quote from Sai Baba's discourses in April and May, 2005 issues of 'Sanathana Sarathi' and for quoting from Charles Penn's book "My Beloved". I also thank Professor Skolimowski for his kind permission to quote from his book "Dancing Shiva in the Ecological Age".

My gratitude to Nandagopal for thoughtfully gifting me a very valuable book "Ayurveda: A Life of Balance" by Maya Tiwari, now known as Swamini Mayatitanandaji and to her for kind permission to quote from her book.

Thanks to Werner Weber, a Swiss friend, for reminding me of Tesla. My gratitude again to Werner and his wife, Erika, for the patient hearing they gave me while I read excerpts from the manuscript. To Dr. Ranjan K. Panda, I owe the word 'Maha Shakti' (the Primal Energy), and I am grateful to Ranjan for the suggestions on some sections of the manuscript. I thank Tarun Mittal for his comments on some portions of the manuscript. I am greatly indebted to Naomi, my Japanese daughter-in-law, for assuming full responsibility for the final typing with some editorial assistance from Vinod. Had Skye Farris not indirectly introduced me to Braden, there would be no book, and for this my gratefulness.

Although my youngest sister, Dr. Savitri Purshottam, M.D., Ph.D., has no direct connection with the book, indirectly she is more than linked. She has been a constant support for more than half a century since my arrival in India, and has shown great caring for an elder sister whether she was at Harvard, Worcester, Mass., in California or Calgary, Canada. For her love and support, I shall always be grateful.

Sustained efforts to contact the heirs and publisher of the book "Sathya Sai Baba—The Embodiment of Love" by the late Peggy Mason and Ron Laing ended in failure. All letters written requesting permission to quote from the book were returned, some of them stating that the authors were deceased. Letters to the publishers were also returned as well as letters to the home of the authors and to "Whom it may Concern". The only option left was to quote the passages giving the name of the authors and the book and not to include it in the bibliography. Hence this acknowledgement.

And finally, my gratitude to C.J. Ramcharan for kindly giving me his consent to publish his experiences with his ailing wife and his close encounters with the hurricanes in Orangeburg, South Carolina, U.S.A.

And last but not least, my grateful appreciation for the Editor, Mr. Om Anand's understanding of the unusual message I have attempted to convey. Accepting the work instantly placed him among the ranks of the transformational population described as 'cultural creatives' who constitute only one-fifth of the planetary inhabitants. For this evolved soul my greatest esteem.

I would like to end these acknowledgements by expressing my deep gratitude to the publishers of New Age Books and to members of their staff, particularly Ms. Jyotsna and Ms. Pragya Jain, for their forbearance and understanding in dealing with an elderly author and for overlooking some of the idiosyncratic comments I made. I am deeply grateful to all of them for their kind and sustained co-operation during the publication of the book. And last but not least, my grateful appreciation for the editor's understanding of the unusual message I have attempted to convey. Accepting the work instantly placed him among the ranks of the transformational population described as 'cultural creatives' who constitute only one-fifth of the planet's inhabitants.

List of Illustrations

Sri Sathya Sai Baba

Sri Sathya Sai Baba in the *Abhaya hasta* pose. (the hand indicating 'no fear')

In a pleasant mood

Sri Sathya Sai Baba

Performing *Narayan Seva—feeding of the poor*

Distributing clothes to needy women

Distributing clothes to needy men

Contents

Sri Sathya Sai Baba

Introduction

The Wake-up Call

The devastation that was caused by a severe earthquake west of Sumatra in Indonesia measuring 9.3 on the Richter Scale and the giant tsunami that followed it was sufficient to jolt the writer out of her complacency and to goad her into starting the writing of this book. An earthquake of this magnitude has not occurred since the Alaska earthquake in 1964 with a magnitude of 9.2. According to U.S. geologists, the earthquake that unleashed deadly tidal waves on Asia was so powerful that it made the earth wobble on its axis and permanently altered the regional map (*The Hindu* December, 2004).

It was the most powerful in the world since the last forty years. Most destruction was caused by seismic waves or a tsunami hitting India, Sri Lanka, Malaysia and Thailand within twenty-four hours of the quake. This was the first time a tsunami wave had hit India, causing extensive damage across the southern coastline and killing thousands of people. Geophysicists cannot predict earthquakes because they occur with no warning or foreshore activity. The peculiarity of the tsunami that results from earthquakes or volcanic eruptions is that it has a long body and a short crust and can travel thousands of kilometres. It would be unnoticed by boats and ships. When the wave reaches the coast, it becomes a large wave and can reach up to thirty metres in height (*The New Indian Express* December, 2004).

What are the Causes

We may wonder why these natural occurrences take place from time to time in Nature, which has been sustaining and nourishing us throughout countless millennia. One explanation is obvious; there may be others, but this we have to acknowledge with a guilty conscience—that men of greed and arrogance swear that Mother Earth was created to be used, misused and abused and to be 'conquered', come what may—to satisfy their insatiable greed, self-interest and corrupt practices. Now after a few hundred years of being victimized by technological advances and the misuse of hi-tech gadgets to suck out her wealth and rich resources which are the life-breath of Nature, she, in rage, like the Goddess *Maha Shakti* (Primal Energy), has turned her wrath on her erring children, determined to teach them a lesson for all time to come. The Sumatra catastrophe is only the beginning. Others are on the waiting list; none will be spared; all are equally guilty. It is the inexorable law of Karma, the law of cause and effect, and Nature seems determined to have her pound of flesh.

About calamities occurring on the planet, Sri Sathya Sai Baba said that man's inhumanity to man (and all kingdoms) expresses itself in the form of natural catastrophes, like earthquakes.... God does not decree these calamities (such as earthquakes, floods, droughts, famine, epidemics) but man invites them by way of retribution for his own evil deeds. Again, he said that we must remember, these calamities occur not because of what God has made of man, but because of what man has made of man. And again, the world is the body of God. There is a cancer in the body, and it must be removed.

So, man is the culprit, accused by no less a person than the Cosmic Avatar Himself.

Throughout the past three hundred years, and with the advent of the industrial revolution, man's rapacious exploitation of earth's rich, abundant and seemingly inexhaustible resources, consistently ignoring the cries and warnings of Mother Nature in the form of natural calamities, has brought the situation to a point of no return. The results are there for all to see. Commenting on the destruction that has taken place in the body of the Earth, Tiwari says, "When we inflict damage to the food body, we are breaking down a system that has been stoic and almost impenetrable.... As Earth's magnetism loosens and her electrical impulses weaken, we drift away from the core of remembering... Smell is created by the Earth. When we smell the Earth's natural fragrance we remember all time."[4]

Is it necessary to enumerate the countless insults we have heaped on Mother Nature in the form of toxins, pesticides, pollutants of all kinds, chemicals, industrial wastes and dangerous solvents among others? Are not these foreign bodies sufficient to inflict damage to her food body? Tiwari explains that the natural shifting and decline of a planet does not adequately account for the abnormal seasons and other global disturbances being experienced at this time. These are propelled by humankind tampering with its own nature. Once the food body is diseased, the *prana* (vital) body suffers.[4] The pranic or vital sheath, the one next to the food sheath, is the second of the five sheaths which constitute our body. It is responsible for a variety of functions relating to the human body as well as the universe. Tiwari says "*Prana* moves the air, water, nerves and memory cells and controls expansion and contraction of the earth's surface. The ebb and flow of the oceans and the moon's orbit around the earth are propelled by *prana*."[4]

With the information described above, we begin to realize that our actions and behaviour towards the planet are intimately connected to its behaviour and activities; and most important of all, to its balance. Whatever we do appears to have a direct effect on the functioning of the planet. Shall we ever be able to estimate the wholesale damage we have inflicted on the Earth during the past two centuries, and at the present time are still engaged in doing; and that too, at an enhanced rate and intensity, plundering and destroying any and everything that hinders our industrial and so-called progress and development.

As Tiwari says, "When the food body of the planet and its inhabitants is violated and plundered, the whole balance of *prana* (the universal life force) is disrupted, both internally and externally. Outside, the inevitable harsh storms and killing winds begin bringing with them the swift karmas of...diseases within our bodies."[4] Tiwari emphasizes the importance and functions of *prana*, and as it is a subtle energy, is vulnerable to human interference. "*Prana* is the kinetic force of the universe. It causes the earth's movement around the sun.... She (Earth) is made alive, and in turn generates life for every organism that dwells on her, whether human or one-celled."[4]

Calamities due to Man's Interference with Nature

We understand from the above information that the abnormal conditions currently obtaining on our beautiful planet are due to man's deliberate interference with Nature's laws due to gross ignorance coupled with self-interest. Tiwari goes on to say "*Prana* alone controls the breath of the planetary heart.... this eternal breath moves the entire Universe.... The breath of the planet is the source of vitalization and renewal. When this layer of energy is sickened, the earth exudes fear, pain, tremors and spasms. These are indications that her stalwart food layer has been pierced."[4] It is therefore, not difficult for us to understand why Earth and her inhabitants have reached a critical point; and unless something gives way or breaks down to allow something more healthy to replace it, humanity is doomed, and as Tiwari says, can disappear within 300 years. She further states "... the system of vibrations is the first to deteriorate within the pranic body because of disharmonious noises and impulses. The vitiation of universal *prana* is directly responsible for the enormous increase of planetary insecurities."[4]

It seems that only man can restore what he has so wantonly destroyed. As the Hopi prophetically says:

When the heart of man and the mind of man become so distant that they are no longer one,
Earth heals herself through the catastrophic events of change.[2]

The remedy lies thus within man's heart and mind. After the cataclysmic changes, it is he who has to put the pieces together again, with heart and mind in unison.

Sri Sathya Sai Baba's Role

In His divine pronouncements Sri Sathya Sai Baba has been making over the past several decades, He has been drawing the attention of humanity to the changes imminent in the future and has tried to focus its attention on the immediate necessity to change its way of life. He has been addressing a world of human beings hypnotized by the illusive and delusive lure of materialism, hedonism and sensual pleasures, so much so that it is unable even to conceive of itself as being in imminent danger of destruction and change. We as a race of human beings, the most highly evolved of all living creatures, according to Sai Baba, with a core of divinity and being endowed with consciousness, capable of realizing our oneness with the Creator Himself, have become hopelessly enraptured by the enticements modern technology has brought into our lives in the guise of creature comforts, material possessions, and the whole gamut of technological gadgets that cater to our every whim. Under these circumstances, perhaps, it is natural to consider God as someone redundant to our way of life. Because of this complete absorption with worldly things, we have become blinded and deafened to the higher aspects of our nature as potentially spiritual beings. This is the burden of Sai Baba's numerous discourses for more than half a century of His life on Earth. But we are not impressed. The lure of the material world and the call of the flesh are too great to resist, and therein lies our downfall.

What Sai Baba has expressed in purely spiritual language, Braden and Wise, the two authors with whom Sai Baba's sayings have been compared, have written in a manner that the agnostic, the atheist and the rationalist may understand and hopefully accept.

Earth Electromagnetic Changes

Gregg Braden's book "Awakening to Zero Point—The Collective Initiation", was the first to alert us to the phenomenal changes taking place within and around the planet. Braden says, "Events of unprecedented change are occurring upon the earth right now and are seen as dramatic shifts in the historic behavior of social, political, economic, military, geological, meteorological and atmospheric patterns of energy."[2] These events are being brought about by two parameters that are undergoing changes simultaneously, one of magnetics and the other of frequency.[2] Firstly, the earth's magnetic field is decreasing because of slowing of the earth's rotation, and secondly, the basal resonant frequency of the earth or the 'earth's heart beat' is increasing. These two parameters indicate the Shift of the magnetic poles and "heralds the beginning of the singlemost significant event to occur in conscious human history, signalling the completion of a 200,000 year cycle of experience."[2] Quoting Braden again: "The 'Shift of the Ages' has begun; it is happening now, and may be completed within our lifetime."[2] Accompanying the Shift will be devastation, destruction of much of what we hold dear; and after the cataclysmic changes are over, a New Age will be ushered in which Sai Baba describes as the

Golden Age, the *Sathya Yuga*, the Age of Truth. The events described by Braden after the Shift would include a change in the manner in which individuals, corporations, governments and nations relate to themselves, others, their lives, their jobs, career, and family. A general sense of loss of control or lack of values for tasks completed. These patterns lose their meanings without the blueprints of the structures they were based upon, that is, the old world structures that had existed before the 'Shift', wherein values had been different and social and moral norms completely at variance with the new reality. There will be geological, meteorological and social changes such as seismic activity, new types of faults, earthquakes etc., unusual weather, winds, ocean currents, extremes of rainfall, flooding and social unrest with chaos leading to political and economic arrest in some areas.

The precursors of the above changes as Braden sees them are two digitally measurable parameters which are currently undergoing changes that will affect the Earth and its inhabitants in more ways than one. These two parameters are earth's magnetic field and the basic resonant frequency or earth's heart beat. Because of the slowing down of the earth's rotation earth's magnetism is undergoing a rapid decline; dropping from a magnetic peak 2000 years ago by 38 per cent to the present. As magnetics are a function of planetary rotation, a decline in the intensity of magnetics seems to indicate a lessening in the rate of earth's rotation. This is actually happening within the core of the earth as well as the overall rotation of the planet making the days and nights longer. The earth's magnetism is dropping to a point nearing zero at the present time. When the zero point is reached, the magnetic poles of the earth will automatically become reversed, the North pole becoming South and the South pole going North.[2] It will be obvious to anyone that such a reversal will have drastic repercussions on the functioning not only of the earth itself but of its inhabitants as well, since humanity is linked in more ways than one to Mother Earth. This process is currently underway and the Indonesian catastrophe is a warning sign that changes in and on the earth are, indeed, taking place.

Apart from the magnetic field decreasing in intensity, the other parameter known as the basal resonant frequency of the earth is rapidly rising from 8 cycles per second at present and will most likely attain 13 cycles per second when probably the magnetic field reaches zero. This resonant frequency represents the pulse or heart beat of earth and can be measured by scientists. This resonance is increasing rapidly and as it is occurring simultaneously with the decrease in earth's magnetics, can produce far-reaching changes on earth, the most important being the instant reversal of the magnetic poles, which the ancients have referred to as the 'Shift of the Ages', causing drastic changes which will affect our everyday lives. The earth's normal rotation from west to east will be reversed and earth will rotate from east to west. This will result in the sun rising in what we now know as west and setting in what we used to call the east.

According to Braden the increase in earth's resonant frequency will have far-reaching consequences on humanity as a whole. Because of the increased frequency, all life forms on earth will have to change their vibratory rate if they are to survive. This means that each and every cell of the human body will have to increase the rate of its vibration to harmonize or become resonant with the enhanced earth's resonance. This increased frequency will produce changes of a transformative nature in human beings as the increased vibratory rate of their cells will transform them into new beings with shifts of "thought, feeling and emotion."[2] As to the decrease in earth's magnetism this too will have a direct effect on our thoughts and the crystallization of such thoughts. The consequence of a thought will become instantaneous or almost so, due to the decrease of magnetic interference between thought and the product of thought.

We may wonder why such phenomenal occurrences are due to occur or as Braden states have already begun. For example, the earth's magnetism is already weakening as can be digitally measured and her heart beat or resonant frequency is increasing which can also be measured. To ignore this factual piece of information is to bury our heads in the sand like the ostrich which will in no way stop or decrease the process now in motion. Isn't the devastation following the Sumatra earthquake and the resultant tsunami a current example? Should we not consider this catastrophic event as a wake-up call or a warning signal? The scientists are reported as saying that this phenomenon comes in clusters and we may expect to experience some more such calamities in the near future. Such catastrophes have taken place several times before, Atlantis being the most recent, occurring 11,000 to 13,000 years ago when it disappeared beneath the waves of the Atlantic Ocean.

Again, we may ask why do these things happen. We have to question ourselves and make objective enquiries into our actions as human beings inhabiting the planet. Could we be responsible in some way for Mother Earth going berserk and 'out of gear' as it were, and if so, what have we done to irritate and unnerve her? We have only to turn to the prophetic sayings of the Avatar, Sri Sathya Sai Baba, to find the answer. On being asked about the future of the planet, Sai Baba had this to say: "There will be physical repercussions because of growing selfishness, minor adjustments to the planet and a certain clear out."

According to the U.S. Geological Survey, relating to the Sumatra earthquake, the energy released as the two sides of the undersea fault slipped against each other, made the Earth wobble on its axis. The Survey stated that they can detect very slight motions of the earth and they would expect that the earth wobbled in its orbit when the earthquake occurred due to the massive amount of energy exerted and the sudden shift in mass. Tsunami waves which hit India for the first time were caused by the massive earthquake in the Indian Ocean. Such waves are usually triggered by seismic disturbances, coastal earthquakes, volcanic eruptions or undersea landslides, that jolt the ocean floor (*The Hindu* December, 2004). Often tremors displace ground surface, sending an entire column of water in motion outward from an earthquake region, with disastrous results thousands of kilometres from the origin.

Prana as the Underlying Cause

Seeing that the scientists can neither predict nor prevent earthquakes, it is incumbent upon us to ask why should the earth move suddenly for no apparent reason, causing its plates to hit each other, producing a break and increase of pressure resulting in an earthquake. Going back to what Tiwari described in the previous pages of this chapter, she stated that the "vitiation of universal *prana* is directly responsible for the enormous increase of planetary insecurities."[4] Utilizing this piece of vital information, it may not be too far-fetched an idea to assume that it is probably the reduction in *pranic energy* which could cause the shifting of the plates resulting in earthquakes both undersea and on land. Since *prana* is involved in controlling the expansion and contraction of the earth's crust, it is conceivable, to this writer at least, that any abnormal movement of the crust could have its origin in the disruption of pranic energy. Once *prana* is "sickened", according to Tiwari, the earth exudes "tremors and spasms" and the vitiation of *prana* causes "planetary insecurities". This eternal breath, that is, *prana*, moves the entire universe.[4]

The presumption that *prana* is responsible for cataclysmic events on earth needs some sort of investigation. The subject is worth pursuing and only the scientists can approach it from the objective point of view; but they will have to broaden their scope of looking at things with a tubular vision, and to adopt some of the tactics of a person like Nicola Tesla, taking cues from the leaves of his notebooks. As for the spiritual scientists, they have no difficulty in explaining the reasons for Nature's periodic backlash, since they can see the direct relationship between cause and effect, in this case, man's gross abuse of Nature and her resources being the cause, and the occurrence of natural disasters, the effect. Sri Sathya Sai Baba, the Avatar of this Age, and who is our contemporary, has already drawn our attention to our role in this situation.

Another ambiguous area relates to the slowing down of earth's rotation; a lessening in the intensity of magnetics seem to indicate its slowing down, as magnetics is a function of earth's rotation. This is, in fact, precisely what is happening within the inner and outer cores of the earth, as well as the overall rotation of the planet; one indication of this being the decreasing magnetic field and another in the lengthening of the days, which are becoming longer than the clocks can account for.[2] It is doubtful if even the scientists know the cause for this slowing down of the planet's rotation. Again, one is obliged to think that the same universal energy which probably triggers earthquakes could also cause changes in the rotation of the earth. How can this be explained? This energy, *prana* is the universal life force, known to the Chinese as "chi" and to the Japanese as "ki". *Prana* is the kinetic force of the universe. It causes the earth's movement around the sun. "This heap of dirt called earth becomes a mobile dynamic entity, vibrating with complex life because of *prana*. She is made alive, and in turn generates life for every organism that dwells on her whether human or one-celled", as described by Tiwari.[4]

It is the contention of this writer, that since *prana*, being the kinetic force of the universe, causes the earth to orbit around the sun and also controls expansion and contraction of the earth's surface,[4] is thus intimately connected to anything relating to the movement of the planet, including her inner and outer cores. It is these cores that are slowing down and thus causing the rotation of the planet to follow suit. It is conceivable that *prana*, could be the cause for lessening the rate of earth's rotation, since *prana* has become "vitiated" and "sickened" due to man's ignorance and his misguided interference with the vital forces of Nature.

It seems to this writer that two important phenomena are intimately related to the action of vitiated *prana*; firstly, the occurrence of earthquakes, whereby the movement of the seismic plates takes place. One can visualize the normal situation with a full-blooded *prana*, holding the plates in place, not allowing them to budge from their rightful position and thus maintaining the integrity and coherence of the entire earth's crust. Secondly, the slowing of the planet, producing a decrease in earth's magnetic field, leading to Zero Point and the inevitable reversal of her magnetic poles, whereby the North Pole becomes South, and the South Pole becomes North, resulting in a reversal of earth's rotation, the rising of the sun in the west and its setting in the east; as well as numerous other changes on earth affecting all of her inhabitants.

The Role of Science

Since we are dealing with an invisible though potent form of energy which science apparently is not as yet acquainted with, any steps taken to identify, analyse and quantify this energy *prana* may not meet with success. The pathway to understanding this force, perhaps, lies not through the well-established experimental approach which has so far proved inadequate to elucidate matters beyond the realm of the five senses, coupled with the inherent fallibility of the empirical approach, but through the unfamiliar path of the experiential, unfamiliar as yet to the scientist. Not so, however, to those who have been able to transcend the intellect and tap higher realms of knowledge and power, namely, the spiritual scientists, known to ancient India as *Rishis*.

However, all is not lost. To the degree that scientists have been able to photograph the human aura, that area of bio-electromagnetism seen by mystics and even some ordinary humans which surrounds the human body, and to study some of its characteristics, to the same degree cannot the physicists study *prana* which is after all, another form of energy? Physicists have been able to study different kinds of energy through the means of sophisticated equipment now available to them in laboratories. Surely, something can be done to bring *prana* into their field of study, considering that *prana* is at the basis of so many of the 'planetary insecurities.'[4] No one ever thought that the human aura could be physically demonstrated, until the discovery of Kirlian photography.

Modern day physicists are no longer embarrassed to mention the word 'consciousness', a forbidden term in the world of science some decades ago; tabooed as belonging to the non-scientific realm of metaphysics. Yet consciousness is way beyond *prana*. Tiwari says that pure consciousness has no attributes, no modification, no differentiation, and is beyond the grasp of intelligence and because it is spatially limitless, all is dissolved in it, the source of sources.[4] Sri Sathya Sai Baba describes consciousness as a vibration. But we are to understand that this form of vibration is far beyond and above the arena of scientific investigation, another word for consciousness being God-beyond all forms of scientific enquiry.

To return to the subject of *prana*, Ayurveda, the ancient system of Indian medicine, whose history is 5,000 years old, has documented the characteristics of *prana* in detail. The Sanskrit word *Ayurveda* means the science of life [ayur (life) and veda (science)]. These ancient scientists discovered that *prana* controls movement; is the breath of the universe, the universal life force, the kinetic energy of the universe, and is responsible for planetary movements as well as earth's rotation and the movements of the oceans etc. With these facts as a starting point, cannot *prana* be brought into the modern scientific laboratory and made the subject of investigation? Otherwise, how will one even begin to understand the cause of periodic earth disasters scientifically, when *prana*, this subtle, mysterious life force is the basis of it all. Were *prana* to become a subject of scientific investigation and were the physicists able to throw a little light on the reason for the vitiation of this universal life force, there will follow a quickening of the awareness that something urgently needs to be done to prevent further weakening of this vital force. In this way man will be able to mend his ways and to avoid doing things that interfere with universal forces.

Nicola Tesla's Example

Nicola Tesla has shown the way and if the modern scientist, particularly the physicist, can bring himself to withstand the pulls and pressure of vested interests, he would certainly be able to establish some sort of connection between *prana* and the earth. *Prana* is also the life force of humans and is also associated with *pranayama* (the science of breath control), a subject more familiar to those interested in yoga, since *pranayama* is an integral part of yoga. With these two subjects intimately connected to *prana*, namely, Earth and Man, any scientific investigation into *prana* would be facilitated as both subjects are readily available to the research approach.

Tesla* said: "Science is but a perversion of itself, unless it has as its ultimate goal the betterment of humanity." A profound statement, indeed, and at the present juncture in the 21st century, needs to be taken seriously. It has been reported that even today, after more than half a century has elapsed since his death, Tesla's notebooks are still being examined by engineers in search of unexploited ideas. Tesla was the pioneer who ushered in the age of electrical power

---

* <http://www.lucidcafe.com/library/96jul/tesla.html>

and at the time of his death he held over 700 patents. Would our present-day scientists care to tread the footsteps of this brilliant man, to study his original approach to problems and endeavour to break new ground by thinking differently?

One

The State of Society Today

The General Situation

Humanity today inhabits a highly endangered planet—a planet wobbling on its axis since the devastating Indonesian undersea earthquake on December 26, 2004; a planet rapidly becoming slower as it rotates on its axis; a planet with decreasing magnetics as its field approaches Zero Point; a planet with an increasing resonant frequency or "pulse"; a planet revealing its instability through frequent Earth Changes; a planet unable to regain its balance due to man's senseless interference with its resources and a planet crying out aloud to its deaf inhabitants to discard their unsustainable life-style if they wish to survive.

To any human being with even a modicum of awareness, it is apparent that something is radically wrong with our present-day society. Something has misfired during the past two or three centuries to place human society in the sorry state it is in today. According to recent studies made in the U.S.A. the above statement may be accepted by only 20 to 25 per cent who are described as forming the "transformational population" or the "cultural creatives", the remaining 75 to 80 per cent, unfortunately, may be blissfully unaware of the actual conditions obtaining in human society today. "Where ignorance is bliss, it is folly to be wise", is the old saying.

The Influence of Science and Technology

During the past three hundred years humanity has been slowly but surely deteriorating, and so insidiously that only the very alert among the society will have noticed it. We have gone downhill in every aspect of human endeavour, and the irony of it all is that we think we have progressed. The dramatic upsurge of science and its loyal hand-maiden technology have brought into our lives an array of multifarious gadgets that we have come to think of as being absolutely indispensable to our 'civilized' way of life. This is not to deny the fact that these 'indispensables' have made our everyday lives on the physical plane at least, less laborious and less time-consuming, in short, they have relieved us of our enslavement to the everyday tasks of looking after ourselves, our homes and families, as also making the workplace easier in which we earn our livelihood. While not debunking the positive effects of the industrial revolution which is mainly responsible for this drastic change in our lives, at the same time we have allowed ourselves to become enslaved in another way—to the very machines that were meant to remove our previous enslavement.

Thus science and technology are the first to initiate the downhill process. Once man surrenders himself to something or anything outside of himself, he loses a certain amount of mastery over himself, commensurate with the amount of surrender made. We have come to depend on the simple calculator to do our little sums and calculations and more recently on the computer to serve our manifold desires. The inevitable consequences are obvious to all discerning persons—school children are forgetting how to do mental arithmetic, even how to write properly. The machine does it all, and, perhaps, better too. Letter writing by hand, a valuable asset of past generations, revealing not only certain characteristics of the writer by way of formation of his letters but also threw light on some aspects of his deeper thoughts, a situation that cannot and does not exist under the conditions of the electronic mail (e-mail) as it is today, where warnings have to be occasionally issued about safe-guarding the secrecy of letters sent by this means. Again the machine does it all, most efficiently indeed, and again something subtle is lost in the process.

There is nothing wrong with the computer *per se*. Because of the computer, science and technology have made a quantum leap to higher levels of achievement; because of the computer information technology has scaled heights of excellence as would have been inconceivable a few decades ago; because of the computer, information technology has been catapulted to such an eminence in world affairs that any country lacking the facilities of this technology will find itself relegated to the backwaters of global economics, politics and intellectual activities.

Wherein lies the fault ! the dependence of man on this modern efficient machine. The way things are turning out it appears that the lap-top has become so much a part of modern man's outfit that one would be inclined to think of it as an extension of his cerebral cortex. Herein lies the fault and hence the danger. It is not what the computer is doing to man but what man is allowing the computer to do to him. Why blame the machine? Skolimowski quotes the columnist Sydney I. Harris as saying: "The real danger is not that computers will begin to think like men, but men will begin to think like computers."[8]

Use the computer by all means. It is a wonderful machine. But man should not allow it to use him, to enslave him, nor should he become over dependent on it. There is nothing wrong with the computer. What is wrong is the way man has allowed the machine to replace so much of what he should do and ought to do in making use of his brain—the biological computer God has gifted him with. Truly, the things the computer can do are mind-boggling, but that does not mean that man should feel so inadequate as to relinquish many of his important mental activities to the computer, a machine which after all man himself has created. This is analogous to the Creator handing over his Creation to man whom he himself created.

The very fact that man has created the computer with all its manifold wonders, bears ample testimony to the infinite resources of man's mind and intellect. And in the final analysis as Sri Sathya Sai Baba has said, "The difference between a human being and a computer is that the former is conscious of the fact that he is spirit; that he is animated by spirit and a computer is not.... A computer will never be conscious of the Self.... Lifeless matter can have the task of being useful to man...."[6]

And more recently, with robots on the upswing, even our everyday chores will be automatically done for us—simply by pressing a button. Today the word is 'automation', the answer to all our human needs. Then what shall we engage our muscles and minds in? The suggestion has been made that we humans will have more time to devote ourselves to and to develop the talents we may possess, as well as to engage ourselves in the study of the higher and more spiritual aspects of human nature. The question poses itself. Have we as 21st century citizens become such integrated beings with coherent ways of thinking as to be able to make this right-about turn away from our hypnotic attraction for creature comforts and the things of the material world and to strive to probe the finer aesthetic and more intellectual reaches of the human mind? As yet, no signs of this mass awakening are in sight. As mentioned at the beginning of this chapter, only 20 per cent are ready, not enough probably to turn the tide of the teeming masses into more positive intellectual and spiritual pursuits.

Science and technology have separated us from ourselves and from those who constitute our environment. The word used to describe this is 'alienation'. We have lost the ability to go within where lies the core of divinity, patiently and silently awaiting our undistracted attention, as well as the ability to integrate our thoughts, speech, actions and attitudes with those around us. We have become strangers, not only to ourselves but to our fellow human beings. And this feeling of separation we extend to all other living creatures and to Nature herself. Hence the wanton, unmindful and heedless destruction of the Earth and all her resources.

What can be considered the classic example of alienation was brought to the writer's attention by Ted Falconar, the writer, who described Hikikomori, 2,000,000 Japanese youths who remain confined to one room in their houses, severing all relationship with society. The writer's Japanese daughter-in-law, Naomi, filled in the details. "Hikikomori is a form of neurosis and the Japanese word means 'silent retreat' or 'social withdrawal'. The group consists of eighty per cent males, the majority being the eldest sons of their parents from middle class families, not including single parents. Most of them were bullied at schools and turned truants. These youths are very sensitive and react to the comments, criticisms and actions of others resulting in great emotional trauma. This causes them to decide to stay at home in their rooms to avoid coming into contact with their taunting peers and thereby hoping to heal themselves.

"The average age at which this abnormal behaviour pattern begins to appear is around fifteen years of age, the average period of isolation is seven and a half years, the longest being 23 years. They do leave their homes at times, but to visit only the vending machines, convenience stores and supermarkets, where they don't have to communicate with others. The situation becomes worse when the adults around them—their teachers and parents, force them to go out or to go back to school. Apparently, the elders lack understanding of their suffering and the traumatic experiences they undergo. These youths need others to believe in them, to love them and to be patient with them while they make attempts to heal themselves."

They occupy their time viewing TV, the internet, playing TV and computer games and reading pornographic literature. Some of them end up by staring at the wall for hours, apparently having given up the fight. Wherever violence occurs, it is usually directed towards the parents, never to outsiders, due to lack of courage on their part. Families having Hikikomori children are singled out for criticism by others, hence the tendency of the parents, particularly the mothers, to conceal the presence of such children in the home as there is a stigma attached to the condition.

This sort of behaviour is alienation *par excellence*, the causative factor being probably the result of living in a highly technological society as exists in Japan today, where cut-throat competition for jobs and professional openings characterizes the work ethics. It is just possible that those young people find it almost impossible to cope with the highly competitive world around them, and seeing perhaps, a bleak future ahead make the final decision to withdraw themselves from what they apparently conceive as a diabolical and macabre society. If this be the cause, the quicker the soulless, mechanistic, and 'every man for himself' society comes to an end, the better for all of humanity. Man is a gregarious being, and any attempt to completely isolate himself from his fellow human beings will have disastrous mental and psychological effects on his psyche, leading in most cases to the disease of the present technological age—alienation. The socializing factor in man undoubtedly stems from the fact that we all have a common origin and any attempt to voluntarily interfere with this collective affinity, although we may not be aware of it can lead to emotional, mental, psychological and spiritual disaster.

Again quoting Skolimowski, "...alienation has become the hallmark of advancing technology" and put in another way "the more sophisticated technology becomes, the more it disengages us from life". He concludes that the whole problem of decline in Western life–style "lay in the very foundation of modern Western philosophy, in the visions and systems of Bacon, Galileo and Descartes."[8] Referring to Descartes, the writer is reminded of his famous saying "I *think*, therefore I *am*", in complete contradistinction to the equally famous Vedic statement, "I *am*, therefore I *think*." (Writer's italics). It is due to this inherently erroneous Cartesian idea that Western civilization made the first great false step and intellectualized every aspect of human endeavour. To all serious–minded persons it is obvious that man's intellect is fallible, this fallibility being apparent in so many of his activities– medicine, engineering, or science and technology; indeed in every pursuit involving the sole use of man's mind. To quote a single example in the field of medical sciences, whatever was considered indisputably factual information half a century ago, is today almost completely outdated and even fallacious. In order to arrive at truth, which is unchanging and eternal, one has to transcend the intellect; hence "I am, therefore, I think or exist."

To give an example of the disastrous effect Cartesian ideas have had on modern Western thought and culture, the writer quotes a true incident that took place in one of the Western medical schools in the first half of the 20th century. The first– year medical student had just completed his course in anatomy after having dissected the entire cadaver allotted to his group for the first-year course. The demonstrator, who was making his rounds, came to the student's table and having seen that he had completed the dissection of the human body, turned to the student who happened to be an Indian and asked him, "You, Hindu? Did you find the spirit?" Before the student could answer in the negative, the demonstrator said, "Do

you know why?" to which the student wanted to say that it
was not possible to find spirit in dead matter preserved in
oil for months or years. Before he had time to begin his
statement, the demonstrator, pointing his finger at the student
said, emphasizing each word, "Because it does not exist."
Stating this, he turned on his heels and walked away, leaving
the poor student open-mouthed and dumb-founded. This
is a glaring example of the havoc Descartes brought into
Western civilization by his erroneous theory, "I *think*, therefore
I *am*". To place the fallible intellect at the top of the body /
mind / spirit complex of the human being, is to put things
upside down, thereby causing confusion. Since the intellect
is subject to change, is prone to error, and is not eternal, it is
not Truth, it is not Absolute, as the "I *am*" principle is, which
is immortal, which is spirit, which is unchanging, which is
the Absolute from which everything is derived—body, mind,
intellect. The Vedic dictum, "I am, therefore I think or exist",
assigns second place to the intellect, where it rightfully
belongs. Even Einstein was quoted as saying that no one
should think that his discoveries were the result of the
intellectual process alone. After listening to a violin recital by
the young Yehudi Mennuhin, Einstein went backstage,
embraced the prodigy, and said to him, "Now I know that
God exists."

Today, such scientists as Fritjof Capra, David Bohm, Rupert
Sheldrake among others have gone so far as to state that Indian
philosophy and religion may have to show the West the way
back towards truth and reality. This is in conformity with what
Sri Sathya Sai Baba has stated on more than one occasion,
that India was for many centuries the guide and guru of
mankind, because the people of India are God-loving and
not much God-fearing. He also maintained that India is a land
where faith in God is imbibed at the mother's breast by every
child since millennia. Baba also warns us that Indians have
forgotten the culture of their own country, Bharat—India—

which is one of the noblest and holiest countries in the world and instead are imbibing Western Culture which is alien to this country.

Some Aspects of Religious Practices

Apart from the decline in science and technology there is a decline in the practice of religion among some groups. In Western countries particularly, this is more so. The people have become disillusioned with religion, the intelligentsia turning away from orthodox teachings, and thus the churches are becoming empty with thousands shutting their doors forever. There is a feeling of disenchantment, of having been misled, or brain-washed into thinking by vested interests in religious affairs, that though 'born in sin' Christians can attain salvation by regular attendance at church and listening to sermons, many of which hardly penetrate the deeper recesses of the mind. To some, there is a feeling of disgust, of having been duped into something that has failed to fulfil the promises made. This attitude has resulted in thousands of people turning towards other faiths to find the fulfilment their own religious beliefs have failed to offer.

The role of Christian missionaries in this sordid affair is known to all in the developing countries where their activities have generated much criticism and even hostility among the people. By enticements, inducements, and at times wholesale bribery, they offer goods, food, money and other incentives to the poorest of the poor, a considerable proportion of the population in all developing countries who provide a soft and porous target for their proselytizing activities, and who can ill afford to resist the temptation to accept the offerings. These missionaries pay little heed to the disastrous effects of conversion on the family as a whole. When only a few members of the family embrace the alien religion, a dichotomy eventually seeps into the social life of the community, disrupting joint families, even nuclear families and bringing unrest and chaos into the lives of people, who though impoverished previously, now become truly pauperized by loss of their ancient traditions, religious beliefs and cohesiveness as an ancient well-established social unit. This is the crime being perpetrated by the missionaries, who despite laws of the land to control their questionable activities, continue nevertheless to ply their illegal trade, the irony of it all being that the new converts have embraced the new religion not from the standpoint of conviction but because of largesse. It is a known fact that wherever the poor is offered material goods, he is more than willing to change his faith, even to be reconverted to his former religion.

Skolimowski expands the theme thus, "Economic bribery is part of the process of conversion. It is a violation of human rights to make other people inferior because of the religious, ideological and economic reasons. The gospel of gentle Jesus is that of love toward the other. This is not what happens in the Khasi Hills (in India). On Sundays, Christian cars go to the Khasi villages to beam Christian messages through megaphones. This is an intrusion, violation of privacy, of their peace of mind, of their culture, of their tradition. One wonders how would Christian villages and communities feel if vans of other religions (Muslim, Hindu or Khasi for that matter) would arrive in their midst and started to beam messages trying to convert them. Wouldn't they feel outraged? They would— and rightly so. Don't do unto the other.... I think that UNESCO should declare that religious proselytizing should not be allowed among tribal people. We must cherish their heritage and learn from them rather to try to convert them to our rather destructive ways. The Khasi forests are natural sanctuaries in which the human soul breathes freely along with Nature. We need more such sanctuaries, not less. We need to make their religion more universal rather than wipe it out through our short-sighted religious convictions."[8]

Christian missionaries have done the greatest disservice to Jesus and Christianity, bringing disrepute to a religion more than two thousand years old, by their indiscreet approach and in some instances by covertly carrying out their activities despite public objection. Skolimowski describes the head of a local middle school and a writer who succinctly sums up the role of the Christian missionaries, when he said, "There is an onslaught of Christian churches on the traditional Khasi people, and the traditional Khasi people are terrified by it." He questioned the statistics according to which a big majority of the Khasis are Christians.... He also said, "When I go through Khasi villages, I do not see this Christian majority". Then he turned to me directly and said, "Why do you Western people tell us to forget our past and start everything anew? We cannot do that." I told him, "Listen to your heart, and obey your Gods. Your destiny must be shaped by your conscience." He was visibly delighted and asked me, "Are you sure, Sir, you come from the West?."[8]

Politics and Politicians

As for politicians and politics, what is there that has not been justly said about them? But has this even so much as made a dent in their attitudes and behaviour? It seems that if there is one creature on the face of this earth immune to the severest form of criticism regardless of how derogatory it may be, it is the politician, no country excluded. One is inclined to think that something in the genetic makeup of these people has either gone awry or probably, is missing from their chromosomal constitution. The greatest calumny, slander, blackmail, grossest insult, criticism of the worst kind are shrugged off as water off a duck's back.

During the past few millennia several systems of government have been tried out and experimented with such as, monarchy, totalitarianism, Nazism, fascism, socialism, communism, etc. All of these have failed to provide the ideal form of government people desire. With the introduction of the democratic form of government, many felt that this was the answer to all political ills. Democracy has been lauded for centuries as being the ideal form of government—the role of, for and by the people. The British Parliamentary System of democracy provided the model, particularly for the countries once comprising the British Empire. The British Parliament was a respected body of politicians, both in the House of Commons and the House of Lords. The newly independent countries of the erstwhile British Empire moved with alacrity to adopt the form of government of the Mother Country.

The writer recalls very vividly the atmosphere pervading the first general election in India in 1952. The excitement, the mood of gaiety and the intense interest generated by the election had the ambience of an Indian festival, as the people of Tamil Nadu, a state in South India, rushed out of their homes and farms to cast their vote. There was democracy, running on thousands of bare feet through uncut fields, performing high jumps over hurdles and barricades to get to the polling booths on time. What an achievement it was to place the little piece of paper into the little slot in the box and thus to become an integral part of the election process in India. Excitement, joviality and an atmosphere of festivity prevailed. From the illiterate labourer and the most sophisticated to the high profile professional and academician—all were reduced to the same level as they patiently awaited their turn in the queue to cast their vote. Spirits ran high and minds and hearts were collectively focussed on the future of a newly born India, free from the fetters of colonialism after two hundred years. It was, indeed, a heartening sight to see such enthusiasm for the democratic process.

Alas! What a sad state of affairs it is today, after fifty-eight years of independence. Whereas during earlier elections the percentage of people turning out to cast their votes could be anywhere near 80 to 85 per cent, today a political party is considered fortunate to attract even 30 to 50 per cent. This scenario does not augur well for the future of democracy in India and is certainly disheartening when one realizes that the 'great' Indian middle-class, numbering hundreds of millions of voters choose to deliberately remain indoors during voting hours, or preferably to leave their homes for the coolness of the hill resorts, the beaches and other holiday sites—simply to escape the onus of voting. What a sad commentary on the fate of Indian democracy. Not that we accuse the mass of educated, highly qualified and even highly motivated professionals of dodging their duty to the Motherland. Not at all. The state of Indian politics has fallen to such a low level that one recoils from going into the messy details of its functioning. Whom do we see occupying some of the highest positions of authority in the cabinet and councils of the land? Half-educated persons with civil and criminal cases against them, enjoying high positions in the Prime Minister's cabinet, holding important portfolios with such nonchalance and aplomb, that more capable individuals would baulk at handling; ministers with charges against them of corruption, fraud, chicanery, forgery, assault, misappropriation of funds, even the smudge of murder— the list is endless, being lauded and abetted by both the electronic and print media, so much so that one wonders if criminality has become one of the criteria for success and fame and for becoming a politician. Do these conditions obtain only in India? Far from it. All countries today are tainted to a lesser or greater degree with the same polluted political brush, and no one dares to point a finger at the other, except for some developed nations, who out of sheer arrogance turn the Nelsonian eye on the atrocities of their own government while pointing the finger at another country, forgetting that as the finger points to the other, the remaining fingers point towards themselves.

Under the circumstances described above, it is difficult for anyone to cast aspersions on our middle class citizens for what may be described as shirking their duty. There is almost complete alienation between the politician and the honest, idealistic and nationalistic citizen in this country. The separation is almost complete, each content to go his own way. In the final analysis, the country suffers. Moral standards have fallen; corruption at all levels, from the highest in the land to the poorest of the poor is rampant, no wonder the country holds a high position in the list of corrupt countries in the region. An achievement indeed since we achieved independence in the year 1947.

The manner in which the media projects these dishonourable political characters may lead the younger generation to conclude that the sure way to success and fame lies along the pathway of notoriety. The media loses no opportunity to highlight the activities of politicians, however insignificant the occasion may be; glaring faults are at times cleverly side-stepped and what should be considered a politician's duty towards the country is blown out of proportion as an act of goodwill or foresight on his part. Small wonder that the more informed and intelligent sections of society have become disenchanted with the media and some have gone so far as to ignore it altogether. But this amounts to only a minuscule proportion of the enlightened citizenry. The rot seems to lie in the mentality of the people who rule the country. It seems that the land and its people are secondary to their personal interests and this in a country where one of the greatest avatars was born and ruled for decades, according to the strict laws of *Dharma* (righteousness). To Rama, the country was of prime importance and nothing to him was too dear or too precious to be sacrificed for it, even going to the extreme extent of banishing his own beloved wife, Sita, to the forest, when he thought it was in the country's interest to do so. Her absence caused him great grief and suffering and he was heart-broken over what he saw was his bounden duty, but he did it. This is the glorious tradition of India. But does any one care about these noble principles which have been enacted for millennia in this sacred land? Today it is "everyone for himself and the devil take the hindmost." The dishonourable politicians should be ostracized by society; and the masses should refrain from voting for them. They have polluted all aspects of life and because full power lies in their hands, they ride roughshod over every rule or law with impunity, sometimes defying even the constitution that governs the land.

It is this attitude that has further widened the gap between the intelligentsia and the politician. There certainly are politicians who do not fall into the category described above, but they can be counted on the fingers of one hand. Many good, God-fearing people have opted out of politics because of their inability to cope with the average run of politicians and their questionable life-styles. Present-day politics has fallen to such a level as to merit the description of a 'cesspool', a term recently applied to the process that governs us. The well-known columnist, T.S. George, in a recent article describing legislators as India's shame, quotes Nanaji Desmukh of the RSS as saying, "...the so-called representatives of the people are shamelessly increasing their perks and perquisites" and he calculated that the expenditure on a single member of Parliament is about 150 times the per capita income of an Indian per annum. Desmukh continues, "Let us not forget that monarchy became an object of hatred when misrule and the misuse of authority by the kings became unbearable with the rulers spending the bulk of state revenue for their own pleasures and enjoyments." George concludes his column thus, "Hereditary monarchy was easy to get rid of. What do we do with elected monarchy?" (*The New Sunday Express* April, 2005). To this question the brief reply by the Buddha suffices, "This too shall pass."

It is this grim situation that exists today which makes many serious-minded, deeply-thinking citizens in several countries of the world evince great concern about the decline in morals and human values in their societies. The human values of truth (*sathya*), righteousness (*dharma*), love (*prema*), peace (*shanti*), and nonviolence (*ahimsa*)—the values that are the hall-mark of Sri Sathya Sai Baba's mission—are endangered by the rapidly declining moral and ethical standards, as well as the social mores of today's society, both young and old. Sai Baba places great stress on human values and says that the values of truth, righteousness, peace and love which were put into practice in olden days had made India the great spiritual leader of the entire world. He maintains that truth and righteousness have been instilled in the minds of children by their mothers from the time of their birth and that it is these two values that sustain a human from birth itself. In correcting the translation of *dharma* into what He terms inadequate English, He explains that it actually means 'that which sustains', in other words, it sustains human life and in following these two human values of *sathya* (truth) and *dharma* (righteousness), human life becomes sanctified.[5a]

Those concerned individuals in today's society who have been described as the 'transformational population' or 'cultural creatives' and who care for the future of their country, look on helplessly at the deteriorating situation and can only wring their hands in anguish, since their number is too small to turn the tide of events. Many are wondering as to how long this state of affairs will continue. Many wish for something drastic to happen with the hope that change will ensue for the betterment of all. As recently as January 2005, a warning has been sent out regarding recent Earth Changes by the Mayan elders at Guatemala, which has been verified and brought forth by various Mayan elders. It is the 18,000-year-old calendar of the Mayans which has alerted us to the 'Shift of the Ages' and the deadline of 2012. What these ancient people saw so many ages ago seems to be coming into manifestation at the present time, and it is entirely up to us to accept or reject their predictions.

This message is taken from the Mayan elder's "World Earth Changes Prayer Day" and can be found on the internet*, "Through the ancient techniques of divination and tools of prophecy, the Mayan elders are calling forth to humanity at this time to pay closer attention to the messages being sent forth by the mother earth and to immediately take the actions they have been calling for to unite in an effort to bring balance again upon our planet. The recent destruction that manifested in Indonesia is predicted to now occur rapidly upon five continents of earth. This message is not meant to induce fear; to the contrary, it is a call for bravery and for action. The elders are concerned about what has been presented in their recent divinations and they call to all humanity to warn their leaders and to work very hard at a spiritual level to prevent the impending destruction. This message...is for all humanity. The hurricane in the U.S. and the earthquake and tsunami in Indonesia have been warnings and we must now pay attention to the floods in Europe, Los Angeles earthquakes and other efforts of the mother earth to awaken, will manifest quickly." It would be relevant here to draw attention to the recent statement of Sri Sathya Sai Baba: "Today we find many nations, religions and castes in the world. No. No. Within a short period of time, the whole world will have one race, one caste and one religion."[5b] How many more wake-up calls do we human beings need? We have to remember, however, that before this unification of humanity takes place, the catastrophic changes will have already occurred to purify and heal the planet and to clear the way for the New Age.

---

* <http:/www.earthlink.net/-lifespirit23/solar.htm>

Relating to declining values, Skolimowski says concerning the Flower Children of the U.S.A. in the late sixties, that they appeared in Los Angeles on Sunset Boulevarde in 1968 with nothing to offer but a single flower which they were giving to passers-by. He said that this was a revolution, and that what they were offering was LOVE. He continues, "What was beautiful in these young people in the late 1960's was that they saw through the whole thing—the whole fallacy of Western rationality, the whole hypocrisy of Western life-style, the whole dance that was supposed to bring us to the gates of Paradise, and instead was bringing us to the gates of unmitigated, existential hell of individual and social alienation."[8] The very fact that not only Sri Sathya Sai Baba but also seismologists and geophysicists are aware of the current calamities occurring throughout the globe and now and then issue warnings of the possibilities of further occurrences, should bring some comfort to those worried about the future. It seems that only natural phenomena of a severe variety may right the situation and bring erring humanity back to its senses. Sai Baba assures us that this state of affairs will not continue and that changes will take place sooner than we expect. He warns us to take note now and to effect the necessary changes He has outlined. Skolimowski sums it up nicely when he says, "In retrospect we can now see that we made a serious mistake some three centuries ago when we decided to make things easy for ourselves. In making things easy for ourselves we have been cheapening our status as human beings. This mistake has not been a technological mistake but a philosophical one". And further he laments, "The world is in pain, because older values have collapsed and newer values have not yet emerged. The world is in pain because values are a part of our psychical nourishment—to deprive people of right values is to starve them psychically, is to cause pain. The world is in pain because our psyches are disarranged, as our values are in a disarray."[8]

The Effects of Industry on Human Society

We are now living under a pall of smoke, soot and dust, inhaling particulate matter which clogs our lungs leading to a variety of pulmonary diseases, such as asthma, bronchitis, emphysema, etc. Where has the clean, fresh air gone, laden with the fragrance of scented blossoms our forebears used to inhale and keep their lungs pink, soft and healthy, instead of black, brittle, and diseased as so many lungs appear today, particularly in some countries, to any medical person exposed to these organs either on the post-mortem table or in the operation theatre. Young children growing up in cities and towns engaged in industrial pursuits can hardly escape the deteriorating effects of industrial effluents on their developing bodies. These wastes contain harmful materials such as toxins, traces of chemicals, heavy metals, poisonous solvents and a host of other materials hazardous to human health. The air, soil and particularly water from shallow wells, lakes, ponds, streams and other water bodies open to the atmosphere are contaminated directly by these effluents.

The Asian Asthmatic Development Board reported at the World Asthma Meeting held in Bangkok in February, 2005 that due mostly to urban development, particularly in Asia, the prevalence of asthma has increased steadily over the past twenty years. Asia's rapid urbanization, dangerous pollution levels and poor medical treatment have triggered an alarming increase in asthma which affects 300 million people worldwide according to the experts. They warned that sufferers in Asia are particularly at risk because doctors are failing to address the chronic conditions. It was reported at the Conference that asthma is becoming more of a concern in Asia...and there is a growing problem with asthma related to people living in cities. Urgent and immediate attention is needed in the region to close the widening gap for the growing number of Asian asthmatics. Another expert remarked that undoubtedly one of the factors could be the use of motor vehicles and their emissions (*The Hindu Business Line,* December, 2004).

With stricter laws being enacted in the developed countries it is possible that close adherence to these laws has eliminated many industrial hazards. Not so in Third World countries where the law is at best more honoured in the breach than the observance, and where municipal and metropolitan authorities who are supposed to ensure adherence to the rules can be easily bought by vested interests. Thus the environment deteriorates, the soil becomes polluted, water bodies are made unfit for human consumption and the air suffocates. Under these conditions is it surprising that diseases due to industry and to vehicular emissions in the metropolitan areas are on the increase and since growing and developing bodies are more prone' to the dangerous effects of these noxious substances, children are the greatest sufferers. This is not to ignore the situation where factory workers and others engaged in individual firms dealing with the manufacture of materials hazardous to human health are any less liable to develop acute and chronic disorders relating to the lung, liver, kidney and other vital organs. The most recent discovery, that of nanotechnology and the possibility of toxicity resulting from the manufacture of goods using this technology has become the subject of debate, many experts claiming that while there may be no actual harm to human beings or animals using the products, there remains the question of deterioration during use and of dissolution of the product after use with the possible further degradation of the environment already chock-full of harmful wastes from existing industry.

Concerning the damaging effects some industries can have on the health of the population, one has to consider the cola companies which operate throughout the world, providing soft drinks to developing countries. While observing the rules of health governing the manufacture of these products in their own countries, a different set of norms seems to govern their activities in the Third World countries where the consumer lacks awareness and is ignorant of the manner in which these multinationals ply their trade. With an unsuspecting and porous population, influenced by high-pressure salesmanship and attractive and misleading advertisements, both in the electronic and print media, catering to the uncontrolled tastes of people who lack knowledge of the situation, the companies ride rough-shod over the health rules in these countries to get their products on the move. Only recently, a scientific laboratory in India carried out analytical tests of the cola products and disclosed an alarming proportion of contamination of the drinks which also did not conform to the required standards of manufacture. Also in India, there was a popular uprising against a cola company to stop their operations because of the withdrawal of large volumes of water from the soil, so badly needed by the people of the local area, where water scarcity is a perennial problem; in spite of this the court granted permission to the company to continue their manufacture of the drink which allows them to withdraw the water they need.

In a particular area in the state of Kerala the situation assumed alarming proportions as there was acute shortage of drinking water due to over-exploitation of ground water by a cola company. In this area the land has become polluted, the water contaminated, and agricultural operations had to be stopped. A gleam of hope is to be seen in the attitude of the local village governing body (the *Panchayat*) which has appealed to the Supreme Court against the decision of the Kerala High Court. But it remains to be seen how a small village body can fight legally a mighty multinational company. The latest report describes the determined will of the environmental activists whose leaders led by the well-known Vandana Shiva, have called for a boycott of these companies and are in the process of amassing the aggrieved people to vehemently oppose the companies in a collective move to compel them to stop their operations and to vacate the State. This is the state of affairs as it exists today, and it is hoped that *vox populi, vox dei* will emerge victorious.

There seems to be no escape for the human community from the vicious circle created by the rapid development of industry all over the world. The more sophisticated the manufacturing industry becomes in technology and know-how, the greater the threat to human and animal life. Here once more crops up the problem of progress and development versus the ecological deterioration and permanent damage to the eco-system. Where lies the solution? May we suggest that there should be some limit to the manufacture of useless articles, particularly of synthetic goods which only end up cluttering up the environment, confining industry only to those products that are absolutely essential to living, both practical and aesthetic and taking industry out of the realm of competition, where not the financial gains but the effect on human life are of prime consideration. In other words, capitalism as practiced today, has to be eased out in some way or the other, making place for co-operative bodies oriented primarily to the production of material goods that serve human needs rather than those that cater to and pamper human greed. Since there is no end to man's manifold desires and lust for things material it is essential that the manufacturing companies re-orient their programmes with this end in view. Only those products that are practical, useful, of lasting value and at the same time appeal to man's aesthetic sense should roll out of the factories. The fact that industry deliberately produces goods that are non-lasting, brings the consumer again and again to the market-place to replenish his stock. What is his alternative? Isn't this the basis of the capitalistic system? This vicious system that keeps the wheels of industry rolling, like a Juggernaut, crushing the consumer financially and even morally, as they relentlessly move onwards.

The author finds it difficult to refrain from describing a personal experience illustrating the tricks of the trade as practised by the people who constitute the world of capitalism. As an undergraduate medical student at the University of Toronto in Canada in 1945, she had bought a new typewriter at a trade fair in the city, only to discover to her horror, after the lapse of only six months, that the machine had become obsolete because an advanced mechanism had been introduced into the new model which was already being sold. On enquiry she was told that the old model had lost its resale value; that the new machine was easier to handle and to manipulate; and that it made typing faster than ever. The temptation to either trade in or abandon her 6-month outdated machine for the new one was too great to resist, when a communist acquaintance who was employed in a factory enlightened her regarding the *modus operandi* of capitalism as it functioned at that time, some sixty years ago. It was the tradition of the capitalists, she said, to withhold new technology resulting from research, even though it had been developed and waiting in the wings when the old model was being made and could have been incorporated then and there. The company would await the trend of the market and as soon as sales of the previous model began to dwindle, the new one would be introduced accompanied by the customary high-pressure advertisements and salesmanship, regarding the virtues of the marvel incorporated into the new model. The communist further informed her that this method of hoodwinking the public was nothing new. She discovered this as she herself was a worker in a factory making nylon rain-coats. She uncovered the trick when the vents under the armpits of the coat were withheld until the company decided to use them in introducing the new model to the market. This was part of the trickery and fraud by which capitalism survived, she said. There is no reason to think that it is any different today.

With the new approach to the production of material goods for human consumption and the primary aim being to serve humanity at all costs, which we are told will be the method of approach of the New Age, we can look forward to Aldous Huxley's brave new world. The main consideration under the new system will be the welfare of humanity, based on compassion and love and not the pursuit of money for its own sake. Some have even gone so far as to state that money will cease to have value and that human beings will share with each other the things they need, somewhat like the barter system of olden days.

In discussing the tremendous gap between the developed and the developing countries and the disparities between them, Wise said during an interview on the Internet that this is how it has been up to now in our mindset of dualism. Referring to a ten-dollar shirt that the interviewer mentioned as being inexpensive in the U.S. because someone in Malaysia or China was paid ten-dollars a day to work for fourteen hours, Wise replied, "Yes, you could have that ten-dollar shirt, but is using someone the only way you could have it? Under our current system, the people that we could use became used. If in fact, we were treating the world population in a more soulful way and using world resources in a more creative way, you could still have beautiful blouses and you could still have them for ten-dollars. However, it doesn't mean some one also has to suffer unless we chose to operate under the system of false inflation and money like we do. There are a million ways to create abundance. We're just stuck in this model of usury. The 'have' and the 'have not' is critical to the game."[11]

This attitude on the part of industry will have to change. The New Age will certainly not countenance any sort of exploitation of human being by any one whomsoever. The key-note of the Golden Age will be love, compassion, empathy, service and Oneness of all beings. There will be no place for the feeling of separation between man and man, man and animal, or man and Nature. All will be an integral part of the Cosmic Web. Nor will there be scope for the feeling of 'alienation' since people will be more integrated both with themselves and their fellow human beings, indeed, with Nature in her entirety. Wise comments thus, "Only you can free yourself from vested interests and learned positions to live as you feel. Only you can invent your future integrity. In changing yourself you create a fertile environment within which others can grow and change.... Those who succeed in aligning their heartfelt values with their actions are way-makers, bridge builders to an integral way of life.[3]

Today, because of the exposure of humankind to the negative effects of science and technology, to the narrow-minded tenets of orthodoxy the breeding ground for fanaticism, to the feeling of separation that characterizes each and every aspect of the business of living, to the practice of overt segregation between different peoples based on colour, class, creed and status; to the racialism encouraged among some classes of society in some countries of the world—because of these manifold factors, man has become steeped in duality. The fact that segregation and separatism are so extreme even between the rich and poor of the same race or community, how much greater will it be between the races of the world, among whom there are such glaring differences. "Unless religion and ecology are fused together in a meaningful manner, we do not have a chance of preserving either our spirituality or our environment."[8]

With the establishment of Sai Baba's Golden Age these anomalies between man and man, race and race and even between male and female will automatically disappear. The changes occurring in Nature and the greater changes within the body/mind/spirit complex of the human individual will ensure this removal, and in its place will be love and compassion, with each cell of each human body emitting the "purest frequency of energy"[2] which we understand as Love. This will be the Utopia of the 21st century.

And in the final analysis, Man, the Universe and God, the Creator will be identical, will become One with the Totality which He is. The feeling of duality will disappear for a thousand years, or undoubtedly for all time to come. In the Golden Age or *Sathya Yuga*, the Age of Truth, vested interests will become an alien concept. This practice is so rooted in duality, that it will not be able to synchronize with the new world order and will fail to survive. The products that emerge from business houses based on vested interests will naturally be manufactured from synthetic materials if present conditions continue in the future. These products will not be able to preserve their integrity and, will in all probability disassociate and return to their original elements since the parameters under which they were produced no longer exist under the new paradigm. They will automatically disintegrate and disappear. Also the individuals who visualized and produced such products will be removed for the simple reason, that with a feeling of separatism defining duality in their mental make-up it is inconceivable that the vibratory rate of their cells will ever be able to approach the pitch of earth's high resonance. Those who fail to increase the vibration of their cells will not be able to survive in their present physical bodies. Thus the swan-song of vested interests, the bane of existence of entrepreneurs, original thinkers, researchers and others with brilliant minds and more brilliant ideas, such as Nicola Tesla was. With the connivance of vested interests, his newly erected apparatus out-of-doors for research purposes was completely demolished, compelling him to abandon the project.

The Economic Situation

The economic situation worldwide seems to be somewhat similar in many respects. Most people, perhaps, know that the Stock Market can be manipulated, has been manipulated and is being manipulated. Those who innocently invest hard-earned funds in the Market discover to their dismay that they have been 'conned' and taken for a ride, whereas the smart 'guys' have gone off with the prize. This happened some years ago with the Bombay Stock Exchange when a big 'scam' broke out over the manipulation of the Market by a *single individual*. In commenting on the economic system Wise says, "Your challenge is to transform the systems already in place. You do not have to dismantle your existing structures and organizations and begin anew. There is nothing wrong with these structures. What is necessary is to raise their functions to higher levels of integrity. To accomplish this, all technology needs to be fully compatible and the information purveyed needs to be updated. The language can no longer be mechanistic, competitive and centred in economics. All mechanistic information is already outdated. Competition is making you better at what does not work. And the economy is a completely illusory value system even in its own context.... The new language derives from energy, integralism, love and compassion. The tools you need are currently in for development in your society. Some are already available for application. Some are temporarily thwarted from application by vested interests and established momentum."[3]

Many economists across the world seem to agree on one point—that the economy of the U.S.A. is going downhill and should in the normal course of events collapse. But this does not seem to be happening. How then does the U.S. economy continue to function in the face of near collapse? Several economists have attempted to explain this enigma.

A well-known economist, S. Gurumurthy, offers the following explanation. Writing in *The New Indian Express* (April, 2005) he says, "The Anglo-Saxon world seems worried at last. For more than a decade savings have become an unfashionable economic idea in the West...." He says that

Americans now save hardly one per cent of their post-tax income which he describes as a myth, because only the Hispanics and Asians in the U.S. save. The other Americans are actually in debt on credit cards for two trillion dollars. While Americans used to save 15 per cent of their income twenty-five years ago, and 7 per cent fifteen years ago, today thrift has become outdated. Gurumurthy maintains that "while the Asians saved, the West spent or invested.... The West got loans at low interest from the Asian savers and spent merrily, even invested back in the savers' economies, as FDI to us! He said that Japanese, Chinese, Indians, Koreans and Taiwanese sank millions of dollars of their savings in the West at some two per cent interest! However, the West now seems to be rethinking and investors have begun doubting the borrowing model of economy. Now a call goes out for a return to higher interest rates to boost savings, thus the U.S. and the West seem keen to drift back to thrift."

Bharat Jhunjunwala in his article entitled "Making of a Multipolar World" in *The New Indian Express* (May, 2005) writes that the President of India, Abdul Kalam, states that a "global economic war is taking place today between India, China and developing countries on one hand and the United Sates, the European Union and rich countries on the other." The truth is America has already lost the war. Our businessmen are more efficient than their American counterparts. Our exports to America are more and imports less. Conversely, America's imports are more and exports less. This is the pattern of America's trade with most developing countries, India and China. The American economy should have "collapsed spontaneously in this situation." However, the author explains that the U.S. economy is surviving only because developing countries like India and China support the U.S. economy by buying U.S. treasury bonds with forex earnings in large quantities thus preventing the collapse. Were these countries to stop buying bonds, the dollar will lose value and the U.S. economy will collapse.

This time, a western economist, Jeffrey D. Sachs, explains the present economic impasse of the U.S.A. He affirms that George Bush's economic policies have failed and global financial markets are reacting negatively. It was the super-rich who benefitted by the tax-cuts of the Bush administration. The policy failed because the tax-cuts could not be balanced with reduction in government spending which was never explained to the public. It was only after re-election victory that they revealed that large budget deficits caused mainly by tax-cuts revenue required sharp cuts in social securities, health-care spending, etc. Sachs went on to state that the annual U.S. budget deficit reached 5 per cent of the GNP with an enormous part of the gap financed each year by Asian central banks, which now hold about two trillion dollars in claims against America. He states, "The dollar is weakening as financial markets understand that the U.S. will need to borrow huge sums from abroad for years to come"; also the willingness of foreign central banks to lend to the U.S. looks likely to end, "for why should the central banks of Japan, China, South Korea and other Asian countries accumulate vast holdings of U.S. treasury bills if the dollar is likely to lose value in the years ahead?" There is a rise in imports and a yawning trade deficit but U.S. politicians are blaming China and other countries for 'unfair trade' even threatening them with sanctions. "This is lashing out at its own banker, even as it asks the banker for yet more loans. Bush's gamble was a loser from the start, generating costly results—mainly for the U.S., but for most of the world too—for years to come" (*The Economic Times*, May, 2005). Such are the devious ways the Western countries, particularly the U.S., have adopted to prop up their collapsing economy.

Sai Baba's Remedies for the Economic Ills

How can this sort of economic fraud on the part of the West be made to change? It is obvious that this attitude of those who direct, control and actualize the economies of countries, have to change their approach. But how? Since their minds are conditioned by the feeling of duality, that is, the lack of the knowledge of the Oneness of all humanity, and as this attitude predominates the human psyche, the ills arising from the economic system, in spite of reforms, will continue to harass countries across the world. The only alternative appears to be that we have to revert again to the teachings of our spiritual masters, since we have got ourselves into such a mess that there seems to be no way out. Sri Sathya Sai Baba has given the prescription for change in His numerous discourses over a period of sixty years, and He says "None can claim ignorance." To reiterate, He exhorts us to change our materialistic ways of living; to get on to the spiritual pathway which will help us to realize that we are all— everyone of us—sparks from the Divine Flame and hence none can claim superiority over the other; to become aware of the reason for our birth as human beings, which we have unfortunately forgotten in our mad rush for higher and higher standards of material living. We have to ask ourselves, he says, four relevant questions without which life makes no sense, and these are, "Who am I? Where have I come from? How long shall I be here? and Whither am I bound?" All of us should ask ourselves these four questions, He asserts. If we can change ourselves sufficiently to achieve these goals Sai Baba has set for our own spiritual welfare, then we are on the road to realizing that we are all *Amritasya putrah*—that is, 'children of immortality' as the Vedas declare, and as the Upanishads exhort us to believe, *Vasudaiva kutumbakom*—"The world is one family."

Is it possible for any sentient human being to adopt the above two principles and still remain in the hypnotic state of duality? If we all possess the same Divine Spark within us which is exactly the same in each and everyone of us, how can we suppress the freedom of others, economically, politically, socially, culturally or spiritually for that matter. How can we then subvert the economies of other nations to serve our own selfish ends? How can we engage in the production of spurious, inferior goods for human consumption that may affect adversely the health and well-being of others? It is necessary at all times for us to remember our common origin, and to ignore all other differences that may intrude into our mental makeup. Since we are all endowed with the power of thought; since we all possess consciousness at the highest level of all living beings on earth; since we all feel pain, endure suffering, entertain hopes and fears, have ambitions and are the givers as well as the receivers of love and compassion, it should not be too difficult for us to bond together as a unified human race inhabiting what is probably the most beautiful planet in our solar system. It needs a collective effort and a collective consciousness to bring about this brave new world that Sai Baba says will be here sooner than we think. If we lag behind, He warns us, and if we cannot or *will* not accept the changes that are imminent, we shall fall by the wayside and perish, losing the golden opportunity for which we became embodied as human beings, and that He says, is to become enlightened and to gain liberation in this very lifetime.

At this stage in human evolution, it may seem too much for humankind to achieve what Sai Baba is requesting it to do. However, we are told both by the ancient peoples and by those who are now observing the current Earth Changes, that if we are not able to affect the necessary changes that will be incumbent upon all beings living on the Earth in the near future, when Earth will undergo such changes as have not been experienced in 200,000 years, and never in the history of conscious human living, then we shall have to make the transition to other realms, and leave the planet to others who have been able to effect the required changes. This is the bleak future for those of us who are immune to change, to adopt a completely new life–style, basking in the mistaken idea that the *status quo* is the best thing that could have happened to us making us loathe to yield to anything that threatens it. If, however, we are unable to accept the predictions and prophesies of the old and new seers, we are in for the greatest surprise in our little lives. Were we to perish, we shall have no one to blame but ourselves. Let us try to visualize what the poet saw, "The old order changeth yielding place to new/And God fulfils himself in many ways/Lest one good custom doth corrupt the earth."

Communism as it is Today

Communism, the questionable 19th century gift to humanity, appears to have had its day. Seeing that Marxism has been rejected by the Fatherland, the former USSR, which has since reverted to its old name of Russia, one wonders how much longer this perverted view of a single individual will continue to mislead the societies which mistakenly adopted it. The Russians, who embraced, bred, developed, sustained and finally dismantled this lop–sided inherently despotic system of Karl Marx, who erroneously thought he had found the panacea for all of human ills, deserves three cheers and a standing ovation for their far–sightedness and courage to throw off the yoke of one of the most oppressive regimes in all of human history. Marxism bespattered the pages of the history of this ancient land with the blood of many of its honest and innocent citizens, from the highest in the country to the lowest in rank. No one was spared for the simple reason that he or she refused to kowtow to a system so obviously against higher human values that humanity has held so dear for millennia. These valiant souls refused to toe the line of their communist masters, to see red as they saw it. Today some assert that the country was much better off under communist rule, and the economy more vibrant and they bemoan the conditions of their run–down economy. But this is to be expected when a stabilized system is suddenly demolished to make way for a new regime which fortunately, was put into place without bloodshed and oppression of the people, an important fact which should not be overlooked. The communist regime had curtailed freedom in many ways, restricting speech and action and even the thought processes of the people, undermining their status and dignity as human beings. The soul of Russia has been resurrected and once more breathes the air of freedom and liberty. Nothing on earth can stop this highly intelligent, innovative, energetic and hard-working people from once again becoming a leading global nation, something Tolstoy himself would be proud of; and this time devoid both of the imperialistic might of monarchy as well as the stranglehold of a cruel despotic system of government. When asked by a group of East Germans visiting His Ashram at Puttaparthi for the first time when their country would be rid of communist rule, Sai Baba with His usual homespun humour simply said, "come-u-next". It was not long after that the Germans threw off the stifling rule of the communists.

A flash-back to another communist state, this time not a country, but a state within a country. The state of Bengal in the Eastern part of India at the time of the partition in 1947, by the departing British rulers, was divided into West and East Bengal, the latter forming part of the new country of Pakistan, ultimately becoming an independent nation known as Bangladesh, with the military aid of India. The people of West Bengal, after years of Congress rule, took their struggle for a change of government to the streets of Calcutta, fomenting unrest and riots, holding street processions, waving the red flag and shouting 'zindabad' (revolution), instigating violence, strikes, picketting of factories and big business houses, which were obliged to move out to other Indian states. Eventually, the Congress government was voted out to be replaced by the communists in the late seventies which rules the roost up to the present time.

The mind is perplexed to understand how a land steeped in spirituality as West Bengal was, could have opted for such a godless regime; a land that produced spiritual giants like Sri Ramakrishna and no less a spiritual stalwart than Swami Vivekananda, who strode like a colossus throughout the length and breadth of India, then undivided, to spread the knowledge of the Oneness of religion, of Vedanta and its philosophy of many pathways to the Infinite; and to sound his vibrant call to his countrymen, "Awake, arise and stop not till the goal is reached." This was the land that elicited the slogan, 'What Bengal thinks today, all India thinks tomorrow'. This was the land that gave birth to Paramahansa Yogananda, Sri Aurobindo, Sri Chaitanya, Anandamayi Ma, all spiritually enlightened beings each of whom had something refreshing and novel to offer humankind. This was the land which was the first to denounce child marriage, the ill-treatment of widows, and to support their remarriage, to denounce the practice of *sati*—of widows throwing themselves on to the burning pyres of their dead husbands; this was the land to support the education of girls and establish some sort of equality between the sexes.

A possible explanation for this dilemma is that in the pursuit of such an upsurge of spirituality, less attention was paid to the impoverished among the masses. And that is where communism scored a victory. They won the elections by appealing to the poorest of the society who formed the majority. True, they brought about land reforms and relief to the landless, they clothed the naked, fed the hungry and sheltered the homeless. Praiseworthy actions, indeed, but it has to be borne in mind that man does not live by bread alone. As a potentially divine, multidimensional being he is made up of a body/mind/spirit matrix and satisfying only one component of this complex does not solve the problem but compounds it. Indeed, the mind may be re-conditioned and brain-washed to accept new ideas, but what about the spirit, the one and only thing that informs matter, the body as well as the mind. Without the appeal to the spirit, the only unchanging, eternal, imperishable, birthless and deathless being, man becomes restless and unfulfilled. Eventually, like the Russians and East Germans as well as so many of the countries of Europe, the spirit in man will propel the people to cast off the atheistic and godless regimes of the communist and revert to its true nature—the integration of man's body with his mind and spirit, as his Creator intended him to be. Today, some people are beginning to realize that the body, the senses, the mind, which is only a bundle of thoughts and ever changing, and the intellect, without the controlling influence of the spirit or higher Self, Cosmic consciousness, which is the divine core within us, is like a ship sailing in unchartered waters without captain or compass, lost and doomed forever. This group, according to recent surveys carried out in the U.S.A., comprises 20 to 26 per cent of the population of the country and can be applied to all other countries of the world. What of the remaining 75 to 80 per cent? Do they include the communists, atheists, agnostics, rationalists and others, making up the sum?

It is apparent to many people that the days of communism are numbered. For how long can the few countries left waving the red flag, continue to do so in the face of a human community becoming rapidly enlightened, albeit 20 to 26 per cent, with a collective consciousness geared to the pursuit of the divine in man—the divine that no sentient being can deny if he is honest with himself. The mere contemplation of man, Nature, the Universe and the creation as a whole should leave any rational being with a feeling of awe and wonder as to compel him to question himself, 'Who made all this?' It is this question along with others such as, 'Who am I? Where have I come from? How long shall I be here? Where I am heading for?' that set man on this quest, the answers to which lie within the depths of his being, leading to knowledge and ultimately to the Higher Self or the Spirit in man.

No doctrine on earth, flaunting a theory or philosophy based solely on the premise that man is a material being and that all his motivations are based on his material desires and needs, can survive in this day and age of a rapidly awakening spiritual awareness, in which consciousness plays the greatest role, which Marx had considered as being secondary to man's material needs.

China, a country that embraced communism with open arms and practised it with all its flaws and limitations for decades, has recently undergone a sea-change. The Chinese communist government has rolled out the red carpet for the multinationals who have walked into this one-time closed country to a royal welcome embellished with its traditional oriental courtesy to practice their profit-making business. Whether this political move by the Chinese Government is for the good of the country in the long run remains to be seen. It is said that all heavy industry and big business concerns are in the hands of foreign industrialists. Capitalism in the form of multinationals, at one time anathema to the Marxists, have taken over the country's industry, the Chinese people comprising the labour force that keep these companies running and funds pouring out of the country into the coffers of other nations. After having said all this, Western capitalism has earned our gratitude for making inroads into the heartland of communist China and it is hoped, may act as a leavening agent to enliven the society and make it sufficiently porous so that new ideas may penetrate their brain-washed minds and who of their own accord will rise up and throw off the yoke of a despotic regime to replace it with a more humane form of government.

To return to the subject of West Bengal. After the independence of India this state was the industrial hub of the country, a thriving centre of trade and commerce. Subsequent to the take-over of the government by the communists, industry started deserting the state on account of interruption of their operations by the frequent strikes, pickettings of their offices, go-slow movements and other activities not conducive to the healthy growth of industry. The result—only a few years later the state began to deteriorate and came to the brink of joining the backward states of India. Airlines, shipping companies, the tourist trade, and of course, business houses, shunned the capital city of Calcutta, now known as Kolkata, as if it were a leprous entity, once the mecca of numerous activities in India. What a dismal fall from grace of a once vibrant, intellectual, cultured, philosophical and spiritual people where academia was one of the gods the Bengalees worshipped and adored. Today, apparently having second thoughts the communists, like China, are making all-out efforts to woo the capitalists, both Indian and foreign, to attract investments where the infrastructure is least conducive to the functioning of modern industry. However, we shall have to wait and see the outcome of this venture.

So, what of the future of Marxism in India, when even in its stronghold, the state of West Bengal, its shaky foundations are beginning to rumble? The writer makes no apologies for the juxtaposition of material describing an atheistic, godless system which considers religion as the opium of the masses, with a concluding section of this chapter on spirituality.

Some Aspects of Spirituality

It can be stated without fear of contradiction that a section of humanity today, albeit a small proportion, has evolved to the stage where spirituality has become devoid of complicated ritualistic rites, narrow orthodox, sectarian religious beliefs and a more rationally oriented approach to the subject. The established idea that only one religion or a particular system of beliefs is the sole pathway to the Absolute does not form part of the mentality of this group. The rigid, fanatical approach towards things of the spirit has no place in their way of thinking. This allows them to investigate, examine, question, enquire and search for the answers in their quest of the spiritual. It is this group of people with the awareness of the Oneness of all beings and the acceptance of all spiritual teachings as genuine pathways to the Totality which we call God who will act as an inspiration to the rest of the population, be it slowly and painfully, until the Earth Changes that are occurring even at the present time, reach their peak anytime now, we are told, to replace the old and worn-out systems of religious and spiritual beliefs and practices.

In 1996, as described by Wise, the results of a survey carried out in 1994, became available to the public, sponsored by the Institute of Noetic Sciences and the Fetzer Institute. The Survey estimates the size of the 'transformational population' and identifies many of its shared values and concerns. Characterizing those who represent transformation values as 'cultural creatives' the Survey estimated there are 44 million cultural creatives in America alone. In five years it increased to 55 millions, 26 per cent of the population of the U.S.A. Wise states, "This study is a landmark for the world. It gives the transformational population a powerful position in the world's marketplace from which to influence the correct, dominant material reality toward integralism—if these individuals bond and initiate collective action."[3]

Relating to the awareness of human beings in general at the present time to the changes that are occurring on Earth and in the society, Wise, in an interview on the Internet says, "More than a fifth of the population is consciously attuned. And when I say consciously attuned I mean they could recognize the shift and address it. But a much greater number is attuned just by their own inner value and integrity without having the language of consciousness or the discernment of the psyche to label it. The population—and the number is growing phenomenally in the magnetism of our field — is really intensifying. We are now building these stories about what it takes to get us out of the competitive 'mode'. The interviewer intervened to say, "You feel that a fifth of the population is attuned to a shift in consciousness at this point?" To which Wise replied in the affirmative.[11] When questioned about the 65 per cent of the population that is starving and how they can be attuned to this consciousness, where those in war, drought and poverty zones all over the world, where people can only be aware of where the next meal is coming from, Wise replied, "Look at India, which is probably the classic model, where there is a central placement of spiritual integrity in the lives of the people so even in the worst situations people are living in an honest, enlightened and non-violent way. This I would put into the group of a fifth of the world population." To this the interviewer questioned, "So even though they are living in physical poverty, they are universally attuned to spiritual principles," to which Wise replied in the affirmative. Wise went on to state that there is a much larger number than even 20 per cent which have awakened to the internal recognition of these values. She says, "There's a spiritual drive inside us guiding us towards integrity and wholeness and love and devotion and creativity and joy and expression."[11]

Spiritual groups are mushrooming all over the globe, particularly so in India, where currently many television channels are beaming twenty-four hour spiritual programmes all over the country at which massive crowds are in attendance. This is an encouraging sign especially during these times when the masses are distracted by the trappings of consumerism and materialism which as it were have moved to their doorstep. It is hoped that this mass interest will act as an inspiration to enliven and enthuse the society, especially the upper classes, to have another look at spirituality as separate from religion. After all, we all possess a divine core and as Sai Baba has repeatedly reminded us, we took birth to realize our divinity—that we originate from the Divine, that we subsist in the Divine and that it is our destiny to return to the Divine, the source of our origin. This, He said, we have conveniently forgotten. "Earth Changes* that result in natural disasters tend to bring people together for support emotional as well as physical. Once the crisis is over, we return if we can, to our previous patterns of living. Until spiritual communities become commonplace, I suggest we all work within our existing communities, sharing our spiritual principles and recognizing the Oneness in all creation." In her discussion on the transformational population, Wise has remarked that 20 per cent of the population is attuned to a shift in consciousness, and that the number is growing at a phenomenal rate. In this respect, it is interesting to note that she singles out India as the 'classic model' of what she describes as having 'a central placement of spiritual integrity' and this she would put into the group of a fifth of the world population. This certainly places a responsibility on the people of this country and it is hoped that they will continue to live up to this assessment of someone who as a multidimensional being has a clearer insight into and a unique clarity of vision of the world situation as it is today, than any ordinary human being.

There are some people who attempt to alienate indigenous people from their traditional ways of life and convert them to alien religions, particularly Christian missionaries operating in developing countries who are the only religious persons on the face of the earth to have appropriated to themselves the sole divine right to save the heathens of the planet. This they do paying scant heed to the dangers involved in their mission, especially to disruption in the societies they interfere with. Western society has caused disruption not only in

---

* <http://www.matrixinstitute.com/index.htm>

things spiritual, but in all aspects of life in general, not only
in their own countries, but particularly in developing nations
where the introduction of technology, their industrial
activities, their mode of economics, their social life–style and
their cultural and moral norms have wrought havoc among
the people of these countries, who in their mistaken
endeavour to keep up with the Joneses, copied lock, stock
and barrel the Western way of life, now apparent to all
discerning minds as having gone amuck, leading their own
societies into a steady decline and bringing about chaos
and disruption in people's lives, especially among the
younger generation. The Flower Children of America of the
late sixties tried their best, but in spite of their noble intentions
and the millions of flowers they might have distributed,
society has continued downhill.

This state of affairs is nicely summed up in the following
lament by the lonely African from Colin Turnbull's book (1962)
quoted by Skolimowski, "I have tried hard to understand the
white man and his ways, but I can see only harm. What
happiness have they brought us? They have given us a road
we did not need, a road that brings more and more foreigners
and enemies into our midst, causing trouble, making our
women unclean, forcing us to a way of life that is not ours,
planting crops we do not want, doing slaves's work.... At
least the Bhagwan left us our beliefs but the white man even
wants to steal them from us. He sends us missions to destroy
our belief and to teach our children to recite some fine-
sounding words; but they are words we believe in any way,
most of them. And we live according to our beliefs, which is
more than the white man does."[8] What an indictment! And
by the member of a race Western man describes as backward
and uncivilized, living in a dark continent.

Skolimowski describes his idea of ecological spirituality
and includes in its tenets the following ideology: the
sacredness of nature, consciousness becoming reverential,

appreciating the universe in its entire glory and with sufficient depth, extending human values to all beings and creating an all encompassing ecological ethics. He writes, "Ecological spirituality is the celebration of the celestial union of all beings by the Reverential human consciousness. It invites and heals the entire web of life—of which it is a part and to which it bows in awe and reverence."[8]

It has been estimated that the world population will be reduced to one and a half billions after the reversal of the earth's magnetic poles leading to the Golden Age. Since approximately 20 per cent of the population is what is termed the "transformational population or cultural creatives" it will number 1.3 billion souls, if we consider the population on the planet today to be approximately six and a half billions. This approximates the estimated 1.5 billions who will be left. These findings seem to fulfil the predictions of Sai Baba when He says that only few, very few will listen to his warnings about the future. He also maintains that there will be a 'clear out' or a weeding out and sorting out, referring presumably to the large proportion of human beings who are destined to be removed and will not survive to see the New Age. He also affirmed that there is not much time left for us to change our material life–style. Sai Baba declared that His aim in coming is to re–establish *Dharma* (righteousness) and to repair the highway to God, because we have forgotten the pathway to blessedness.

Spiritual and other predictions throughout the world assure us that the time of reckoning is at hand and that the current chaotic conditions we now live in will pass away. All the inharmonic energies extant in society today will disassociate and disappear. Scientists have confirmed that the North Pole is shifting every year and many people have come to accept that the predicted reversal of Earth's magnetic poles will take place. When that will happen is anyone's guess. However, according to Mayan predictions the deadline seems to be 2012 or thereabouts. At this point in time the Mayan calendar, which recorded events for 18,000 years, came to an abrupt end.[2] Furthermore, the earth changes occurring at present are strong indications that a major change is expected to occur on the planet as the two parameters of magnetism and frequency are undergoing rapid changes which will completely alter the earth and affect changes in her inhabitants. These two events, namely, the Mayan predictions and the present Earth Changes appear to coincide, hence the assumption that the changes may occur sometime around 2012.[2]

Also the Voice of the Avatar, Sri Sathya Sai Baba, based on His omniscience, has alerted us to this change. He declares: "Man is living at the dawn of a Golden Age and he himself will determine the timing of the transition by his own acts and thoughts.... The new Golden Age will evolve gradually. The day of awakening is here and the day of reckoning or weeding out is not far away. The cleansing of the world will take place and only those awakened souls will be left to experience life in the divine state. Others will fall by the wayside, left behind and lost in a world of illusion and darkness."[1]

It behoves us therefore, to take heed of these timely warnings which are in harmony with current Earth Changes, and it will be at our own peril to ignore these collective predictions.

Two

Sri Sathya Sai Baba's Warnings About the Future

Sai Baba's Warnings

"The time has indeed come for a great awakening when the days of ignorance and illusion are replaced by a new Golden Age."

"The Golden Age is here now for those who are ready. How can anyone want to continue a life totally identified with the body and become a victim of his own actions."[1]

The above quotations alert us to the changes ahead of us. We learn from no less an authority than Sai Baba that a new age is awaiting us. We ignore these warnings at our peril. Sai Baba repeatedly warns us that those who cannot accept the changes that are taking place and who do not change their life-style by giving up attachment to material things, worldly pleasures and sensual attractions that hinder one's progress along the spiritual path, will fall by the wayside, become victims of illusion and will perish, thus losing a golden opportunity to get on to the spiritual path and to realize the goal for which they became embodied, that is, liberation.

The Shift of the Ages

Braden sounds a somewhat similar warning when he says: "Science may be witnessing events for which there are few points of comparison but ancient traditions have preserved the understanding that during key moments in human history a wisdom has been offered allowing individuals to experience rapid change without fear. This is one of those moments. This wisdom is now being passed down. Your life is preparing you for the 'Shift'. The recorded and predictable time-table is intact; the time is now. For those frightened of change, who equate dull with secure, this is meant as a curse.

"The world that you have always known, your world, is changing very rapidly. The structural guidelines that determine the way you think, perceive and act toward yourself and others are changing, not only around you. They are changing within you."

"The effects of the 'Shift of the Ages' are reverberating throughout each and every aspect of creation."

"The time of the Shift is not about death and endings. Rather the Shift mirrors our choice of life. The 'Shift of the Ages' is a new expression of life and the birthing of a new integrated wisdom. The opportunity of Earth is the opportunity of experience. Your life is your greatest tool of mastery."[2]

Commenting on the same theme, that is, the advent of a new age, Wise's approach is one of conciliation and tolerance. She says: "Those of you who have spent the better part of your life working toward the transformation ahead, take solace—the window is opening. There is no need to push it. The resistance of old and unenlightened ways is not an obstacle; it provides critical controls to the rhythms of transformation. Humanity must be able to survive this process without the breakdown of all physical bodies, and without dissolution into personal and social chaos. Those who overpower or devalue your efforts or who write you off as 'powerless', 'immature' or 'idealistic', are not your adversaries. They are your collective immune system—empowered by the same values that empower your individual immune system...their entrenchment in resistance, duality and control serves you at this juncture."[3] This reminds us of Sai Baba's assertion that the Golden Age will evolve gradually and that there are chinks of light appearing throughout the world.[1] Wise is saying the same thing in her own way. She says about the transformation that is to take place that we should not push the window as it is beginning to open. In other words, there is no urgent necessity to forcibly dispense with the old regime and try to break it up, before the new dispensation is ready, established and equipped to replace it. She is requesting us to ride piggy-back on the old order until the new one is in place. Showing great tolerance and understanding, she describes our adversaries—those who ridicule and deride us for supporting the new order, as our 'collective immune system'—their resistance is useful to us at this juncture.[3] This approach is quite unusual, original and rational at the same time. But then, as a multidimensional person, Wise is an unusual being. Compassion seeps through all her statements.

Both Braden and Wise have apparently refrained from describing the tragic consequences that will inevitably arise from whatever catastrophic events may take place. They have, it seems, deliberately avoided spelling out the loss of lives and destruction of Nature that are certain to occur prior to, during and following the cataclysmic events. Sai Baba, on the other hand, in no uncertain terms, and like so many of His predecessors, has spared no language in pronouncing what will happen if humanity persists in pursuing its present evil and ungodly ways. This is the prerogative of the spiritual masters. Sai Baba knows down to the minutest detail exactly what is going to happen, and, perhaps, when it will happen; and considers it His bounden duty to tell us so, not mincing matters or concealing facts.

The Situation Today

Commenting on the situation in India today He says: "The

greed and selfishness that are affecting this country are tragedies for humanity, for India has the role of guiding and leading mankind to the goal of self realization.... Youth is growing up in India in the hothouse of faction and passion, not as in the past in the cool bowers of reverence and humility. Elders indulge in fights, wrongful litigation, in corrupt means of earning money, and cut-throat competition. Their low behaviour, in the home, the village, in clubs, in the civic bodies, in the legislature, in all walks, set the standard for youth."

Let us consider some of Sai Baba's specific warnings to humanity: "The day of awakening is here and the day of reckoning or weeding out is not far away. The cleansing of the world will take place and only those awakened souls will be left to experience life in the divine state. Others will fall by the wayside, left behind and lost in a world of illusion and darkness."

"When the Lord incarnates in human form it is a time of great opportunity for those who are ready. All of you here today have that opportunity, but that alone is no guarantee of liberation.... Much effort is required, also an irreversible commitment to the spiritual path, leaving behind forever the life of illusion with its worldly desires, attachments and false values. So long as desire remains, you cannot firmly establish your feet on the spiritual path."[1]

"I have given the warning. I have given My message a thousand times and no one who hears My words can claim ignorance. Do not delay action to put right your own life-style and to change it to the way of God. *There is no other way*" (Writer's italics).

"But change will come. The day of awakening is not so far away, and when it comes there will be a revelation of the true power of God, a manifestation of the omnipresence of the Lord. This will be the signal for a great move forward and the weeding out of those who are not ready to accept the challenge of the moment. It will be just so, mark my words. *But few will listen, very few*"[1] (Writer's italics).

While reading Sai Baba's warnings to us, we begin to realize that in spite of more than six decades of teaching, lecturing, giving discourses, writings, informal talks, during thousands of interviews to thousands of individual devotees and private advice to so many others, we have not really come to our senses about the seriousness and importance of what He has been saying repeatedly. What has come over us, we should question ourselves seriously. There is self-complacency and a feeling of smugness about our own future; or is it ennui, a lackadaisical attitude to the things we do not wish to consider since they threaten our present comfortable life-style. That Sai Baba has to literally point the finger at us, warn and at times threaten us about our dismal failure to change our present life-style and turn Godward is a sad commentary, indeed, on the times we live in. Why this lethargy to change? Why this foolhardiness in failing to listen to the words of a great spiritual Master such as Sri Sathya Sai Baba who has specifically incarnated Himself in human form to save us from ourselves, as it were. Knowing the weaknesses and failures of human beings, He tirelessly repeats His message; but somehow, the full import of what He says always seems to elude us. And He is fully aware of this. He knows that the people living during the *Kali Yuga* or the Satanic Age—our present iron age—are spellbound by the lures and attractions which the age offers. He knows that we have long forgotten the reason for our presence here on this beautiful planet. He is aware that we have long lost touch with our Divine origin— that we originated from the Source; that we subsist in the Source; and that we are destined to return to the Source. All this we have conveniently forgotten and worse still, we are not even aware that we have forgotten. Hence His repeated warnings and more recently, threatenings so as to jolt us out of our stupor, to administer shock therapy by His harsh words. Apparently, according to Sai Baba, in spite of all this, 'few will listen, very few'.

Jesus took recourse to casting out those who desecrated the temple in Jerusalem by means of buying and selling in a holy place and polluting holy ground through commerce. He overthrew the tables of the money changers, and the seats of those who sold doves, accusing them of making the temple into a den of thieves (Mark 2, 15). However, it surpasses one's imagination to think of the gentle Sai indulging even in the mildest form of violence, though it be meant to admonish and punish his flock for their own good; but when it comes to verbal whipping, He is merciless—without an equal.

The Havoc caused by High Living Standards

What then is His alternative? He has spelt out in no uncertain terms what we are expected to do to change this situation. Turn away from worldly things, He admonishes us; leave aside the temporary attractions of materialism, of sensual pleasures, of the lust for wealth and power, position and status, pomp and pelf. These are transient and perishable and subject to change. Whatever is subject to change is not Reality, not Truth and like passing clouds obscuring the light of the sun. But we seem to be hypnotized by what we see around us; in stupor like the drug addict, by the baubles of the material world. We seem to have a totally insensate attitude to the fact that we have enclosed ourselves within the material comforts of the hi-tech style of modern living. We have brought the cinema into our homes; at the touch of a button we bring the sights and sounds of far-flung places on the globe into our sitting rooms and bedrooms; at the touch of a few more buttons we can create the environmental conditions that cater to our sophisticated tastes for temperature, humidity and air control. Basking in the luxury of this ersatz way of life, we get a smug feeling of having arrived, not realizing that we have become prisoners of the materialism and body comforts of the technological age we live in. Sai Baba affirms that the ideal of a higher material standard of living has played havoc with society.

Present day human society has become so immune to the urgent necessity for change—positive change—that nothing short of some sort of shock therapy is absolutely essential to rouse them out of their complacency or shall we say stupor. For society to change its present ways, mere talking and persuasion will not produce the desired results. Hence Sai Baba's repeated warnings to humanity to change its life-style from that of hankering after worldly possessions to that of the spiritual pathway. He affirms that there is no other way; no other alternative. If mankind refuses to listen and to reject their materialistic ways, they will not survive to see the Golden Age. There is not much time left, He says. The change has to be effected now. Delay will only mean disaster and doom for such individuals.

We have forgotten that we are children of Nature; forgotten how it feels to walk with bare feet in contact with Mother Earth; to sniff the invigorating cool, fragrant fresh breeze of the outdoors; to listen once again to the chirp and twitter of bird-song and to feel the fresh rain-drops on our faces. We have become prisoners of our desires, our greed and our life-style. When shall we learn to break the shackles of our serfdom to materialism and emerge as free souls as our Creator meant us to be. Perhaps the time has come for change; and if we are not able to effect the changes ourselves due to complacency, self-satisfaction and arrogance, Nature will be only too willing to oblige us by doing the needful, of course, with disastrous results.

Warning of the Storm and Wave

Sai Baba has warned us that the 'storm' and 'wave' will come without fail—the former we can rest assured to destroy much of what we hold dear, the latter to wash away the remainder. Perhaps, only after a catastrophe of this kind shall we open our eyes and clear our clouded sensorium to take stock of what has happened around us. Today the unfortunate victims of the Sumatra disaster through earthquake and tidal waves are experiencing what Sai Baba has forewarned us about. If such occurrences do not shock us out of our present state of lethargy, stupor and gross unawareness—nothing else will. The consequences have been spelt out by the Avatar Himself. We shall fall by the wayside, swept away, blinded by illusion and shall end up in darkness and perish. Others more attuned to the dangers of the times will survive and emerge to see the Golden Age waiting to come into being.

The recent catastrophe affected as usual the poorest of the poor. According to the prophets of doom subsequent disasters may not be confined to certain sections of society. There will be a weeding out, according to Sai Baba, of the undesirables, and since this group of humans is ubiquitous, it is foolhardy to conceive of any class or particular social group being spared. Nature has become enraged because of man's foolish ways and disastrous activities and it is inconceivable that she would distinguish between the 'haves' and 'havenots'; so also the law of karma which is inexorable will make no distinction between rich and poor, high and low, qualified and unqualified. There will be a levelling effect and as Sai Baba says "a clear out", meaning a certain amount of destruction of the population. All this will happen prior to the establishment of the Golden Age, He affirms.

Regarding the cause for natural calamities we repeat what Sai Baba has said: "Man's inhumanity to man expresses itself in the form of natural calamities, like earthquakes.... God does not decree these calamities such as earthquakes, floods, droughts, famine and epidemics, but man invites them by way of retribution for his own evil deeds." When Peggy Mason, the author of "Sathya Sai Baba: The Embodiment of Love" asked Sai Baba about the planet, He said: "There will be physical repercussions because of growing selfishness,

minor adjustments to the planet and a certain clear out."
About a possible nuclear holocaust, He says, "The calamity
which has come upon mankind will be averted. A new
Golden Age will recur. I shall not fail; it is not in the nature of
Avatars to fail."

Man's Inhuman Actions

Twenty-first century Man, heedlessly indifferent to the
incalculable damage that could result from his nefarious
activities to the health and well-being of all forms of life on
the planet—plant, animal, man—continues to inflict his
atrocities regardless of the obvious damage caused by his
industrial activities, ignoring the cries of Mother Earth in the
form of earthquakes, storms, flooding, droughts, famines,
etc. and the cries of woe and pain of humans and animals.
So long as his pockets continue to jingle with the comforting
sound of filthy lucre, his physical comforts more than
surpassing his needs, his palatial hearth and home catering
to his every desire bestowing pomp and prestige on his
family name—he is at peace with himself. Nothing else and
no one matters. Now, the time of reckoning has come. Long-
suffering Mother Earth has awakened and is poised for
revenge. The Sumatra Earthquake (9.3 is the latest figure)
and the subsequent tsunami are the warning signals. Nature
is on the warpath and no power on earth can stop her. She
has given several warnings to errant humanity—all
unheeded. None can accuse her of a pre-emptive attack.
The future is hers—and the goal - to heal once and for all
the bruised and battered Earth, so that human beings can
again live and move and have their being on the planet as
the Creator fashioned them to do. Like the Godess *Maha Shakti*
she will level the unrighteous and establish righteousness.

We have dwelt at length on man's cruel treatment of Mother
Earth; but what about man's inhumanity to man—his own
species. The sort of behaviour he exhibits toward his fellow

human beings is based on his feeling of separation; not being aware of the common divine origin of humanity. Regarding this attitude Sri Aurobindo explains it thus: "Our nature, our consciousness, is that of beings ignorant of each other, separated from each other, rooted in a divided ego, who must strive to establish some kind of relation between their embodied ignorances; for the urge to union and forces making union are there in Nature."[13] And again, "Sri Aurobindo and the Mother, however, say that though humanity has at present arrived at a critical situation, it is only a few individuals who realize that it is an evolutionary crisis and the only way to resolve it is to break the present limitations of human consciousness and rise to a higher spiritual stature of being. The common mass of humanity and even most of the modern thinkers have no true understanding of this situation and of the right way in dealing with it... It is only some exceptional individuals who have the adequate capacity to meet the demand of the evolutionary Nature, who have the intrepid courage and resolute faith to accept its challenge and to answer the present call of the Hour of God.[13]

Pari passu with this feeling of separation, man had long ago extended it to his dumb brothers. If he considers his fellow creatures as separate from himself, how much greater would be the feeling of separation between him and the animal kingdom. It is because of this attitude that animals from time immemorial have been the target of man's greed and inhuman treatment. They have been shot at, killed and skinned, sometimes alive, stuffed and exhibited, eaten cooked or raw, roasted whole in barbecues, some gigantic enough to roast a whole cow. Apart from his gluttony for animal flesh to satiate his bizarre tastes, he uses almost every part of the animal to satisfy his greed for exotic material things—horns, teeth, skin, bones, claws, feet, feathers—name it—man's ingenuity knows no bounds in utilizing all parts of an animal to meet his materialistic and hedonistic demands.

It is in this context that the author recalls the following experience still fresh in her mind, although more than half a century has elapsed since it occurred. She still remembers with great vividness her visit to one of Chicago's famous stockyards which she visited as a post-graduate student, having just completed her Doctor of Medicine degree (M.D.) at the Toronto University Medical School. To say that she was horrified and emotionally traumatized on witnessing the gruesome and bloody scenes in that sophisticated slaughterhouse in the heart of Chicago is to put it mildly. An unsuspecting robust pig, pink with health, was brought up to the second floor of the building by an elevator which landed at the head of the assembly-line where pigs were reduced to their separate parts. Without much ado, its throat was slit and the blood flowed. The inert carcass was then thrown on to the first part of the assembly-line where the butchering began. While writhing in mental agony to see the manner in which one of her dumb and helpless brothers was being subjected to such indignities, even in death, she caught herself simultaneously having a sneaking feeling of admiration for the slick, swift, efficient and highly organized manner in which the carcass was segmented, disjointed, sliced and slipped along the moving assembly-line in record time. No waiting, no lapse, nothing to stop the relentless movement of one part of the animal to the other succeeding sections of the line—nonstop. She wondered about the mental state of those assembly-line workers carrying out a single movement, repeatedly, for perhaps six to eight hours and that too, having to do with handling dead animal flesh. Besides the questionable appeal to the sense of sight, there was the question of smell certainly. What a way to spend one's life on earth, she thought. If Freud had not established the discipline of psychiatry and provided psychiatrists, they would have had to be invented to deal with the problems of such workers. Such were her dismal thoughts as she kept watching intently, not wanting to miss a single move.

Eventually, after the passage of what seemed to her an age, although it must have been over in less than half an hour, she was escorted to the basement, where the different parts of the pigs were being packaged into bacon, ham, salami, sausages, pork chops, etc. readied to be shipped through the exit door for sale just close by.

What efficiency! What an organized approach! What monetary returns! All because of man's feeling of utter separation between him and all other forms of life, including his own species, of course. She recalls glancing over her shoulder as she left the room to take one last look, only to see with a wave of horror, another of her dumb brothers being thrown on to the assembly-line where the process started all over again. She wondered if he had witnessed part of the previous proceedings and whether he had seen the gruesome end of one of his comrades. We talk about man's inhumanity to man. How do we describe man's attitude to the animal kingdom where dumb, innocent and helpless creatures, with a consciousness of their own, are subjected to such physical, mental and emotional torture, all for no fault of theirs but only to satisfy the lust for taste and the greed for flesh by individuals who call themselves humans.

Mahatma Gandhi has said that the appeal of the lower order of creation is more forceful because it is speechless. Sri Sathya Sai Baba sums it up by saying that animals did not come for the purpose of supplying food for human beings. They came to work out their own lives in this world.

Three

The Arrival of the Golden Age

A Gradual Change Over

According to Sai Baba the change over from our old world order to that of the Golden Age will not be sudden. Regarding the present state of turmoil, chaos and confusion, of not knowing which way to turn, modern society, buffeted by the pros and cons of moral laws which seem out of place in this sensual, permissive age, where wrong is equated with right and right sometimes identified with wrong; in this current world of confused thinking, and where 'sounds the clash of race and clan', Sai Baba says: "The transition from that unhappy state to the state of bliss cannot be achieved over night; but the changes have begun and the seeds are sown. Man is living at the dawn of a Golden Age and he himself will determine the timing of the transition by his own acts and thought.... The new Golden Age will evolve gradually."[1]

We are told by Sai Baba that the New Age which is imminent will be so entirely different from what we have been accustomed to that we would be unable to conceive of such a life. However, not all of us will qualify to move into this new world order. Certain changes have to be made within our lives, our thinking and our relationships if we are to survive to see the new world. He says, "The time will come when the light will spread with ever increasing intensity throughout the world. It will herald the time of the great awakening, a new era, a new beginning, a time when man becomes aware of the existence of God and the true nature of each individual soul. Man will also realize his own individuality and the reality that there is only the One, the divine Creator, the Totality."[1]

Beyond All Comprehension

"The time is approaching when all humanity will live in harmony. That time will be there sooner than one expects. Before it arrives be prepared for whatever is needed to reveal to every human being the true purpose of existence. It is not what anyone alive can imagine. It isn't something that one can aspire to. It is beyond all comprehension. I can say that its beauty is magnificent beyond all dreams."[12]

These statements of Sai Baba find somewhat of an echo in the observations made by Braden when he says, "To the degree that we are able to see the events of life through the single eye of the heart, as opposed to the polarity of the logical mind, to that degree we heal our illusion of separation. 'Seeing' the events of life for what they are, rather than 'looking' at the same events through the lens of what is expected, serves to heal the feelings of separation in polarity. In our heart there is no polarity.... The greatest of gifts that we may offer to one another is the gift of ourselves, in wholeness, completeness and truth."[2]

When man becomes aware that God exists in each individual soul and that there is no difference in the degree of divinity between man and man, whether he be rich or poor, high or low, caste or casteless, without duality, then will the stage be set for the dawn of the New Age. Because we have failed to realize this Oneness due to the 'polarity of the mind' where differences exist based on colour, caste, creed, status etc. we have the 'illusion of separation.'[2] About this feeling of separation Wise explains it thus, "...duality will recede. At this time there is radical discontinuity between your inner essential and your outer material dimensions. Your development in one does not necessarily correspond with the other, leaving many among you material-rich and love-poor or love-rich and material-poor. In your forthcoming expansion the integrity gap will close.... Separatism will be replaced by integralism."[3]

Commenting on the disturbances in the world Sai Baba says, "What has happened to the balance of the world? At present it is being tossed from side to side, from top to bottom, and there is no sign of stability anywhere.

"The present condition of the world is man's creation, the result of his misuse of the gift of life given to him by God. Man has drifted far away from the source and has pursued his own ambitions and pleasures, regardless of the consequences to Mother Earth. He does not realize that Mother Earth herself is divine, God's creation for His own pleasure.

"Man finds himself in a glorious earthly paradise and he has forgotten his origin and the purpose of his life.

"The world will not recover its stability until man himself changes his way of life and his destructive and selfish acts."[1]

Sai Baba emphasizes that "the time has come for a great reconciliation of mankind, a reunion on a vast scale so that once again, the whole world becomes one, with no separation or segregation." "But", he says, "the world today is not so perfect. Yet there are chinks of light appearing out of the darkness, and those tiny rays are the beginning of a great surge of love and light flowing down from God, the fountain head, to light up the world and cleanse it of evil.... The time for change has come, a moment of great awakening, and the opportunity for man to realize his own divinity, for that is what he is, divine."[1]

Separation of Mind and Heart

The Hopi in its ancient wisdom perceived the danger when the mind and heart of man ceased to be one and realized that Earth under these circumstances healed herself by cataclysmic change.[2] Even thousands of years ago it seems the human heart and mind were the same as they are today. Hence the importance of the coming Age, which we hope will bring about this union that we all long for. Without the controlling effect of the 'feeling heart'[2], man's mind takes the downward plunge into avariciousness, greed, lust for power, arrogance, hostility, and unmindfullness, resulting in dangerous and destructive acts such as the senseless and lunatic felling of the rain forests—the most recent being the granting of permission to destroy parts of the Amazon rain forests for selfish gain—a forest that God has gifted to man since time immemorial and which is absolutely essential for maintaining the ecological balance, not only locally but globally. This sort of butchery of Mother Nature is possible only because of our great feeling of duality. We are painfully unaware that man and Nature have coexisted for countless ages, and that there is a symbiotic relationship between them, an interdependence that is inherent, having been put in place by no less a being than the Creator Himself. Why should we come between them to satisfy our greed and self-interest? For countless millennia Nature has coexisted with man without either encroaching on the rights of the other. For ages past the ozone layer was intact; the soil and water and air remained pure and unpolluted, so that man could slake his thirst merely by cupping his hands to drink from stream, brook, river or lake, without fear of disease. Only a few hundred years ago the situation changed to present the grim facts of polluted water, poisoned soil and vitiated air. We have arrived at the point of no return and unless something drastic occurs to stop these suicidal acts of man, we may all go the way of the dodo.

Tiwari sums up the matter thus: "The power of the mind has been greatly misunderstood. It was never meant to make us exclusive, superior beings. We have simply evolved by our own karmic actions. We are all one consciousness... The

Earth is awaiting our conscious evolution. She has endured epidemic proportions of our anger, jealousy and hatred. The time has come to sustain our goodness and know that our minds are of one mind."[4] Sathya Sai Baba drops hints as to the solution of this impasse between man and Nature. He says, "One day a great wave will come and sweep away much of what exists today.... It will be a time of great awakening and enlightenment, as a new era is born."[1] He emphasizes again the role of man in the future society, "The future of the world itself lies in the heart of man. Every thought and every action plays some part in his own future as well as the future of the world.... The integration of all in the world will come, the timing depends on you."[1]

What is to be Done?

Sai Baba places the onus on us as to the timing of the arrival of the Golden Age. What could He mean by this, we wonder. If we examine His teachings carefully and note the details of what He says, this may throw some light on His meaning. Here are some of the guidelines for our consideration: Harmony and love should flow; hatred, fighting, scheming, evil, all negative emotions should disappear; we should become aware of the existence of God and the true nature of each individual soul; we should also realize our own individuality and the reality that there is only the One, the Totality, the Creator; the choice of free-will to decide our future; to realize the truth; not to be identified with the body; not to wander from the Path; to experience life in the divine state; irreversible commitment to the spiritual path; to forsake forever the illusory worldly life with desires, attachments and false values; to avoid the feeling of separation; to find peace within ourselves; to awaken to the truth that God is love, to be able to see the beauty of the Absolute Truth; to play a part in bringing forward the transformation; to prepare ourselves for the change; to try to know ourselves; to establish our true relationship with God; to banish all thoughts of differences; not to become part of the confusion that surrounds us; to avoid evil thought, selfishness, greed and jealousy; to change our thought pattern, values, ideas, level of consciousness; by becoming closer to God; to entertain no fear about the future; to use these to accelerate the arrival of the New Age.

What a prescription! And these are only some of what He has decreed that we should strive to do; strive to become; strive to influence others to follow, and in so doing hasten the arrival of the Golden Age, which He says is waiting for us to open the door and allow it to happen. Are we prepared to accept Sai Baba's challenge; for indeed, it is a real challenge to us who have so securely ensconced ourselves in our own life–styles of creature comforts, of body consciousness, social status, and in our ambitiousness to get ahead, paying little heed to trampling on others' rights. Are we prepared to change all this and to adopt at least some, if not all, of the remedies detailed above which will ensure our survival and qualify us for becoming citizens of the new world order?

The Key Word—Individual Effort

Sai Baba Himself has said that this decision depends solely and wholly on each individual. None can coerce, tempt or induce people to forsake their present state of what they consider to be secure and permanent in a world which they fail to realize is fleeting and rapidly changing with every passing day. Change and decay are not in the spectrum of their awareness and any attempt by anyone to dislodge them from their citadel of security and permanence will only result in failure and hostility. How then can these eternal verities Sai Baba has placed before us for immediate execution be brought into actuality? He Himself has given the remedy—by actually living these values ourselves in our everyday lives; showing by example that a change in our life–style is possible, and that a switching over to other patterns of living based on the spiritual values He has outlined will in no way endanger our future. But we shall have to prove this quickly, as there is hardly anytime left to consider the pros and cons. Sai Baba has warned us not to allow the chaos and confusion surrounding us to affect our peace of mind, and that we should steadily forge ahead and pursue the spiritual path without allowing any external influence to obstruct us.

He says "Mankind can and will be saved.... The integration of all mankind will come in the course of time and it will result from a better understanding of the truth.... The Golden Age is the creation of man, not of God."[1]

Braden's findings are in tune with this when he says, "Each individual now living upon the Earth is an integral part of the Shift process."[2] Wise has elaborated on this theme, "As individuals integrate the increasing amplitudes of their own axial values, and all frequencies that constitute their reality, their insight and behaviour will further align with universal values. Such a population will change the social environment and, eventually, what is called reality."[3]

Conditions for Survival

Adding to His pronouncements on the dawn of the Golden Age, Sathya Sai Baba says, "Although the Golden Age lies in the future, man can prepare himself by turning to God and living his life in complete harmony with the Infinite. That is possible now, if you surrender your will to God and dedicate your life to Him. You will become His instrument and in that capacity you will find fulfillment through service to humanity", He said that life is a change and change is taking place all the time.[1] Continuing, He says, "It is a process which takes time and the new Golden Age will evolve gradually. So you should live in hope, live in love, live in purity of heart and thought and above all be true to your own self. Let the divinity within shine forth and become one of the great beacons to light up the world and hasten the arrival of the new Golden Age."[1] And again He reassures us that we should not have fear, that all will be well, and that love and light will replace the darkness and a new era will be upon us very soon.[1] So He exhorts us to look ahead, not backwards, and know that the divine awakening lies ahead. The path is through God, with God, in God, always remembering that God is love.[1] He continues: "The reawakening of man is at hand, reawakening to the certain knowledge that man himself is God.... But you must learn to give up attachment, to forget about self, to conquer ego; to lose all sense of desire, and then you will have prepared yourself for the future."[1] However, He sounds a warning, "The dawn of the Golden Age is at hand but everyone will not experience it. The age of preparation precedes the Golden Age and it is during this time that the sorting out process takes place. So seize the opportunity that all of you have been given to rise above the material level and manifest once again in the divine state. Only then can you enter the Golden Age and experience the omnipresence of the Lord."[1]

It seems from the above pronouncements of Sai Baba that all of us may not remain to see this awakening for the weeding out process will take place before the dawn of the New Age. This sorting out will ensure that no one or not many of us will be left to interfere with the process that is being initiated to provide the right atmosphere for the Golden Age. Mother Nature will ensure our removal so that the pathway to goodness, love, light and peace will be unhindered. Right now we are witnessing the onset of the Earth's cleansing actions. The first tsunami originating from Sumatra in Indonesia alone affected seven countries of South East Asia and swept away hundreds of thousands of souls. About future calamities, Sai Baba has this to say, "The evil must and shall be removed before such a catastrophe (destructive war) takes place. There will be minor wars and skirmishes, of course; these cannot be helped in the existing state of affairs."[1] Continuing, He says, "Today the seeds are still in the ground, slowly germinating as the teachings of the Lord begin to spread throughout the world and infiltrate the mind of man. Soon these seeds will begin to grow and what emerges will brighten the world as the beauty of the absolute truth begins to reach so many people."[1]

According to Kishoo Gandhi, "The world conditions at the present moment are increasingly becoming so chaotic and blindly destructive that they have created a widespread feeling of acute anxiety and distress. Some great catastrophe which may engulf the whole world seems not a far too distant prospect to many people. Faced with such a formidable and overwhelming situation, they find it extremely hard to believe that the birth of a new age of some great Light and Truth is imminent."[13]

A Slow Change to the New

As the old order like a ship, is reduced to a dot as it disappears over the horizon; the new one, also like a dot comes into view, at first partially, then larger and larger as it approaches land, until eventually the entire ship is seen and recognized as such; so will the old dispensation under which we are living at present also gradually disappear, giving way to the New Age—the Golden Age of Sri Sathya Sai Baba. "Change and decay in all around I see", laments the poet and so it is with our present system. Wise has postulated that we shall have to live with the old paradigm for some time until the new order is firmly established.[3] The Golden Age will not be established overnight and Sai Baba asserts that it will take place slowly, giving the old regime time to fade away. Nothing in the universe happens suddenly, except perhaps, natural disasters which occur without warning. Nature takes her own time to effect positive changes. Consider the seed in the ground, which takes time to swell, burst, sprout and pierce the soil as a seedling, taking time to produce its leaf buds, then its blossoms and finally the fruit. Even some trees take decades to attain their full stature. Also we have to remember that Rome was not built in a day.

This slow process is necessary, since man is not ready for the change. The mass of humanity is still not aware that the earth beneath their feet is undergoing drastic changes within, that the society around them is rapidly undergoing changes and most important of all, that changes surpassing all the others are occurring within themselves. To all this man is innocently oblivious due to his pre-occupation with and hypnotic attraction for the material world around him—a world of glitz, glitter and glamour, of irresistible sights and sounds, of malls and super-markets, shops and department stores, chock-full with so many tantalizing, eye-catching goods, the gew-gaws and baubles of the material world—as to turn the head of the most sober and self-controlled human being. Filled with desires for the multifarious material things of the world, heeding not his own welfare, man crazily and unheedingly plunges into the morass of materialism, and unmindfully becomes a victim of consumerism, spending recklessly without thought of tomorrow, filling his hearth and home with perishable, useless articles of the irresistible market-place, his mind filled with ever increasing desires, little realizing there is no end to this insatiable, restless craze for worldly possessions.

Some of Sai Baba's advice for changing oneself to become fit for the future:

- "Today you have an opportunity for your own awakening, and you alone will decide whether you are now ready for that experience, or whether you prefer to continue living in the world of illusion, a life where false values are attributed to things which are really of no value at all, here today, gone tomorrow. Yes, much of what you value so much will end up as dust, just like the body."[1]

- "You are here on a visit, one lifetime, one of many lives, when again, you have an opportunity to go through those experiences which will help you to achieve your goal, the ultimate realization of the truth and your own divinity, the fact that you and God are one. Many of these experiences may seem difficult, even traumatic, but they are all there for a purpose."[1]

• "Today, man continues to search in outer space for the source of creation and imagines that giant telescopes will soon reveal the mystery of creation. But man will never reach that goal unless he learns to look within."[1]

• "Today there is much suffering in the world, so much disillusionment. And so it will continue, as long as man is motivated by his senses and all the desires which they create."[1]

• "What is the real challenge? It is life itself. What is life? Life is divine, the creation of man by God in His own image. Man himself is innately divine but where is that divinity today? Where has it gone? Where has man gone to and what has he done? How is it that man has not recognized himself as innately divine?."[1]

• "The wondering process began several aeons of time ago, when man first found himself with a body. His experience of matter proved a fascination which was so strong that it obscured his vision. He lost sight of his divine origin and became more and more obsessed with the material and the sensuous pleasures and demands of the body."[1]

• "The world is in turmoil and the vast majority of those souls who have incarnated at this time have chosen to follow the material path and to remain oblivious of the truth. They are not even aware of their own identity.... But all is not lost. The divine spark is always there waiting patiently within every living soul, ready to manifest itself, as the divine principle, once the inner awakening has come."[1]

Four

Changes in Vibration and the Level of Consciousness

Consciousness is a Vibration

According to Sri Sathya Sai Baba the earth has consciousness, just like every human being, and that consciousness is also in motion. As people on earth live more consciously, the greater the collective consciousness of the earth will become the less mistakes will be made on earth. Then the earth will be sanctified. He also said the time for that to occur is nearer than we think.[6] He states that consciousness is a vibration. The consciousness-vibration of minerals is infinitely slower than that of people. The consciousness-vibration of a plant is again much slower than that of an animal, and the consciousness-vibration of an animal is again much slower than that of man.[6] As for the existence of suffering, He says it acts as a sting to make our consciousness optimal. At the time of death consciousness leaves the body, separates itself from the soul, and does not form a unity anymore with the soul. Consciousness of the *Atma* is at the same time the soul.[6] He affirmed "It is of interest to note that the amount of accumulated consciousness never gets lost from many lives, wherever you may incarnate."[6]

Few will Listen, Very Few

These are priceless announcements of Sai Baba, but do we take the time to understand what He is saying? In spite of everything Sai Baba says, we continue to cruise along the labyrinthine ways of our minds and to plod along the mundane pathways of our little lives, paying not much heed to what the Avatar is saying in language so simple even a child can understand. Out of His great love and compassion for errant humanity, He has warned us a thousand times over a period of decades, "But only few will listen, very few", He laments.[1] Why is it that with a Divine core, extensions of the Creator Himself, we fail to heed advice given in our own interest and by no less a Being, in this Iron Age, than the Avatar Himself who has taken birth for the specific purpose of bringing us back to the Godward path from which we have long strayed.

Sai Baba on the proper use of intelligence from His discourse in *Sanatana Sarathi*, May 2005, "It is said that out of all beings, human birth is the rarest. Ants, though tiny in form, are able to acquire food, share it with other ants and also store for the future. It is surprising that human beings are unable to provide food for themselves in spite of their intelligence. In fact, there is no being superior to man in intelligence in this world. But he is unable to make proper use of his intelligence. He conducts himself in an unworthy manner because of his selfishness and self-interest. Humans do not lack anything in their life. Everything is at their disposal. But they lack the discrimination to make proper use of the resources available. In spite of having everything in plenty, they are not able to give up their pettiness. There are many lessons to be learnt even from ants. When an ant bites you, you feel the irritation and immediately try to kill it. But you do not make efforts to kill the evil qualities within yourself. Deep-rooted selfishness and self-interest are making man's intelligence perverted and leading him astray. When you give up selfishness then your power and intelligence will become manifold."[5b]

Sai Baba's sayings are couched in simple language but pregnant with meaning. In many cases He refrains from going into the causative factors or giving details to clarify His statements, but hints at what is in store so that the individual will use his own ability and ingenuity to think and work out for himself what the Avatar is saying, as man has the divine spark within him which he can address at will for information and enlightenment. He said it is not the custom for spiritual masters to spell out every point to the aspirant. He is expected to use effort and free-will to come to the right decision. He is not to sit and wait to be spoon-fed spiritual knowledge. Like all other areas of human endeavour effort is absolutely essential for progress along the spiritual path.

The simplicity of His language may tend to camouflage the profundity and depth of the message He wishes to convey to us. This may be one of the reasons why many of us do not take the teachings seriously and thus make no effort to put them into practice. This, however, is only conjecture. The reality is we turn a deaf ear to what He says simply because the teachings threaten our life-style and were we to put them into practice, our present mode of living would have to be drastically altered, something many of us are not prepared to do; are loathed to carry out or are just not interested in doing. How much easier is it to listen to Him or read His sayings and then put them out of our mind and carry on with our life as usual. The omniscient Sai certainly knows all this. Hence His statement, "Very few will listen, very few".

To elucidate some of His important pronouncements on topics relating to the Golden Age recourse has been taken to the information provided by Braden who goes into great details to explain scientifically the reasons for the Earth Changes we are at present witnessing. For example, Sai Baba simply mentions changes in vibration, values, ideals, and of consciousness and thought patterns, which will govern the society of the New World order. These crisp, terse statements leave us wondering as to their meanings. To understand how these changes will come into actuality, Braden and to a certain extent Wise describe the mechanisms by which these changes will be brought about. The chapters of this book have attempted to elucidate some of this information. Thus a comparison of Sai Baba's statements with those of Braden and Wise complement each other and gives the reader a general over-view of the New Age all three say is imminent.

Marx's View of Consciousness

Contrast Sai Baba's statements on consciousness with what Karl Marx has said on the same subject. According to Marx, the entire aspiration of human beings, be it social, cultural, ethical, political, spiritual or religious, is the result of man's quest for material comforts and materialistic desires. These aspects of society have their basis not in the higher echelons of man's spiritual aspirations, and certainly not in man's consciousness. Marx asserts, "The mode of production of the material means of existence conditions the whole process of social, political and intellectual life. It is not the consciousness of men that determines their existence, on the contrary, it is their social existence that determines their consciousness."[13] Marx will be remembered for having misled a large portion of humanity for several generations, and more grievously so, the intellectual elite of society, who, already turned off from the spiritual way of life, found a new avatar in the person of this erring human being. One consolation is that a large majority of people have already discovered the utter emptiness of Marx's communism; a misfit philosophy created by a misguided person and adopted by those who were searching for a panacea to assuage unfulfilled aspirations and the lack of solace that characterize a mind bereft of divine thoughts.

Change in Vibration

Sai Baba has stated that there will be many changes when the Golden Age dawns. There will be, for example, "a change of vibration."[1] What the Avatar has stated in three simple words, pregnant with meaning, has left us wondering as to the exact implications of His statement. He has said that the Divine does not reveal everything that is going to happen. This is the nature of divinity. In order to throw some light on Sai Baba's statement, we turn to the scientific explanations given by Braden, who has dealt at length with the subject. He states that the basal resonant frequency or the heart beat of earth will increase during the time of the Shift; and that all the cells in the human body will try to catch up with this increased vibration, resulting in an increased vibratory rate of each cell. This change alone will produce a drastic transformation in the make-up of our bodies, changing us into advanced human beings. This increased frequency of the earth is a digitally measurable parameter along with the other parameter which is also digitally measurable, namely, planetary magnetism, which is decreasing to approach Zero Point; these two parameters alone will have a "far-reaching and a profound effect upon human consciousness, human thought and perception specifically and the behaviour of matter in general."[2]

Putting it another way, Braden says, "Each cell of your body is constantly shifting patterns of energy to achieve harmonic resonance to the reference signals of our planet."[2] In other words, each cell of our body is increasing its vibratory rate, seeking to match earth's rhythmic heart beat which has risen to a high pitch. He says this time is experienced as dramatic shifts in the Earth, mirrored as changes in our sleep pattern, relationships, the ability to regulate our immune system and perception of time—a process of initiation that is preparing us to accept tremendous change within our body. This change, he asserts, is happening now as science witnesses events for which there are no reference points of comparison[2]

Changes within the Earth's body affect our bodies because the two are tied in subtle ways, according to Braden. With the increase in earth's frequency, each cell in the physical body—mind—matrix must arrive at this enhanced level eventually. "This is the balance of peace, well-being and union that is historically the goal of the spiritual disciplines."[2] Elaborating on the human-earth relationship Braden says each cell within the physical body of each human living upon earth at present is attempting to align itself to a higher range of information, a zone of frequency operating at a greater pitch than that which has been experienced within the last 2000 years of human history. This zone of high frequency information represents an awareness that each individual is striving to attain.[2] These are the goals spiritual aspirants endeavoured to attain since time immemorial and succeeding only after a life-time or indeed, several life-times of great endeavour. "A physicist may call this period of time an electro-magnetic null zone or a time of Zero Point, an idealized state of consciousness that is the goal of many meditative practices."[2] This is Sai Baba's Golden Age, referred to by others as the Fourth Dimension, The Aquarian Age, and 'The Shift of the Ages', among others.

Changes of Level of Consciousness

Following the Shift or the period which corresponds to Sai Baba's Golden Age, Braden says that human awareness will be experienced consciously on multiple levels simultaneously. This, he describes as a new state of consciousness with no name as yet. What is going to happen is that instead of compartmentalizing our experience into the conventional brain states we know now as alpha, beta, theta, delta, etc. all of these states will be in "simultaneous union providing an awareness of the totality of being."[2] Could this possibly be the supramental state described by Sri Aurobindo which he said is the next state in the progress of spiritual man? Braden says that this is the beginning of the time referred to today as the 'New Age' or by some as a fourth-dimensional experience. With the above information, we are able to see the relationship between vibration and different levels of consciousness.

Continuing on the subject of consciousness, Sai Baba says, "What you are witnessing today is a sad reflection of man in his present state. In spite of appearances and many words, he is not motivated by love, only by personal ambition. All that must go. But do not despair. There are many levels of consciousness in man and what you are witnessing today is just one of them. Other levels will be revealed in the years ahead as man evolves and the Lord's creation will be seen in all its glory."[1]

According to Wise, "The consciousness of the future is already functioning among you, but it has not yet been successfully formulated for societal embodiment. The future is still developing, using the resources of the current unenlightened collective body."[3] And about consciousness Tiwari states thus, "Pure consciousness has no attributes, no modification, and no differentiation. It is beyond the grasp even of intelligence. Because it is spatially limitless, all is dissolved into it, the source of all sources. The consciousness body (in man, the *anadamyakosa*) is beyond the elements. This non-state is often referred to as "the abiding happiness and complete fullness."[4] Continuing His remarks on consciousness, Sai Baba says, "One should be conscious of oneself, of the Self that permeates everything. In-so-far as everything is permeated by Spirit—the *Atma*—a computer is also the Self. A computer, however, will never be conscious of the Self....Lifeless matter can have the task of being useful to man.... Besides, when consciousness is still at an initial stage, it is not even able to know its own housing."[6] He continues: "The difference between a human being and a computer is that the former is conscious of the fact that he is spirit; that he is animated by Spirit and a computer is not."[6] He goes on to say: "It (consciousness) is not a step by step process. Only when consciousness has been fully realized, will everything and everyone be known. Suddenly, in a flash. It is not so that when consciousness is growing, the insight into everything and everyone is growing too.... For the growth of consciousness God divided Himself into Time/Space.... Consciousness is that part of God which wanted to be revealed through creation."[6] Commenting on change in general, Sai Baba says, "Changing is inherent in matter. The moment matter is not subject to change anymore, it would cease to exist.... There is never one moment that something is not different from what it was before, and the speed of these changes, brought about by the person himself or by the other person, is faster than the speed of light."[6]

About the change at the cellular level, Sai Baba says, "Eventually every cell in the body will become filled with God-consciousness. The person who does not think in terms of 'mine' and 'yours' anymore has a divine consciousness. He has liberated himself from the bonds of separation. Only when man has a divine consciousness does he know that there is no difference between him and Me."[6]

Regarding the different levels of consciousness that humans in the New Age will manifest, it is analogous to the differences between members of the same family, all of whom share the same chromosomal constitution and genetic make-up of the parents; so will there be differences in the state of consciousness among humans which will seem to occur at different levels. Since this development will depend on the vibrational level of each individual and the degree to which his body cells have been able to increase their vibrations depending partly on the will and choice of the individual in the attempt to attain resonance with earth's enhanced vibrational state, it is obvious that the eventual level of consciousness each of us will attain will depend on our ability to catch up with Earth's zone of frequency, operating at a high pitch. This will, of course, produce differences in the society, but it is to be hoped that since the entire human race will have attained by that time an enhanced state of awareness characterized by love and compassion, we need not fear the emergence of a new type of class consciousness, since each human being will be accepted at his own level of consciousness and respected and loved as such, love being the keynote of the new society.

A New Race of Humans

There will be a new race of human beings—*Homo sapiens* functioning at a level of consciousness such as he had never attained in thousands and thousands of years, except, by the realized souls such as sages, seers, saints and the rishis or spiritual scientists of Vedic times. With the existence of such a superior race of beings, one would expect the emergence of a superior society out of this transformation. Sai Baba assures us that the changes occurring after the establishment of the Golden Age will be so stupendous that we are not able at this stage of our development to imagine what it would be like. It will be truly the Golden Age, the *Sathya Yuga* or the Age of Truth, the highest and most idealistic of the four *yugas* (ages) of Indian philosophy. The earth will then be populated by a race of humans, motivated by love and compassion, understanding, kindness, tolerance and acceptance, to whose mentality notions of segregation and separation will be alien.

Let us consider this scenario: Imagine the planet devoid of its slaughter-houses, ostrich farms—where the largest bird on earth is reared for the table, chicken farms, ranches, other types of animal farms such as sheep, goats, pigs, etc., prisons, red-light districts, orphanages, old folks' homes, civil and

criminal courts, juvenile delinquency, child and women
battering, sexual abuses of all kinds, corporal punishment,
capital punishment, crimes of all sorts—murder, rape, cruelty
to animals, man's inhumanity to man, separation and
segregation based on caste, creed, colour, race and
nationality; a world devoid of wars, nuclear weapons, missiles
and bombs, nuclear power plants; cheating, stealing, fraud;
corruption in government, commerce, politics, the military,
religion and all other levels of society; the commercialization
of medical services, education, housing; cloning, artificial
insemination, manipulation of the genetic material, as if
playing God, in an attempt to produce custom-made humans;
usurpation of another's property, military take-over by force
of another country etc. etc. The list is endless. Other kinds of
atrocities which will certainly not be countenanced by the
new race of humans could include the misuse of animals in
such questionable activities as cock-fights, bull-fights,
performing animals in circuses or on the street, to provide
cheap entertainment laced with sordid drama and contrived
excitement at the expense of the animal's freedom and dignity.
One wonders at the perverted mentality of such individuals
and winces with shame and disgust to think that we also
belong to the same species.

Sai Baba's Weeding out or "Clear Out"

The establishment of the Golden Age will bring to an end such
atrocities. How? The answer is simple. Where will be the
humans with such depraved mentalities, even to think of
much less to perpetuate such evil and cruel acts? Since the
"clear out" as Sai Baba describes it, will have already taken
place before the onset of the Golden Age, with millions and
probably, billions of us making an unceremonious exit from
the planet either during catastrophic disasters such as
earthquakes, tsunamis, the "wave" and "storm" also referred
to by Baba, flooding, volcanic eruptions and other natural

Sri Sathya Sai Baba in the *Abhaya hasta pose*. The hand indicating 'no fear'.

disasters due to the imbalance of Nature, Earth's population will have decreased to a mere fraction of what it is at present. Only those who deserve to survive will be the occupants of the planet. Some reports predict a reduction to 20 per cent of the population, leaving the planet with a mere 1.5 billion souls to usher in the Golden Age. The other factor contributing to Sai Baba's 'weeding out' could possibly be the inability of some of us to get into resonance with the earth's high-pitched frequency. We shall simply not be able to survive under the new conditions of increased vibratory rates, were we to fail to increase the vibration of our cells. As Sai Baba has said, we would fall by the wayside and perish.

In His discussion in *Sanatana Sarathi*, May 2005 issue, Sai Baba has advised students to make certain changes in their lives and to better themselves. This advice can be taken by all of us, students or not. "Students today read all sorts of books and fill their heads with useless information. There is little use in studying a *Pustaka* (a book) if the *Mastaka* (head) is filled with rubbish. Students should acquire the knowledge which will help them to lead a noble life and save them from the cycle of birth and death. They should acquire that knowledge which will make them immortal. Modern students have become proficient in bookish knowledge. They have the intelligence to answer any question from text-books. But they are not making efforts to translate their bookish knowledge into practical knowledge."[5b] Continuing He says, "The knowledge one acquires should be utilized for the benefit of society. You should utilize your wealth and knowledge not for selfish purposes, but for the welfare of others. God has given you the human body not merely to eat, sleep and enjoy worldly pleasures... (the human body is meant to do good to others). Of what use is your education and intelligence if society is not benefited from them? Presently, man is making new discoveries and inventions but till this day he has not really understood the purpose of human birth.... It is only by grace of God that man acquires intelligence, knowledge and wealth. Man should understand this and lead a sacred and divine life.... But man is acting contrary to it and thereby ruining himself. Animals like bulls and buffaloes render service to man in a number of ways. It is unfortunate that man is not able to understand even such a simple tning...one can attain divinity only by serving society."[5b]

The survivors who will be in harmony with earth's resonance will wonder how it was possible for a man to so enrage a bull in an enclosed arena, and to be considered heroic for having killed the animal. The 'valiant' toreador will be thus consigned to oblivion, along with cow-boys and their wide-open spaces—the ranches—rearing cattle by the thousands for slaughter, to supply tons of beef for human consumption. They will be the mythological figures of the New Age. Such a world will be nothing less than Utopia, the world visualized by dreamers of the 20th century as something never to materialize, the world described by Bahaullah of the Bahais—one world, one government, one people, a universal faith; and the world of Sri Sathya Sai Baba, described in His now famous pronouncement:

There is only one caste, the caste of humanity.
There is only one religion, the religion of love.
There is only one language, the language of the heart.
There is only one God and He is omnipresent.

The rapid decrease in planetary magnetics, *pari passu* with Earth's ability to sustain higher harmonics of her base pulse marks the beginning of a new paradigm in conscious human awareness.[2] The "intensity of Earth's magnetic field is dropping—38 per cent lower than it was 2000 years ago."[2] According to Braden, "Now as the intensity of the fields decrease, the lag-time between a thought and the realization of that thought is decreasing proportionally."[2] In other words, when the magnetic fields decrease, the veil between thinking and the crystallization of thought is lifted, so that the gap between a thought and the consequence of that thought becomes decreased. Magnetism creates a barrier, as it were as "dense magnetics lock in emotional and mental patterns from generation to generation."[2] With lessening of the magnetic fields, the 'lock-in' mechanism loosens up, allowing us to attain easier access to higher states. Braden states that human experience is and has always been intimately tied to the strength or density of the magnetic fields surrounding earth; so that decrease in planetary magnetism seen today has a profound effect on all life.[2] To reiterate one such effect is the relationship of thoughts and their consequence. As the density of magnetics decreases, the barrier between thought and its materialization becomes less, so that a thought may be realized more quickly than heretofore. It is possible that as the fields decrease further and interference of magnetism becomes still less we may experience nearly instantaneous consequences of our thoughts.

Since no privilege comes without its attendant responsibility, we are expected to constantly monitor our thoughts. The onus is on us to avoid altogether stray, negative thoughts, particularly those that can cause harm both to ourselves and to others. This has been the teaching for millennia by the spiritual masters of all religions, and has been the stumbling block of the spiritual aspirant. Even Arjuna on the battlefield of Kurukshetra, five thousand years ago, complained to Sri Krishna that it was as difficult to control the mind as the wind. This controlling of thoughts is a great responsibility and it's to be hoped that with the higher vibrational velocity of our cells allowing us to direct our will "consciously toward the life parameters of choice"[2], we would automatically choose to think rationally, positively and without fear. Through a realignment of two digitally measurable fundamental parameters, those of planetary magnetism and planetary frequency, they have a far-reaching and profound impact upon human consciousness, human thought and perception, specifically and the behaviour of matter in general... Each parameter has a dramatic yet subtle effect upon the cellular body, human consciousness, and the manner in which that consciousness expresses itself.... The relationship between Earth, the planetary magnetic fields and cellular function of the body is a key component to the understanding of the conscious evolution and the process of the Shift.[2]

Consciousness and Future Calamities

Regarding the role of consciousness in relation to future calamities Sai Baba has this to say: "Today as I told you, the evil is so widespread that humanity itself would be destroyed in a nuclear holocaust in the event of a world war. It is to prevent such a catastrophe that the Avatar has come to raise human consciousness above the existing syndrome of anger, hate, violence and war and save the world from disaster. This can be achieved only by the establishment of the brotherhood of mankind through the Vedas, the Shastras, and all religions with their evangel of dharma to liberate the human race from the chains of karma (the cycle of birth and death)."[7] Sai Baba has told us that He has not come to establish a new religion or to announce anything new; nor has He come to gather around Him devotees or disciples or to make converts. He has come, He said, to remind us of the Shastras and the Upanishads and all the other religions and to show us that they all say the same thing. He has come to remind us of the one God from whom we have taken our origin, and that we are all one possessing the same Divine spark with no separation between us; to remind us that we are 'children of immortality' as the Vedas affirm; He has come to tell us of God as love; that there is only one caste— humanity; only one religion—love; only one language, that of the heart and only one God who is omnipresent.

Regarding consciousness, Wise says: "Until your consciousness is collectively coherent, however, the caterpillar will try to fight you off, defending its survival, as if you were a cancer."[3] Sai Baba affirms that birds, beasts, and trees have not deviated from their nature; they are still holding it valid. Man alone has disfigured it, in his crude attempt to improve upon it. Thus He says that the Avatar has to come as a man among men, and move as a friend, well-wisher, kinsman, guide, teacher, healer and participant among men. He has come to restore righteousness. And so when man follows righteousness, He is pleased and content. About dying consciously He says: "...the more completely we experience things, the more completely we go towards death...until finally we die consciously... until life and death have become one process of Being... until no distinction is made anymore between life and death" And commenting on karma, He says: "I take karma away when the individual is open to my Grace, when his consciousness is in tune with mine"[6], and that all things that take place in a lifetime are valuable lessons to thus arrive at Sai consciousness which is the same as God consciousness.

Sai Baba states thus, "The Lord said, 'Let there be light.' and there was light. Let that light shine through you so that you yourself become a beacon of light and rise to the highest level of consciousness where you and God are One. That is God consciousness."[1]

Five

Change of Values, Ideals and Thought Patterns

The Keynote is Change

About changes that will take place when the Golden Age dawns, Baba says, "Eventually the world will change, but only when love and light replace the darkness and ignorance. All of you can play a part in bringing about the change that is so necessary and the opportunity lies in front of you at this moment."[1] He continues to describe these changes. "The time will come when the light will spread with increasing intensity throughout the world. It will herald the time of the great awakening, a new era, a new beginning, a time when man becomes aware of the existence of God and the true nature of each individual soul. Man will also realize his own individuality and the reality that there is only the One, the divine Creator, the totality. Changes lie ahead, God's plan is perfect and those who are ready will play their own part in these plans."[1]

Sai Baba reiterates the warnings that without effort liberation cannot be guaranteed. Apart from effort, there should be an irreversible commitment to the spiritual path leaving behind forever the life of illusion with all its worldly desires, attachments and false values. So long as desire remains, you cannot firmly establish your feet on the spiritual path.[1] He affirms that although there is chaos everywhere, fighting, scheming, hatred, evil, with the negative emotions in the ascendant, eventually the change will come.... "Do not delay action" He warns us "to put right your own life-style and to change it to the way of God. There is no other way... You must learn to give up attachment, to forget about self, to conquer the ego, to lose all sense of desire and then you will have prepared yourself for the future.... The storm is not yet over and the process of change will continue as a new awakening comes to the world."[1]

Human Values

Regarding human values He said that if they could take root in the educational system, the emerging products from our institutions will have the following attributes: They will want peace with justice in a world that acknowledges the rule of law and in which no nation or individual need live in fear; they will want freedom, not being born to have someone's foot over their necks or hand over their mouths as also freedom at home and in the world; they will want the dignity and work of every individual to be recognized and safe-guarded, they will subscribe strongly for the tenets of equality before the law and equality of opportunity for all.[7]

According to Wise, during the transitional stage—a period of subtle, conceptual and energetic change—awareness will expand, values will organize and there will be amplitudes of consciousness. She says, "As the transformational process progresses, fewer people will hold as reality the ideas and beliefs that currently govern your civilization. When new models emerge people will feel safe, acknowledging that what they have always called reality is just one set of choices from a menu of possibilities,"[3] again echoing what Sai Baba describes as changes in values, ideals and patterns of thought. According to Braden "Lower magnetic fields provide the opportunity for change through the rapid manifestation of thought and feeling.... Ancient traditions remind us that we are living a cycle of change that began nearly 200,000 years ago—'The Shift of the Ages'. You are part of that change." He asserts that transcending religion, science and mystic traditions, this time is experienced as dramatic shifts in the Earth mirrored as changes in our sleep pattern, immune system, relationships and perception of time. He continues, "Individually we experience each day as an opportunity to affirm life" and that together we are bringing into being a new wisdom in the process.

Change of Thought Patterns

About the effect of a lesser magnetic field and higher vibratory rate on us Braden says, "It provides the opportunity to more easily change the patterns that can determine how and why we love, fear, judge, feel, need and hurt.... The world that you have always known, your world, is changing very rapidly. The structural guidelines that determine the way you think, perceive and act toward yourself and others are changing, not only around you. They are changing within you."[2]

We have no option but to conclude from the opinions expressed above—both secular and spiritual—that our present world is going to become topsy-turvy and that we shall have to restructure our lives to be able to survive and to deal with the drastic changes that are about to take place. The one word being emphasized here is 'change'. Braden says that our restructuring and realignment result in profound effects, radical shifting of thought, feeling and emotion. He states that "human experience is and has always been intimately tied to the strength or density of the magnetic field surrounding earth" and so "the decrease in planetary magnetism seen today has a profound effect on all life", and that "Living in this time of transition is where we have the greatest opportunity to demonstrate our strength, wisdom and compassion as we live our mastery of two simultaneous worlds in the presence of one another."[2]

Again, the onus is on us to change ourselves as Sathya Sai Baba repeatedly exhorts us to do—to change our life-style, to eschew the attractions of the material world; to decrease our desires, to show compassion to others, to be guided by the voice of our conscience—the divine spark within us; to follow the pathway and the teachings our spiritual masters have laid down for us from time immemorial; to live above the confusion we see around us so as not to become embroiled in the chaos, to always remember why we were given birth, to keep the goal of life always in mind—that birth in a human body is something very precious that even the gods desire, and that the goal of life is to return to the Source from which we took our origin.

About thoughts Sai Baba has said that if you want to have good thoughts, you must resort to the spiritual path. The starting point for the spiritual is Satsung, holy company, and that thoughts are contagious. He said that if we want to reach the ultimate truth of our being and be immersed in the bliss of the Atmic principle we need to develop complete control over our desires. The moment any thought arises, we should enquire into the nature of the thought. We should ask ourselves: "Is this thought desirable or is it harmful for my spiritual progress"; and also that bad thoughts should not remain in the mind.[6] He has said that faster than light is thought. Thoughts are as powerful as actions and that thinking good thoughts is better than thinking bad thoughts. Not thinking unless there is a necessity for it is better still. He emphasizes that thinking about others without being asked, whether they are good thoughts or bad, carries risk. Even if the thoughts are good, such a thought reaches the other person faster than light and it will always change him; since we do not understand what a good thought really is it is better to desist sending even a good thought, since such a thought is always subjective. The only kind of thought which should be sent disinterestedly and objectively to another person is that of light. Send light, love and peace to the other person. With it you send it into the cosmos where it will live eternally, Transform every thought about the other person through light.[6] He goes on to say that also faster than light is the transformation process, which is, in fact, an extension of the previous process referred to above. Everything another person picks up consciously or unconsciously, transforms him.... This transformation takes place at the same moment as the thought towards the other person, as the intention of a certain action towards the other person and transforms that person through a crystallizing out of that fact which goes infinitely faster than the speed of light. It takes place as it were at the same moment.[6]

Sai Baba says that everything we think and do changes the earth, for example, every blade of grass that is picked gives the earth another look; each step that is made, each sentence that is written, and therefore, each thought that is thought.

He also said, "Everything is related. The evil thoughts of one man are not confined to himself, but they spread out into the universe, just like a virus. However, those dark clouds can be cleared away in the course of time if and when positive loving thoughts begin to flow."[1] This process of everlasting change implies the underlying unity which it is all about— that is, the *Atma* which never changes, which is unchangeable.[6] Continuing on the subject of change, He says that change is inherent in matter. The moment matter is not subject to change anymore, it would cease to exist. Just as the molecules and atoms are always in motion, so do the energetic processes of thought and transformation and their attendant metamorphosis. There is never one moment that something is not different from what it was before and the speed of these changes brought about by the person himself or by the other person is faster than the speed of light.[6] About the light we may send to others, He said that this is the light of the Self which we can send through our thoughts and which gives cause for transformation in the other person; it travels through the thought-process which is faster than the speed of light as we have seen—in combination with the process of metamorphosis. The inner light, the light of the *Atma*, is faster than light on earth because this light-source is of divine origin and God is light and is beyond the light. The light is from God. The light of the *Atma* is *Atma*, is God. In sending light to the other person we are sending God to him and as he is also God, the light reaches him in the same moment that it is sent. Bad thoughts also reach him in the same way, but they obstruct the divinizing process of both he who receives and he who is the sender.[6]

Change of Ideals

About the place of ideals in life, Sai Baba insists that we should live not for the sake of *Annam* (food) but for the sake of *Adarsham* (ideals). Ideals are always supreme and everlasting. If one person becomes an ideal he can influence the lives of many others for the better. To lead an ideal life, it is essential to have love of the nation and love of the spirit (Atma) as well as love and respect for parents.... Parents as well as teachers should serve as ideal examples for students.[7] Wise seems to be saying the same thing, in her own way: "Only you can invent your future integrity. In changing yourself you create a fertile environment within which others can grow and change.... When you who embody and express the values of the future come together to effect a common purpose, you will be irresistible... Humanity and its reality will change form without dying."[3] Braden describes some of the changes that are expected to take place as the Shift is completed. He said that individuals will experience tremendous difficult challenges as they draw into their lives worst fears to be balanced and healed. The fears will be unique to each as a result of individual experience. For some it may be loss of finance, loss of spouse or mate, or loss of health etc.... Further he says that old patterns lose their meaning without the blueprints of the structures they have been based upon; that there would be a perceived increase in the passage of time. Events may feel as if they are speeding up due to the body's attempt to match the increasing rapid pulsations of earth's fundamental vibration. He also states that quicker vibration in a field of lower magnetism allows access to our emotion of unresolved experience stored within our bodies, and that "Our restructuring and realignment result in profound effects, radical shifts of thought feeling and emotion". He says that those parameters of frequency and planetary magnetics alone have a far-reaching and profound impact upon human consciousness, human thought and perception specially, and the behaviour of matter in general. The Shift marks the closing of the current cycle of conscious evolution. "Though the Shift to Zero Point is a rare event by any standards, please remember that it is part of a very natural process, good, healthy, and vital to conscious human evolution."[2]

Sai Baba says our pain is His pain, even the pain of animals and that He also answers the call of animals in trouble. What a colossal burden He has to bear willingly undertaken for the sake of the Creation for which He is responsible. Sri Aurobindo describes in his famous epic poem 'Savitri' the heavy task of the world-redeemer. He says that the world itself becomes his adversary and that his enemies are the very beings he came to save. Man's cruelty to man and also to animals has continued for millemia and has caused much pain to all right-thinking people who have had to bear this anguish for untold centuries, knowing that there was no way to terminate it. This sort of behaviour will have to change as it will be incompatible with the Golden Age. Mankind has lost its human values of truth, righteousness, love, peace and non-violence, which are the basis of Sai Baba's teachings, so he can resort with impunity to any form of cruelty to any form of life, be it human, animal or plant, all of which possess consciousness, be it at different levels, as described in Chapter Four.

Man's Inhumanity to Animals

A current example of man's cruelty to animals can be seen almost anywhere in this country. Just think of the fate of old cows who have gone dry and are no longer of use as money-makers to their owners, after having produced milk for all of their productive lives. Those aged cows who need rest after prolonged years of faithful service and who need food to remain healthy in their last days on earth, are assembled, placed in rows, and made to march to their death along the roads whether in grilling heat, severe cold, or pouring rain, ending up in the abattoirs several kilometres away. To see such animals quietly wending their way, in perfect disciplined formation, showing no resistance, reaction or restlessness whatever and with their passive bovine features, ribs sticking out, a silent indication of having been starved since they no longer deserved a square meal, walking innocently to their death in complete silence, can be a most painful experience which nothing can assuage, since nothing can be done to stop this form of barbarism. One such sight was witnessed as we drove down the mountain road one day, and the writer's foster son who was driving, said to her, "Please bless those cows, Ma". There was too much fullness in the heart to allow an audible reply. As we continued driving downwards to the plains those poor doomed creatures were plodding upwards to their death.

Another recent example of man's cruelty to animals. This happened in Newfoundland, Canada, in March. *The Guardian*, 2005, described the gruesome situation as a 'carnage' on a scale the frozen vastness of the ice floes of Newfoundland have not seen for more than fifty years. The barbaric act begins about two weeks after the seal pups are born and their fur changes from white to grey, having been abandoned by their mothers after two weeks of being fed. At this stage they are unable to swim and when the ice melts they fall into the water and beat it with their flippers to keep afloat. Before this happens they present an easy target for seal hunters, as they have no means of escape. The carnage started when from seventy boats, hundreds of seal hunters disembarked on to the ice. The harvest consisted of 15,000 harp seal pups, most less than six weeks old, all clubbed to death and skinned to provide coats, hats, handbags and other accessories for the European fashion market. An observer from the U.K. office of the International Fund for Animal Welfare, stated that the seals were clubbed, turned over, and sliced down the middle to remove the skin. Previous tests had shown that 42 per cent were still conscious when skinned. The Canadian Government has put forward the argument that the action will protect fish stocks and bring in much needed revenue and employment!

Another recent report, this time emanating from London, describes the highly expensive specially processed beef from Kobe, where the cows are given beer to drink, massaged and allowed to listen to sweet music in order to produce the tender succulent beef the world market requires at a price only the more affluent can afford at the rate of four English pounds per bite. How much more does man desire to satisfy his bizarre taste both physical and aesthetic. A pity that it is mainly the animal kingdom that is exploited to achieve his ends. Isn't it obvious even to the most unaware among us that such mentalities as described in the three foregoing examples relating to man's cruelty to animals will be out of place in the Golden Age and will somehow, someway have to be removed? Will such individuals be able to change their mentality before the New Age dawns? It is in circumstances such as these that the utter lack of human values reveals man's diabolic nature.

Man's Plunder of Nature

Nature has silently borne man's misuse and abuse, not only of the creatures that walk, live and repose on her bosom, but also of her five elements. All the elements for survival—earth, air and water—have been so polluted with dangerous pesticides and poisonous chemicals among other hazardous substances, it is amazing so many of us can still move, live and have our being, enjoying relatively good health. Many of the diseases today are man-made, and because of his greed to possess and enjoy more and more of the material benefits denied to the majority of humans, he continues to ravish and despoil Nature, rapaciously exploiting her rich, abundant and seemingly inexhaustible resources. It is such acts by human beings that have brought Nature to her present state of unrest, imbalance and lack of equilibrium. Sai Baba has said that Earth has consciousness, just like human beings. Many species have gone the way of the dodo mainly because of man's manipulation of Nature's resources to suit himself by encroaching on the natural habitat of animals, reducing their fodder and water sources and limiting their space, in the name of progress and development; in the process producing permanent, incalculable and irreversible damage to the eco-system. At the time of India's independence there were at least 30,000 tigers in the wild if the official estimate of tigers in the wild is to be believed. This figure has dropped drastically to 3,500, again causing much disbelief in the minds of the citizens that the figure may be fictitious. It is possible that the tigers in India have as good as disappeared. Who is to tell us the truth? The animals are killed for their bones, teeth, skin, fat and even their genitals. Only recently newspaper reports published photographs of the forest officials setting fire to hundreds of tiger skins as a warning to poachers to stop their illegal and nefarious activities in the forests of India.

Nature has tolerated these atrocities and acts of barbarism for two to three hundred years. Her time, however, has come and indications are now becoming apparent of her long pent-up unease and pain, in the form of earthquakes, tidal waves, volcanic eruptions, storms, floods, droughts and famines. Earth certainly has consciousness, and that consciousness is also in motion, as Sai Baba has told us. Nature therefore, has the ability to teach us a lesson. She has started the process, the Indonesian earthquake being the first, recent and memorable example. Many more are in the pipeline according to the geoscientists, and it will be foolhardy for us to ignore her warnings. The truth of the matter, is, however, from all indications out there, that man does not seem to be listening. A recent example of the practice of discrimination, the result of a feeling of separatism, was demonstrated by the survivors of the Sumatra tsunami that recently devastated a large part of the southern coasts of India, leaving thousands dead, and many more injured, hungry, naked and homeless. Relief materials, immediately dispatched by the Government of India, non-governmental and private organizations were publicly and without caring for others' feelings received and distributed by the survivors, only to those belonging to their own religion, sect or community. Even among the fisherfolk, the hardest hit by the tsunami, relief supplies were distributed according to caste distinction. Even in the midst of a great calamity, this feeling of separatism could not be overcome.

This only confirms the feeling that man has not learned the lesson in spite of Nature's repeated warnings. Thus, he continues to misuse her, leaving her disrobed and despoiled, inflicting wounds on her body, removing her flesh and draining her blood. He has made cavernous spaces deep into her bowels, has drilled huge holes into the depth of her bosom, and this for centuries, without experiencing even a twinge of remorse. How long one wonders, can anything with even an iota of consciousness withstand such unabated abuse. The reason for man's rapacious destruction of Nature seems to stem from his complete unawareness that the Earth is a living entity. She gives birth to trees and forests by sustaining them with the food, water, air, and heat they need for healthy growth. Her very soil supplies the nutrients required for the seed to swell, burst and shoot upwards, pushing its way through her soil to gain access to air and sunlight essential for plant growth and development. Yet man has been heard repeatedly boasting that Nature is meant to be conquered and harnessed to meet his requirements. Somewhat like the same feeling he has when getting to the top of Mount Everest. In his arrogance he acclaims that he has 'conquered' Mount Everest—this massive, majestic mountain—home to yogis, mystics, saints and sages, that keeps standing in all its grandeur and regal splendour and that has withstood the ravages of time and the onslaught of catastrophic changes, completely indifferent to the behaviour of a few men, for having managed at the risk of their lives to reach the top.

The same attitude, with devastating consequences, is shown towards the Earth. Above all this, the main reason for his maltreatment of Nature is the feeling that Nature is separate from him. This feeling of separation stems from his belief that there is no affinity between him and the Earth, little realizing that there are closer links than he suspects. He is closely linked to earth's electromagnetism in two important ways—her magnetism allows him to pursue thought to its rational end and to store memory, her resonant frequency amplitude determines the vibratory rate of his body cells and allows them to be in resonance with her to ensure his survival. Her food sheath which depends on soil and water corresponds to the gross body or food sheath of the human being. When one is affected the other is inevitably affected. In so many ways we are linked to Nature and by plundering her we are only injuring ourselves. Unfortunately, it is this feeling of separation that allows man to continue his destruction of the Earth without a tinge of regret. This calls for a change in man's pattern of thought.

Nature's Backlash

To restore her balance and to regain her equilibrium Nature has no alternative but to churn her soil and shake herself to fill up the gaping holes man has created by his greed for enrichment at the cost of the environment. To put things back in place Nature will have to shift her seismic plates, both on land and sea, thereby producing earthquakes, tsunamis, and tidal waves of unheard severity, some of which are already occurring. At the present time no week passes by without the report of a few earthquakes of varying magnitudes somewhere on the globe, the most recent being in South Japan with a magnitude of 7 on the Richter Scale.

Apart from the foregoing, man has polluted the air which he as much as animals and plants need for survival on the planet. His factories numbering possibly tens of thousands all over the globe, belching black smoke and poisonous fumes, have so polluted the atmosphere that many plants unable to survive in such unnatural conditions have become extinct. Adding to the pollution are the contaminated effluents from industrial plants all over the world. With this constant heavy pollution from his industrial activities man has contaminated Earth's streams, rivers, ponds, lakes, seas and oceans adding to the hazards of human life which is completely dependent on water for survival, simultaneously posing a threat to marine life, many varieties of which have become unsuitable as a source of food. Some developed countries have been obliged to stop fishing in their own contaminated waters and to import sea-food from countries whose waters have so far remained relatively unspoiled.

The soil of the earth has also become polluted due to the enormous amount of pesticides, poisonous solvents and other harmful chemicals sprayed carelessly and wantonly over field and farm, adding to the already polluted water by run-off from contaminated soil and water during the rains.

Consequently, the soil has become unfit for growing uncontaminated food so essential for healthy living. To compensate for this, private homes, societies and various organizations have started producing food grown organically, but at greater cost so that only the well-to-do can afford it. It is not in vain that Sai Baba calls for a change in values, ideals and thought patterns.

What is the Remedy?

Until man becomes aware that we are one with Nature and that man, the universe and the Creator are one inseparable unit, his greed will propel him to continue the devastation that has already reached the point of no return. Until we are able to effect a complete change in our values, attitudes, ideals and patterns of thought, can we even hope to see the light appearing on the horizon? Sai Baba has said that the light is beginning to shine, though only as chinks all over the world, and that it will increase to such an intensity when the Golden Age dawns that some will be so blinded by it that they will not be able to survive. But all is not lost. Nature will come to our rescue, although some among us will consider her actions as calamitous. She holds the trump cards and as close to her chest as possible so that man does not know what to expect. We cannot accuse her of taking pre-emptive action, because she has given us repeated warnings over the centuries. Her remedies? As many as can put right the damage caused by man's senseless actions: Earthquakes of greater magnitudes to break up the soil and turn it over, much like the farmer does before sowing his seeds. In this manner Nature will deposit deep within her bosom the polluted and contaminated soil, including nuclear wastes, allowing fresh, clean fragrant soil to be brought to the surface, thus providing new earth to the inhabitants of the new era. An additional correction to the damage the massive amount of artificially created substances have caused to the eco-system, has been described by Braden, in his description of Earth's healing, "Materials and compounds that are born of and affirm life, experience graceful transition. Frequency filters ensure the removal of toxic, inharmonic compounds as well as the thought process that has allowed them within the conscious matrix. Products of anything other than Earth's resonant materials (substances that have been forced into unnatural combinations under artificial conditions) may disassociate, as the parameters allowing the substances no longer exist."[2]

Braden is saying that artificially produced materials that had been manufactured under the conditions obtaining during the old pre-Shift world, such as temperature, pressure, humidity and other conditions can no longer hold together and will undergo self-destruction as they would not be able to exist under the changed conditions of the new world order. Braden hints that even the mentalities who are responsible for conceiving such substances dangerous to biological life will also share the same fate—they would also be removed. This brings to mind Sai Baba's warning that those of us who cannot or will not change our thought patterns and fall in line with the philosophy of the new world order will perish and vanish from the face of the earth.

To continue with the remedies at Nature's disposal, we can visualize tidal waves and tsunamis of such heights like gigantic walls moving at the speed of a jet engine along the ocean floor and crashing on the coasts of many countries, destroying everything in their path and reaching areas much further inland to reduce to debris unwanted structures and to sweep and wash away polluted areas leaving the beaches clean and golden as Nature intended them to be; also destroying illegal and other encroachments near the water's edge; fierce winds, storms, hurricanes, cyclones, typhoons, tornadoes and what not to destroy over-crowded cities, and to restore the balance, so characteristic of Nature. High rise buildings, in large cities, like sitting ducks, easy targets for the wrath of mega tsunamis, storms and earthquakes, will rumble, tumble, crumble and collapse like a pack of cards, removing for all time those unaesthetic, unsightly and disfiguring structures that only a warped mentality could have visualized and materialized.

Other remedies include flooding, heavy rains, heavy snowfalls, unusual weather patterns causing great disturbance to all life forms, famine and devastation of crops, with heavy loss of life of human and animals, along with much that man holds dear.

Man's Continued Indifference

But man continues with his developmental activities, regardless of the dangers awaiting him, as he relentlessly pursues his search for oil, gas, coal, iron, water, minerals, gems, gold and other earth resources which he has become entirely dependent on for the survival of 'civilized' living. These unceasing attacks on Nature will have disastrous consequences and we shall all have to suffer, and perhaps, give up our lives, since we are an integral part of the current collective consciousness and shall have to pay the price, regardless of our guiltlessness. Nothing can delay or stop the catastrophic changes awaiting us. Only those who have eyes to see will appreciate the impending cataclysmic events as a process to heal the earth. At this stage it is too late to turn the tide in our favour, since only 25 per cent or so of humanity is aware of what is actually happening. To hope that the remaining 75 per cent will be able to wake up during the few years left to us, will be to indulge in wishful thinking. A refreshing thought, perhaps, is that in the New Age, individuals with the mentalities that have brought us to this current state of universal ruin will form no part of the new world order.

In our three-dimensional world, since nothing goes on for ever and there is always an end to everything, even at the present time, we can see the changing of the old order yielding place to the new. Since the greater proportion of mankind has not changed to meet the current demands for survival, there will be no turning back on the part of Nature. Her consciousness has been awakened, and the consequences will be fatal for mankind. We shall collectively have to bear the brunt of the dangers looming ahead in the form of cataclysmic events and catastrophic changes. The process has begun; it will continue. Seismologists from Ulster University in Britain state that a major earthquake may soon strike the western coast of Sumatra as a result of the quake of December 26, 2004. Nature is on the march to get rid of her imbalance due to the removal of her varied materials and she will not stop unless and until this imbalance has been removed. It is Nature's characteristic to be in a state of balance, otherwise she will behave erratically, as we are presently witnessing. Is there any material thing man uses today that has not been taken from Nature's storehouse of resources either by overt or covert means? Even the artificially produced articles and materials are made from her elements. These synthetic products are in such abundance today that they have become a civil nuisance, and human society is still grappling with the problem of disposal of tons of garbage resulting from synthetic wastes. At the time of writing there is still no practical solution in sight.

The Avatar succinctly sums up the problem in His own inimitable way. Sri Sathya Sai Baba says that Nature is God's vesture, and that the universe is the university of man. Therefore man should treat Nature with reverence; and that he has no right to talk of conquering Nature or exploiting the forces of Nature. He said that man must proceed to visualize in Nature its God.

Six

Choice and Free-Will

Sai Baba and Free-Will

Sai Baba has said that God endowed man with free-will. He also said that man attributes everything he accomplishes in his life to his free-will and other endowments bestowed by the Creator, conveniently forgetting that the Creator was involved in the process. Due to his gross ignorance and inflated ego which blind him to the realization that without the gift of free-will by the Creator Himself in the first place, he could not accomplish what he flaunts as due to his own puny efforts.

Man fails to understand that although he is responsible to God for his free-will, the Creator has given him full independence to use that free-will as he chooses to. In no way will the Creator interfere with his plans, decisions and independent thoughts in the process of utilizing this free-will. Somewhat like the computer scientist, having programmed the computer to carry out certain functions, the scientist leaves the instrument alone to do its programmed duty. Interfering at this stage will only confuse the machine and would be an exercise in futility. Hence the Creator will not impose His will on us for a similar reason. He leaves us alone, but watches our every move or thought, word, and action, becoming merely a Witness to our activities. If we fail in our attempts, He will still leave us alone to try again and again, until eventually we accomplish the task. It is at this point that man thinks he is acting according to his own impulses and intelligence, since he is unaware of the silent witness. However, if he fails and calls on God, He immediately comes to his rescue and the work is accomplished successfully.

Concerning this matter of free-will, Sai Baba says, "People believe that every man has a free-will. It is an entirely wrong belief. They imagine that it is because of man's will, determination, *sadhana* (spiritual discipline) and effort that he is able to achieve success. This is all due to aberrations of their *ahamkara* (ego) and the reflection of their false sense of doership."[7] Again, He says, "What are thoughts; they are the creative force within man, and represent the free-will given to man by God. Life should be full of joy, and it will be if you live in complete harmony with God."[7] Elaborating on the subject of free-will, Sai Baba says man has free-will. Governments, Board of Directors etc. also have free-will, making plans and working them out belongs to a person's free-will. As long as the things which are being worked out are not contrary to the Divine plan, the people have their relative freedom to work out plans as they think fit. This concerns comparatively small choices, with comparatively small consequences, even though they may seem very great to the person concerned. He continues to explain why He interferes individually in some cases, "I know the final outcome. I could know the comparatively less important details, if I focus on them, but since I don't, you could say that I don't know them. Or rather, I so choose, because I choose to leave it up to a person to make his own decision. Only when things threaten to go totally wrong, and only if there are no other possibilities of solving the problem, do I interfere."[6]

It seems from what Sai Baba said, that even though man does not call on God for help when things go wrong, He comes to his rescue anyway, and sets things right, if there is the possibility of failure ending up in a totally wrong manner.

This exemplifies the compassion and love He has for us, and which so many take for granted; so many of us are entirely unaware of His concern and caring, thinking that it is by our own efforts that the work succeeded.

Braden approaches the subject by applying it to the changes that will occur in future. He mentions the use of free-will and choice with respect to enhancing the frequency of each human cell, utilizing the state of Zero-Point or 'null-magnetic fields' where the individuals have "nearly direct access to themselves as pure information without the interference patterns of judgment, fear, ego or the buffers of lag-time between thought and the consequence of a thought. With that access comes the opportunity of cellular and core level changes directed through the will of the individual consciously toward the life parameters of choice."[2] Regarding the actions of ancient spiritual aspirants, he says that as the individual chose to think and feel differently, he or she was able to consciously alter the frequency of each cell of the mind, body and spirit complex.[2] Further, on the same theme of choice, he states, "The Shift mirrors our choice of life"; and again about the importance of choice, he says, "Each time we have an experience, there are thoughts and feelings associated with that experience. They are part of us and can never be forgotten or erased. As we interpret those experiences through the lens of our life-tools, we make a determination as to how that experience will be stored. To the degree that we have chosen to place the energy of each experience in its place of balance, to that degree do we become a being of balance."[2]

From Braden's statements we see the great importance of what the ancients called 'The Shift of the Ages' referring to the reversal of earth's magnetic poles, and the increase in earth's base frequency or the pulse or heart beat of Earth. We may recall here that the enhanced frequency has an effect on our cells since we are inextricably linked with Nature both through her magnetic field as well as her frequency. Each cell of each human body and indeed, of all biological life on earth will have to respond to the earth's increased heart rate; our cells will be automatically activated to increase their vibration rate to bring them into resonance with earth's high pitch frequency. As we live our lives according to higher human values, we further increase this rate, and as stated by Braden, we can choose to let this happen by thinking and feeling differently as did the ancients; and by consciously directing through our will we can make the appropriate cellular changes. He asserts that we should look on the Shift not as death and endings, but as a choice to a new way of life. We conclude from this that the changes that will take place on earth will be a renewal of the earth which has been plundered by man's greed and his feeling of being a separate entity from Nature. She will be renewed and resuscitated by the catastrophic changes which are supposed to occur some time before the year 2012. Braden emphasizes the point that we should put the experiences of our everyday life which leave a lasting and indelible impression on our minds and can never be forgotten, in such a place of balance, within the body/mind/spirit matrix so that we become a being of balance.[2]

Free-will in Making our Choice

Although Earth Changes in electromagnetism will take place regardless of what we do and will automatically influence us, because of our direct linkage to Earth, and the changes taking place within her, we are also individually responsible for transforming ourselves to become synchronous with the changes occurring. This effort on our part is absolutely essential if we wish to remain on earth in our present embodied state. Those of us unable or unwilling to co-exist with the new conditions and who have not been able to sustain the increased energy of earth will be removed, and will make the transition. It is our choice. For example, earth's magnetism is decreasing, and scientists confirm that the magnetic pole is changing its position every year, and from their calculations it would be at Zero Point some time in the near future. In this process the human being is directly affected, in that *pari passu* with this decrease there is a proportional decrease in the time between thought and the consequence of that thought. In other words, we shall be experiencing the results of our thoughts if not instantly, at least more rapidly than previously. This reduction in the time-lag between thought and its result is due to the removal of dense magnetics which act as a veil between thought and its consequences. This change has both its positive as well as its negative results. On the positive side, it means that we can direct our thoughts consciously so as to achieve the desired result in the shortest possible time. This is an entirely different situation from what we are capable of accomplishing at present. In our present state we think our thoughts at random, not even caring for the consequences. Thoughts are a product of the human mind and we have come to accept the description of the 'monkey mind' of man, jumping hither and thither without control. This sort of behaviour can produce distressing results because the thoughts are not consciously controlled, not coherent and not monitored, resulting in the production of useless, negative thoughts, with disastrous consequences, the human tendency being to think along negative lines.

Under the new parameter of decreased magnetism, we have the free-will to make a choice, that is, to direct our mind to produce only positive thinking consciously, knowing that each positive thought can have near instant realization of that thought. This is not to deny that prior to the Shift with its decreased magnetism we also had the free-will to make this choice, but did we? Simply because we took our thoughts for granted, indulged luxuriously in thinking all kinds of thoughts, anytime, anywhere, negative, positive or whatever, not caring for the consequences of this indulgence. This could be due to the fact that the time-lag between the thought and its realization was so prolonged that we seldom cognized the relationship between them, in spite of the fact that our spiritual masters always counselled us to be beware of our thoughts and to control the mind from which they took their origin. Controlling the mind and taming it to respond to our will has been the bane of human existence since creation began. Arjuna, on the battlefield of Kurukshetra says, "For the mind, O Krishna, is restless, turbulent, powerful and obstinate. To control it is as hard, it seems to me as to control the wind."[9] And this was 5,000 years ago. The human mind it seems hasn't changed much throughout the ages and is the same if not worse today.

How fortunate are we to be living not too distant from the time when we shall be able consciously to choose to control our minds into thinking only good, positive thoughts such as the great spiritual masters of olden times. In the final analysis it is all about free-will and choice.

Effects of Earth's Electromagnetism

Apart from the decrease in magnetism that is taking place prior to the Shift of the Ages, there is also an increase in the basal resonant frequency of the earth which is heading towards a figure of 13 cycles per second. It is expected that it will attain this figure possibly simultaneously with the drop to zero of the magnetic field. These two digitally measurable parameters even at present are having effects on us in many different ways—our bodies, our senses, our minds, our sleep patterns, emotions, values, thoughts, etc. When the frequency or heart beat of the earth reaches its maximum, this enhanced frequency will have a tremendous effect on human beings and indeed, on all biological entities inhabiting the globe. With the increase in earth's resonance or frequency, we shall be obliged to increase the vibratory rate of our own cells to match that of the earth. This means every human cell in every human body.

As the vibratory rate of the cells increases we shall be able to attain the vibratory state of discarnate souls, and perhaps, communicate with them. Some individuals will have raised, by choice and free-will their vibratory rate to such a high level that they may become invisible to others, yet they will be in the same place, but will not be seen. Such persons may not be touched by those whose vibration is at a lower level. Braden states that each cell in the physical body/mind matrix must arrive at this alignment eventually. This is the balance of peace, well-being and union that is historically the goal of the spiritual disciplines.[2] From this we can understand that while ancient spiritual masters had to spend years of *sadhana* (spiritual discipline) in cave, forest and mountain-top to achieve illumination after much effort and physical discomfort, we shall be able to attain if not illumination, at least higher spiritual states, simply by an enhanced vibratory rate of each of the cells in our bodies. Such humans will necessarily be of a high order of beings, surpassing their peers with lower levels of vibration. However, there should be no question of superiority or inferiority, it will be only a matter of difference between individuals, much as it is today in any family or community. All are not born equal at any time in the history of mankind and this condition will continue, after the Shift. It will be a time of great achievements and with such evolved individuals inhabiting the planet, we can legitimately expect high standards of living, thinking and at every level of society— moral, social, intellectual, emotional and spiritual. A Golden Age indeed!

The New Age

The Golden Age will be so different and of such a high calibre that it will be unimaginable even in our wildest dreams. This is certainly something for all of us to look forward to, and Sri Sathya Sai Baba has confirmed this state as coming into being during the Golden Age. We shall have arrived at the Age of Truth, the *Sathya yuga*, the spiritually highest and most ideal of the four ages in Indian philosophy. We must remember and keep constantly in mind that such a high achievement depends on our free-will to make the right choice. Such a high vibratory rate will not automatically happen simply because the earth's frequency has been increased. The same old qualities of effort, will and choice obtain in such a condition if we are to achieve this highly evolved state. Nothing can ever be achieved without effort on our part. The conditions obtaining in the New Age, however, will facilitate and accelerate our efforts. "The Shift of the Ages is a new expression of life and the birthing of a new integrated wisdom. The opportunity of Earth is the opportunity of experience. Your life is your greatest tool of mastery. You will discover that fear, your fear, is your greatest ally in preparation for the experience. Through discovering your greatest fears you will be led to your greatest healings in your choice to remember your truest nature."2

Ultimate Free-will and Crucial Choice

Taking note of Sai Baba's remarks, we observe that He emphasizes that ultimate free-will lies in the matter of accepting or rejecting God. He says, "At all times God's existence in man can be recognized. I created everything and everyone with free-will.... Free-will to recognize God's existence, yes or no."6 According to Baba, that is the *ultimate free-will* (Writer's italics). Linking the Golden Age with choice and free-will Sai Baba goes on to say, "Everyone has the opportunity to enter the new Golden Age. But each one has a choice, the free-will to decide his own fate, whether he wishes to continue living in the wilderness, a life of illusion, or move forward along the spiritual path and enter the new Golden Age."1

Sri Aurobindo describes in strong language the forces opposing the establishment of the Divine Truth and states, "Every one must come down finally on one side or the other, on the side of Truth or against it". This, he says, "is the *crucial choice* (Writer's italics), but with one indispensable condition—sincerity."[13] And again, "Those who seek for the Divine have to stand firm and persist in their seeking; after a time, the darkness will fade and begin to disappear and the light will come."[13] About the light that will shine when the Golden Age dawns, Sai Baba has this to say, "The time will come when the light will spread with ever increasing intensity throughout the world. It will herald the time of the great awakening, a new age, a new beginning, a time when man becomes aware of the existence of God, and the true nature of each individual soul. Man will also realize his own individuality and the reality that there is only the One, the divine Creator, the Totality."[1]

Sri Aurobindo sums it up succinctly "...In him we are one with all" and again "A new spirit of Oneness will take hold of the human race."[13] Sri Sathya Sai Baba reminds us, "Now is the time of awakening for your planet and all those who reside there. The days of darkness are drawing to a close and the shadows lengthening until they disappear, to be replaced by brilliant sunshine, so strong that it will cleanse the planet and leave it ready for a new Golden Age. Some are ready, some are not."[1] Sri Aurobindo has described the 'crucial choice' as being the decision on our part to accept or reject Truth which is synonymous with God. Thus, whether it be free-will or choice, the object on which we exercise our free-will to make the crucial choice is the same. However, in the process of using free-will and making the right choice, we shall come up against a certain amount of obstruction and rejection by those who do not see the necessity for making the required changes. In such cases, we have to remain firm in our convictions and not to allow anyone or anything to deflect us from pursuing the path we have chosen. Having the courage of one's convictions will be the ultimate test to carry us over the pitfalls and hurdles on the journey to the Absolute.

About the Oneness of all humanity, Sri Aurobindo sums it up thus, "...within we are one with all."[13] Gandhi adds, "It is that Divine Love that holds in its hands the sovereign power of unity because it is itself the all-uniting power of the One Eternal. Its unveiled manifestation upon earth will create the New Age in the earth's evolution and that age will be 'The Age of the One' because it will establish the reign of the one Eternal in time, of the One Divine in the world."[13]

It is apparent from the foregoing information that although we have free-will to make the crucial choice, there is the stipulation that sincerity is an absolute essential. This again depends on choice, and so the matter turns full circle and we are back to square one—to the use of free-will and its role in the making of choice.

The Feeling of Oneness

Sri Aurobindo in describing the feeling of Oneness, says, "...unification is a necessity of Nature, an inevitable movement...only human imbecility and stupid selfishness can prevent, but cannot stand forever against the necessity of Nature and Divine Will". And again, "All mankind is one in its nature, physical, vital, emotional, mental and ever has been in spite of all differences of intellectual development ranging from the poverty of the Bushman and the Negroid to the rich culture of Asia and Europe and the whole race has, as the human totality, one destiny which it seeks and increasingly approaches in the cycles of progression and retrogression it describes through the countless millenniums of its history."[13] Gandhi in elaborating on the theme of Oneness has this to say, "...it has become imperatively necessary for humanity at the present moment to create consciously a real unity without any delay if it wishes to assure its present survival and future development. That it can only do if it squarely faces the basic causes that prevent the realization of human unity and resolutely overcomes them."[13]

Concerning the problem of lack of the feeling of Oneness among human beings, it seems almost impossible to have love for all unless one has love for the Divine. The feeling of separation stems from our feeling that we are all different classes, castes, creeds, colours, cultures, races, etc. We entrench ourselves behind our separateness based on these factors and like soldiers behind their fortifications tend to develop a feeling of security, secure in the knowledge that our caste is the best, our religion the truest, our race the most advanced, our culture the oldest and best and so on. This feeling of smugness, based on the falsity of our superiority over others have become consolidated and crystallized over millemia. Again, regarding the importance of choice, it is here that we have failed dismally in making the right choices. It is a matter of choice between 'We', instead of 'I and you'.

In the realm of Divine Love, the feeling of I and you or duality does not exist. We are all 'children of immortality' (*amritasaya putrah*) say the Vedas; we originate from one Source, the Divine, hence we all possess a spark of that same Divinity. This being so, how is it possible or rational to think of differences between us. If the spark emanated from the same source, then all the sparks are equal to one another. This is in accordance with Euclid's First Axiom which states that things which are equal to the same thing are equal to one another. But do we have to resort to mathematics to prove a point? Isn't it obvious that basically we are all one regardless of the extreme differences among the races of mankind. We all experience joy and sorrow, depression and exhilaration, gain and loss, and the entire spectrum of the pairs of opposites. He made it that way, didn't He? Was this done deliberately so that our universality could be tested on the touchstone of diversity? Only He knows, and if we profess to love Him the way so many of us do, the least we can do to indicate the sincerity of this love is to embrace all of mankind in the all-encompassing feeling of universal love. There is no other way and the more quickly we come to this realization, the greater the chance of peace and feeling of oneness among us. Sai Baba affirms, "There is no separation between God and man, except in the mind of the individual. There is only the One, no other. You are all part of that One, droplets of divinity. See everyone around you in that light, the light of God the Creator. Then unity, love and harmony will come to the world."[1] The Vedas declare, *Vasudaivam kutumbakom*— The world is one family—and this was proclaimed thousands and thousands of years ago.

To make this an accomplished fact, the theme of this chapter returns to haunt us. It is all a matter of choice, based on free-will. To begin with the 'ultimate free-will' as Sai Baba says is to accept or reject God, and Sri Aurobindo asserts that the 'crucial choice' relates to the same two factors. Is it because throughout the history of mankind we have failed to use our will to make the right choice that we have landed ourselves in this thick soup of separatism, factionalism, cultism, sectarianism, fanaticism, proselytism, the clashes of race and clan and all the other 'isms' invented by man, ancient and modern. It is these imponderables that we have to face and question ourselves, truthfully and honestly, as to whether we are guilty or not of these transgressions. No one else can do this for us. We alone can change the situation and the quicker the better.

Sathya Sai Baba has warned us that the time is at hand, that the pending change will take place quicker than we think, and that the time to act is NOW. There is no time for delay. It is either to do or to die, literally. If we take to the spiritual path as He suggests we do, and save ourselves, then again this depends on our choice which in turn is determined by our free-will. Wise, in dealing with choice says, "We need to make choices governed by our inner authority, our inner guidance. Security lives there. Those people who wanted their piece of the future securely invested, put their authority into the stock market that they now discover can fall apart."[3] And on this subject Wise says, "Because there is free-will there is planetary integrity; there is non-invasiveness from the greater universe, there's ethics of non-violence, there's respect for the human drama." And again she asserts, "Only you can invent your future integrity. In changing yourself you create a fertile environment within which others can grow and change.... It is imperative that you make a choice today that preserves your privilege to make choices in the future."[3]

With respect to our role as responsible individuals to cooperate in bringing about the new paradigm, Wise exhorts us to take the initiative; to make our claims; to step forward and assert ourselves as those being aware of their responsibility and having the courage to carry it out. She places the full onus on us to assume this role which is of vital importance to us and the planet we inhabit.[3]

A Frequency and a Value

"You are not only a person", she says, "You are also a frequency and a value that permeates the Universe. When the choices you make in your daily life and the quality of love you demonstrate in your daily life are consistent with your essential nature, your actions impact more than you knowingly touch.... Each time you express your highest truth and support others in expressing theirs, you are moving the world. Each time you allow inner direction to make your path, you build the infrastructure of peace. All the plans and all the dollars in the world cannot do this. This job belongs to each and serves all."[3] Continuing on the same theme, she questions us, "Who will break the momentum by jumping off the wheel of convention? How many will it take? Only one person can break the momentum—only you. Only you can free yourself from vested interests and learned positions, to live as you feel."[3]

Are we prepared to accept her challenges. Sai Baba says that the Golden Age that is about to be born will be of such a nature as to be unimaginable to most of us, and that we shall be transformed beings. But the catch is to act and take part in the unfolding drama NOW. At least we can make an effort to change the status quo as evolving human beings to come forward and not to be afraid to take a firm stand and make our presence felt. For what is there to fear? Once again Wise urges us to act, "Many of you think you need to be more than you are now–before you can make a contribution that will change the world. This is not so. Each of you has enlightenment in your life. Focus yourself in those places where your enlightenment is found. This is your most fertile ground for growth and contribution. All that is unresolved or unknown within you will eventually appear where you stand with enlightenment, because it yearns to become part of that sacred ground of being."[3]

Surrender

In concluding His remarks on free-will particularly in the case of wars, Sai Baba says, "I don't interfere collectively, but I do individually. The collective crystallization of evil must proceed in cases of war and natural disasters. But at an individual level people are certainly helped. And don't forget that whoever finds himself in such a situation has to resolve a specific karma. No birth has taken place without a reason. One is placed where the law of Karma must be accomplished."[6] He says that He interferes individually since His grace can cancel out the law of Karma, and this is put in action as soon as a person surrenders to Him. Then his fate will be in His hands and he can be protected from any violence.[6]

In the final analysis, if we have faith, love and can surrender to Him, who is really our higher Self—the Sai consciousness, or the Cosmic consciousness within us, we should realize that we are not surrendering to another person, or someone out there, in some remote corner of the Cosmos, who like a puppeteer holds the strings tossing us hither and thither like puppets. This act of surrender depends on our 'ultimate free-will', that is, to accept or reject the Divine, which is actually the inner core of all of us, and in rejecting this, we are really rejecting ourselves, and no one else. Once we can come to a firm decision on this vital matter, on which everything depends and make the 'crucial choice', surrender becomes automatic and we find ourselves shifting our burdens on to the Higher Self.

Some Guidelines on Free-will and Choice:

- "...it is man who has created those dark clouds that encompass the world, the inevitable result of negative thoughts and acts over a long period of time. Man has chosen to exercise his God-given free-will in that way, oblivious to the fact that he himself is creating the future of the world and the entire human race."[1]

- "What hope is there for the future of the world or mankind unless there are dramatic changes in man's attitude, belief and behaviour? Free-will exists at all times and man is free to play out his life in whatever way he chooses."[1]

- "...the time for change is now, today, not tomorrow. The past is gone, gone for ever, but the future is there right in front of you. It is a future which you yourself create through the exercise of your own free-will.

- "How are you exercising your free-will at this moment of time? Are you living your life in harmony with God and do you feel you are in harmony with your surroundings? Contemplate such thoughts at this difficult time and send out love to the world."[1]

In a pleasant mood

Seven

Love

Love is not an Emotion

Sri Sathya Sai Baba says that love is of two kinds—divine and worldly. Divine or pure love is not a feeling or emotion, but a form of energy flowing between people. He says that love is the solvent for the hardest of hearts and it can confer peace, joy and wisdom.[7] Love is timeless, eternal, has nothing to do with emotion, with a habit-forming feeling. Mother-love tends towards the timeless, beyond emotions. Father-love is defined by culture. Emotions belong to daily life. Ideally, mother-love is not an emotion. However, it is often defined by culture and then it is of a lower quality.[6]

Sai Baba continues to explain that spiritual love is timeless, unchangeable, not defined by culture; it is not an emotion.... Mother-love comes close to the ideal. The rest is interwoven with emotions and therefore not pure love which is unchangeable and not defined by culture.... Love as an emotion is functional but it is not the universal spiritual love from which everything originated, to which everything will return and of which man on earth is the manifestation.[6] Speaking about compassion He states that compassion is not an emotion. It is timeless. It is love. Compassion is being disinterestedly available for your fellow human beings. Emotionless feeling is true compassion. Offering comfort without emotion but with compassion is the best comfort there is.... Do your work fully dedicated with a willingness to sacrifice. Place yourself in the service of other people. The more unmoved by emotions you do this the more effective you work for others.[6] He also affirmed that every act should be put to the test of compassion; and that if work is done with anger, jealousy, envy, etc., you may as well not do it.[6] He says, "My work is for all things and for all people always. There is no difference. I work in, for and through everyone. I am not limited to my physical body. I work for everything and everyone for sheer compassion."[6] We note from the foregoing sayings of Sai Baba that love and compassion share almost the same qualities. We often read and hear about compassionate love, a strong combination indeed. Sai Baba continues on the theme of love thus, "True love is priceless. It has no trace of selfishness in it. It does not change. It is pure and unsullied. It always grows and never diminishes. It is spontaneous. The love of God is of such a nature.... Where there is love of God, there will be fear of sin. When both of them are present, society will experience morality.... Love does not have birth and love does not have death. Love is permanent and such true love is itself devotion."[7]

On the theme of love Wise sounds a warning, "I encourage you to question any Being who represents greater consciousness without demonstrating it as love. I caution you not to confuse your understanding of the ideas and knowledge coming forth at this time with genuine expansion into a more universal state of being. Ideas and knowledge alone do not expand Beings. Love is the expander. Without it we will have little more than a new information age. With it, humanity will enter the time of its realization—an Age of Inspired Realism."[3]

Adding to the above comments, Braden describes the effects on the human body following the occurrence of the polar shift which in Sai Baba words is identical with the Golden Age. Braden says, "All patterns of life energy within the physical body are at rest-balanced, as each aspect of belief, emotion, thought and feeling shift into harmony with the new reference point. The energy of reference is that of *love and compassion* (Writer's italics), the purest frequency of expression that may be generated and sustained within each cell of the body. The frequencies of love are not bound by dimensionality or time. It is a new expression of the energy of love, that is the object of (fourth dimensional) information vibrating at such a high pitch.... "The body is cleared of inharmonic patterns of energy that result in disease, ageing and deterioration...." Adding to this he says, "Frequency generated through non-judgment, allowing compassion and acceptance is that of love. Transcending the perception of dimensionality, time and space as the distortions of fear are resolved, love is all that remains. Compassionate love is our truest nature and all that remains as our illusions are healed."[2]

It is noteworthy that while describing love as it will be experienced in the new world order, Braden makes no mention of feeling or emotion, echoing the pronouncements of Sai Baba. Instead, he describes love as "the purest frequency of expression" and that this frequency of energy will be emitted by each cell of our body which will have already attained a high degree of resonance with Earth's enhanced frequency. In other words our cells will have increased their vibratory rate so as to shift into a higher level thereby attempting to match the high pitch of Earth's heart beat. We shall have to become resonant with Earth's basal resonant frequency which will be operating at the highest level.

The Changes that Lie Ahead

Relating to the changes that will take place when the old order gives way to the new, Sai Baba says that the time for change is now, a change to the way of God, and to a life filled with love, so much love that the whole world will be influenced by the love that flows through you and all around you. That is the way ahead.[1] Again He emphasized, "The time of awakening is now and the new Golden Age lies in front of you. It is an age of spiritual enlightenment, a time when the whole world will begin to experience the spiritual vibrations of love."[1] We realize that far from being a feeling or emotion, as we have been wont to consider love, it has been variously described above as a "frequency", an "energy", a "vibration" etc. This change alone will be difficult for some of us to accept since from time immemorial we have been brain-washed to accept and practise love as a feeling based on emotion and on personal attitudes.

Worldly love unlike divine love is not pure love, being adulterated with emotional feelings. At the same time since this is the form of love that exists among the broad masses of the people, it cannot be brushed aside, as it is universal in its appeal. However, it must be realized that this is the lower form of love and should not be equated with pure love or divine love which is permanent, universal, stable, unchangeable, steady, unconditional and lasts for eternity. Unlike worldly love it does not become satiated nor does it jump from one object to another. It is not confined to a particular individual or individuals, but flows to encompass the entire humanity, becoming universal in its expansiveness and un-conditionality. There is not the slightest tinge of emotion in this form of love. This love is the purest frequency of energy that each cell of every human being living on the planet who survives the Shift, will be emitting. This love is enduring and flows through the entire creation. Since God is love and love is God and as He is present in all the three kingdoms—animal, planet and mineral—we may wonder how love can exist in inert matter, a piece of metal, for example. The atoms in metal as in every form of creation are in a state of constant motion due to the movement of the electrons in their orbit around the nucleus of the atom; this movement is a form of energy and the love principle resides there. And since love is God, He is also in the atom as energy.

The same principle can be applied to the plant and animal kingdoms whose atoms are also in a state of perpetual motion. Thus love as a form of energy or God flows throughout the whole creation.

Sai Baba affirms as stated previously that mother-love is the only form of human love which approaches the divine form—it is unchanging, endures for life and never reaches for reward for its labour. Divine love is bereft of emotion, no tinge of the adulterating factor to make it impure. Hence Sai Baba's affirmation of "Love...Love...Love" which is His medicine for all human ills. He says, "Love knows no fear, no untruth, no anxiety.... Love is expansion and expansion is divine life; love activates; love fulfils.... Expand into universal love. Man's native characteristic is divine love.... Love cures pettiness, hate and grief.... Love as long as life lasts. My life is my message. My message is love."[7]

Sai Baba repeatedly exhorts us to make the appropriate changes in our lives and thinking now. Any delay in doing so will be too late, as the new order is waiting in the wings to move on to centre stage. But are we ready? One wonders after seeing the attitude of some people who on being briefed as to the forthcoming events that are imminent, merely shrug off the information presented, as if by so doing it will go away and disappear. It is as if the future situation described is too far-fetched and hazy, somewhere in the far-off distance to be of any consequence for the present time; or could it be that the fears generated by the picture of the future changes are too great to allow dispassionate consideration, and like the ostrich, such people simply bury their heads in the sand, this being the line of least resistance, unable to face difficulties with courage and boldness.

The Role of Divine Love

Sai Baba says that we are His forms, all of us. When He loves us, He loves Himself. When we love ourselves, we love Him.

He said, "I have separated Myself from Myself so that I may love Myself". He also said that there are no shortcuts to liberation, as some people think.

Love alone can give liberation, and that the grace of God cannot be won through reason, yoga or asceticism; only love can win it, love that knows no bargaining, love that is paid gladly as tribute to the all-loving Divine. And also that if we develop love, we do not need to develop anything else.

Sri Aurobindo sums up the subject of love thus, "It is the divine love...that extended inward feeling to the Divine in man and all creatures in an active universal equality will be more potent for the perfectibility of life and a more real instrument than the ineffective mental ideal of brotherhood can ever be."[13] Discarding the well-known concept of the brotherhood of man Sri Aurobindo replaces this by Divine love as being more effective an instrument to produce the necessary changes in man's life by pervading his being to the extent that he experiences universal love extending not only to man but to include all living creatures.

Sai Baba expresses His dissatisfaction, "...the Divine comes as Avatar only to teach mankind the truth about love. Oh man, it is because you lack love and are filled with selfishness that the world is plunged into so much conflict and chaos. It is only when you develop love and the spirit of sacrifice that you will realize the divinity that is in the human. The man who has no spirit of sacrifice will be prey to all ills. A man without love is a living corpse. It is love and sacrifice which make man Divine."[7] He continues, "Love also is the fruit of love. Love is its own witness. There is no trace of self-interest in it. Because love exists for its own sake. It has no fear. It is to teach humanity the way of love that Avatars come in the world."[7]

On the qualities of love He says that love is His highest miracle. Love can make you gather the affection of all mankind. It will not tolerate any selfish aim of approach. It knows no fear, no anxiety, no grief and can transform man into a divine being. Love can tame even the most ferocious of beasts. It is the basis of character.[7]

Love in the Golden Age

About love in the Golden Age Sai Baba explains, "When the Golden Age dawns there will be harmony throughout the world and love will flow everywhere. All thoughts of hatred will disappear. Today you cannot visualize such a state because there is chaos everywhere, fighting, scheming, hatred, evil; all the negative emotions are in the ascendant. But eventually the change will come."[1] Continuing on the theme of love in the new age He says, "God is love, you are God and you should awaken to that truth. See the light, live in light and let love blossom in your hearts so that it lights up the world and cleanses it of the evils and the ignorance of the present age."[1] And again, "Let the world be filled with love, loving thoughts pouring out from a million sources. That is the way to cleanse the world and overcome the evil that has soiled the atmosphere. ...Love, Love, Love, that is my Medicine! And it is already there in such abundance, but man is so blinded by his past that he does not see the vast ocean of love surrounding him on all sides. You must become part of that ocean once again, for that ocean is God, the ocean of love and I AM THAT."[1]

Love Walking on Two Feet

Dr. Frank Baranouski, of the University of Arizona, has said that Swami (Sai Baba) has given us the key to success in the simple four-letter word "LOVE", and that if ever he can use the phrase that he has seen love walking on two feet, it is here. Indeed, from all Sai Baba's sayings, teachings, writings, discourses and personal advice, one thing stands out above all else He says and does. It is the word LOVE. There is hardly a discourse or a piece of His writing that lacks this four-letter word. He never seems to tire describing it, singing about it in *bhajans* (hymns) and telling his listeners over and over that in the final analysis, love is all that matters, Divine love that is. He has said that love is the greatest force on earth and can move the universe. There is nothing it cannot do. Yet we as a race of human beings, seem utterly oblivious to what Sai Baba has been repeating *ad nauseum* from the age of fourteen years to the present time. He will be 80 years old in November this year. We are so immersed in our greed for the material goods of the world, in our relationships with other human beings, in our attachment to things temporal and our concern mainly for 'I' and 'mine' forgetting the 'we' part of relationship. But the Divine Life speaks of something else and this is what Sri Sathya Sai has been drumming into deaf ears for more than half a century. He assures us that the time is up and any further delay in turning toward the spiritual path, the way of love, will spell disaster; we shall fall by the wayside, victims of our own selfishness and be lost forever in the darkness of illusion, losing the one golden opportunity for which we incarnated on the planet—to find our way back to the Source from which we took our origin.

In His discourse in the May 2005 issue of *Sanathana Sarathi*, Sai Baba says, "Truly, God has endowed man with immense potential. That is love. It is beyond all description and measure. There is no greater power than this. But man is frittering away this power without realizing its value. He is under the mistaken notion that love means physical and worldly relationship. No. No. This is not true love. True love is that which unites you with one and all. People utter this word repeatedly without actually knowing its meaning. Love does not hurt anybody. It always helps. Hence, consider love as your true property. There is no property more valuable than love in this world. You are misusing the God-given gift of love by diverting it to worldly matters and sensual pleasures. Your foremost duty is to make proper use of love following the dictum, Help ever, Hurt never. There is no greater *Dharma* (duty) than this."[5b]

While Braden speaks of the 'Shift of the Ages', Sathya Sai Baba describes the change as the 'Golden Age' and that all of us "have an important part to play in bringing about that change". Braden echoes this by saying that each individual man living upon the Earth is an integral part of the Shift process.[2]

How Love can Save the World

Sai Baba asserts that love is the energy that will propel us in this task and only the flow of unlimited love can save the world from its present decline. Relating to this theme Braden speaks of the frequency of expression known as 'love'. He says that love is the purest frequency attainable and each cell will be emitting this energy. Sai Baba similarly speaks of love flowing from millions of sources to fill the world with this energy. For love is God, and God is love. Thus both the Avatar and the scientist-cum-mystic are saying the same thing, although from different standpoints—one from the purely spiritual aspect, the other from the scientific point of view supported by information from records of the ancients. It is interesting to note here that again, the spiritual and scientific approach each other, as they are doing in quantum and post-quantum physics. Sai Baba's predictions are crisp, terse and pregnant with meaning. A comparison of these statements with those of Braden and Wise complement each other and give us a general overview of the New Age that all three say is imminent.

Sai Baba says that the Golden Age has already begun and that we have only to look around to see ourselves surrounded by love, provided we have "the eyes to see, and the ears to hear". Braden also agrees that the Shift has started and may complete within our life time. The time-table as recorded by the ancients is intact, he says.[2]

Many past great civilizations collapsed and disappeared when technology raced ahead of philosophy, leaving it limping behind. The same holds true for our present-day world. Hi-tech rules the roost. What has happened to our spirituality? Being possessors of the Divine Spark, what has happened to the 'Spark'? We have become so indolent, lethargic, in other words, so supine and spineless, that we allow the greed and selfishness of others to overwhelm us and smother our finer feelings. This is what happened to Lemuria (Mu) the lost continent of the Pacific and to Atlantis which disappeared beneath the waves of the Atlantic Ocean. Not so long ago this is what happened to Germany, when the German people kept silent and even supported him while Adolph Hitler, the megalomaniac, strutted the land of Germany with his self-adulatory and passionate speeches, lulling his listeners into a half-hypnotic state by his so-called 'charisma', and brought utter ruin and disaster to this great civilized nation. As Edmund Burke has said, "All that is necessary for evil to triumph is for good men and women to do nothing."

Sai Baba enlarges on the theme of love in the May 2005 issue of *Sanatana Sarathi*, "Love is your only true and eternal wealth. But you are misdirecting it towards mean and worldly pursuits. It should be treasured in your heart and utilized for sacred purposes. You may share it with any number of people. It will never diminish. But man today is unable to understand and experience the true spirit of love.... Love cannot be understood from a superficial level. You have to immerse yourself completely in it. Worldly love is such that you can just taste it and give it up. But divine love is not like that; once you taste it, you will never leave it. Love is God's property. Safeguard and protect this property with utmost care. Love is God. God is love. Hence you cannot separate love from God. Live in love. That is the only way you can understand love and experience God."[5b]

The Functions of Love

Sai Baba and His pronouncements on the functions of love. "Love is infectious, and as you pour it out, it becomes stronger.

That love is the God-force itself, and it is this divine love which will eventually cleanse the world of all evil... It is love which will bring peace to the world", asserts Sai Baba.[1] "But today there is chaos and confusion in the world, because man has wandered from the path and drawn further and further away from God. The time for change has come and all of you have an opportunity to play a part in bringing about that change. A new awakening is at hand and you are there to be torch-bearers and spread the message of the Lord. Love is the energy that will propel you in this task. Only the flow of unlimited love can save the world from its present decline." He says, "Today the world is sick, poisoned by man. But all is not lost and the day of awakening will come and lead to a new Golden Age. All of you should play a part in bringing forward that transformation, and the instrument you should use is love". About the arrival of the Golden Age Sai Baba says, "It is there now for some, those enlightened souls who already reached the state of God realization. It is that awakened state which will lead to the New Age."[1]

Is there Love in the Animal Kingdom?

A chapter on love the author feels would be incomplete were it not to include something on the world of animals. Our dumb brothers and sisters, being lower on the phylogenetic scale, do not attract the attention they deserve, as we are inclined to consider them lesser creatures, perhaps without a soul, undeserving of our time and energy. But this should not be so, because in that vast kingdom are individual animals who stand out by manifesting finer and higher feelings that are usually attributed to *Homo sapiens*. This section of the chapter is devoted to such outstanding animals who by sheer courage, boldness, thought, affection and sacrifice, would put to shame most human beings faced with similar situations.

Stinky—the Mongoose

The first of these episodes that come to mind concerns a wild animal—the mongoose. The author can still recall with great vividness, after the lapse of 26 years, the utter commotion, squeaking and squealing, Stinky, as she named him because of his strong smell, would produce no sooner he heard the familiar purring of her car engine as it entered the front gate and cruised along the driveway, and the ecstatic welcome he would give her standing on his two tiny hind legs and wanting to be picked up. The commotion would cease after much stroking and fondling, and following the pacification, he would jump on to her left shoulder to claim his expected ration of the tit-bits of food protruding from her mouth. With his slender pointed mouth he would gingerly remove the food and consume it without the slightest mess. She discovered that a mongoose is a very hygienic creature. This was a regular ritual they both enacted and with mutual enjoyment. He loved to play hide-and-seek among the thick bushes of the beds of gerberas. At time so cleverly concealing himself that it was difficult to find him. Then suddenly appearing as if from nowhere and squealing to attract her attention, he would immediately run into the bed of bushes to hide himself again before she could catch him. It is a debatable point as to who enjoyed this game the most— both were tired and at least the human was out of breath after the invigorating sporting event.

And this enjoyable relationship with an animal born in the wild, born free, described as 'sly' by humans, since cunning and cleverness or slyness, if you prefer the term, are the weapons at his disposal to catch, grasp and kill a snake, regardless of the size of the reptile—the most dreaded creature on earth. Yet he sat on her shoulder as if he belonged there, eating bits of food from her mouth. She brought him up from the age of one week, feeding him like a premature infant with droppers of diluted milk; she must confess that the attachment was mutual and they became inseparable.

Stinky died prematurely after six months, being fed the wrong diet during her absence, although the interval was only a few days, but during this brief absence, irreparable damage was done to his little body. He ailed for several days. Nothing could be done to save his life and he breathed his last at midnight on her lap. She buried him the next morning near the bed of gerberas where he had spent so many enjoyable hours of his brief life.

Stinky had made the long train trip with us from the City of Calcutta (now Kolkata) near the Eastern coast of India to the foot-hills of the Himalayas to occupy a house which had been recently bought in the town of Dehradun in the Doon Valley. We understood that the area we were going to live in was infested with snakes, poisonous and non-poisonous. However, for the six months Stinky lived with us we saw not even the shadow of a snake. After Stinky's departure, within a few months the creatures came marching in—cobras, kraits, green, brown, yellow and black snakes, all varieties to keep us occupied. It was then that we missed Stinky more than ever and we had to co-exist with those creatures for fourteen years until we moved to the Blue Mountains of Southern India.

One snake which probably was washed out of his hole during a heavy downpour one monsoon night, entered the kitchen through the open door, slithered across the author's feet and took refuge inside a kitchen cupboard. She realized it was a snake that ran over her feet only when she saw his tail disappearing into the cupboard. But this is another story. Suffice it to say that as long as our mongoose was on the premises there was not the sight of a snake. The Creator fashioned both the snake and the mongoose; the snake presumably to control the rat and other rodent populations, the mongoose to control the snake population. This is conjecture, but it appears that the Almighty created the

foundation of Nature on the basis of the pairs of opposites—
day and night, hot and cold, dry and moist, sun and moon,
snake and mongoose etc.—the pairs of opposites our spiritual
masters have been asking us for millennia to overcome as
part of our spiritual discipline.

Were the reactions of Stinky just those born of instinct?
This was an animal from the wild, stalking and striking with
cunning and deadly accuracy the deadliest creature on the
planet; missing the target—the neck of the snake—would
probably mean the end of the mongoose. Yet consider the
intensity of his feelings of affection, love, loyalty and extreme
attachment to one human being who reared him from the
age of one week with much love and care.

Surely, this was a feeling of reciprocity on Stinky's part, a
little cunning 'sly' mongoose, rising beyond mere instinct to
manifest some of the most noble qualities we have come to
associate with civilized man. Sai Baba has said that God is in
all that exists. He is intelligence in the insect, faithfulness in
the dog.... There is nothing in the world which has no heart,
which is incapable of feeling joy or grief.

Bambi—the Barking Deer

Another example, illustrating the intelligence and the ability
to think for themselves when faced with gruelling circumstances
beyond their control relates to a barking deer whom the
author had reared from the age of three days. Bambi, as we
named him, grew to such a great size and showed eagerness
to have more space for jumping, leaping and running around
than the fairly large garden could provide, that she was
tempted to think of a way out. All along she felt a certain
amount of guilt in continuing to confine him in such
cramped quarters. She, therefore, decided against all negative
feelings to set him free in the nearby woods where others of
his kind could be found. She knew very well that domesticated
animals from the wild were not readily acceptable to their

wild peers, but ventured to let him loose, there being no alternative. Alter having coaxed him to enter the wilds at sunset for the first time, he voluntarily went towards the woods and disappeared from sight. Bambi had been with us for years and had become a part of the family. That night and for the succeeding three nights sleep was lost thinking of Bambi's fate in that wild and hostile milieu into which he had been thrown. By the fourth day, her anxiety eased up somewhat and she began to relax thinking that he had been accepted by his kind—a most unusual phenomenon. To our great surprise and a sneaking feeling of relief and joy, Bambi was seen patiently waiting outside the closed front gates on the fourth evening. With the joyous welcome of a prodigal son, the author took him in, only to discover to her great dismay and sorrow that he was exhausted, dying of thirst and hunger, with throat, neck and shoulders covered with puncture wounds and clotted blood. So the rehabilitation was as expected a complete failure. Since he could not lap up water the normal way, she fed him by dropping water from a soaked towel on to his tongue which he drank with great avidity. One hour passed by before he stopped drinking, and then she attended to his numerous puncture wounds.

What was amazing was Bambi's courage and daring to take on the frontal attacks of his wild peers who obviously prevented him from slaking his thirst in the river flowing through the woods, and also from eating, for four whole days, demonstrating an animal's ability to think for itself when faced with a dangerous situation and to decide that the only alternative was to find the way back home, if, indeed, he was to survive. One can only conjecture what Bambi had to endure alone and unaided, in the forest, taking on perhaps, single-handedly the entire herd of wild deer and finally butting his way out of the woods to the relative safety of human habitation. Animals, therefore, can think and make plans in spite of what we humans think about them. Whether Bambi acted out of sheer instinct for survival, or of escaping from a situation beyond his ability to handle, surely the fact that he recalled where he belonged and where he had received love and care, indicated a reciprocal feeling of love in his 'deer' heart as well as trust and confidence, so that his four legs brought him to stand and wait patiently and silently before the tall closed wrought iron gates of what he knew as his only home. No one knew how long he had been standing there. No one saw when he came.

Our final farewell to Bambi occurred a few years later. Mrs. Asha Mazumdar, who was our next-door neighbour at that time, very kindly obtained permission through the good offices of Lt. Gen. S.K. Pillai of Trivandrum, to have Bambi transported to a wild-life park in North India. The day he left us he started emitting peculiar noises which the author interpreted as crying, and he gave some resistance to being hoisted on to the truck, continuing his cries and even while we arranged his fodder and water for the long journey ahead. He apparently realized that he was being taken away again from the only place he felt at home in, and put up great resistance. He continued to cry as the truck left the front gate, and as the vehicle disappeared in the distance the author gave a prayer of thankfulness that at last Bambi would be amidst surroundings that were his natural habitat and that he would be free.

Sri Sathya Sai Baba says that birds and beasts need no divine incarnation to guide them, for they have no inclination to stray away from their dharma (right conduct) and that man alone forgets or ignores the goal of life. How can we therefore belittle the feelings, thoughts, love and trust of such creatures? Is it simply because they are dumb, refusing or unable to retort when tortured by man or to fight back as we humans do?

Faithful Mother and her Dead Pup

An example of their capacity to endure discomfort to an extreme degree relates to a canine mother. Vinod, the author's foster son, was driving his two-wheeler following another one of its kind which just then ran over a pup who was crossing the road with its mother. The driver who fatally injured the pup and his female companion saw what they had done. The pup was mortally wounded, blood was oozing from its mouth, and the grieved mother was whimpering helplessly. Both humans looked on unmoved at the tragic scene, and with perfect composure, indulged in vulgar, loud laughter at what they had accomplished and then drove off. The mother continued her moaning while Vinod picked up the pup, saw its hopeless condition, and decided to administer Reiki healing. After a few minutes of healing, the pup expired in his hands, the healing possibly aiding in bringing the agony to a swift end. Since he had an urgent appointment in Ooty, a hill resort some kilometres away, he had no alternative but to place the pup back with his mother, who immediately took up a position beside her dead offspring, remaining there while he drove off.

After the lapse of several hours on his return journey, he was quite surprised to see both mother and dead pup in the same place, the mother assiduously guarding her dead offspring from the hungry crows that were hovering around. It was apparent that she had not left the side of the pup for all the hours since his death. Without food or drink and in the heat of the sun, she did what she considered her duty. He picked up the pup, while the mother continued her moaning and placed it in a plastic bag in his two-wheeler; no sooner the mother saw that the pup was in safe hands she ran off without so much as a backward glance. It is a tempting thought to wonder how many of us would have subjected ourselves to the heat, hunger and thirst, not moving an inch from the post as guard, until help appeared. Or to put it another way, can any human being surpass the concern, caring, love and intense suffering of this bereaved canine? He brought the pup home; dug a grave in the garden that night and buried it with the dignity it deserved. We consider animals to be inferior to us, indeed that they are, according to the phylogenetic scale; but are they in any way inferior to us in the things that matter—loyalty, affection, concern, love and sacrifice?

Tossing the pup into the nearby bushes presented no problem either to Vinod or to the mother, who could easily have grabbed it with her mouth and deposited it in the bushes, and by so doing have solved her problem. Did her reluctance to dispose of her dead offspring spring from a feeling of aversion that such an act was not in keeping with canine dignity? Who knows what goes on in their heads? Certainly there was a thought process in action during those long hours of scorching heat as she stood beside the dead pup. Surely, this was not an act of pure instinct.

This incident brings to mind the behaviour of Rani, the author's mixed-breed Alsatian who delivered a still-born pup at midnight. She left her one hour later to catch some sleep, still licking the dead pup apparently with the hope of bringing it back to life. A short while afterwards, she woke up to find the dead pup missing, and could not locate it anywhere. Rani, however, seemed to be at peace with herself. After several minutes of frantic searching the beheaded body was found covered up beneath Rani's bedding. The missing head? Nowhere to be found. The author concluded that it was comfortably tucked away inside Rani's stomach. Her conjecture was that having licked the pup's head and face for more than an hour, and finding no signs of life, Rani decided to severe the head which was completely covered with the slime of saliva and presented no problem in swallowing it whole. She returned a part of the pup to her body from which it originated after all; and perhaps, according to canine mentality, was in safe keeping. This was her way of disposing of a problem.

What an entirely different approach from the roadside mother. Both were canines, both were faced with the same problem. Do we need more proof that animals use the thought process in solving their problems? The Creator has endowed the denizens of the animal world with the know-how to deal with their myriad difficulties and this is not confined merely to instinct. To repeat here what the Avatar has said—birds and beasts need no divine incarnation to guide them, for they are not inclined to stray away from their path of right conduct. Only man does. The canine on the roadside sat beside her dead without expectation of any kind; prolonged suffering, patiently borne and the only sound heard was her moaning, doing what she considered her duty without expectation of reward. How many of us are capable of this kind of sacrifice?

The Crocodile and his Human Friend

Strange incidents have been reported following the December 26, 2004 tsunami that devastated the coasts of South India and several other countries in the region. Many of the stories relate to the miraculous manner in which people caught in the tsunami were saved. One such incident concerns a crocodile. This reptile used to swim into a private garden everyday and was regularly fed by the owner of the house. After the tsunami washed away his home, he found himself struggling against the turbulent waves and was making frantic but vain attempts to find a piece of wood or a log to hold on to. Just then he saw what looked like a log of wood and attempted to swim towards it, when he saw the log approaching him. It was none other than his pet crocodile. He caught hold of the back of the reptile, who then proceeded to swim towards the shore. Not only did the crocodile take him to land safely; he deposited the human being some distance away from the shore where he would be safe from the turbulent waves.

If any one were to try to convince the author that this behaviour was purely an instinctive act on the part of the crocodile, she would suggest that he or she consult a psychiatrist. The crocodile not only recognized his human friend, but recalled his kindness, realized he was in danger, and without any hesitation, swam to his help. What feelings were this act based on? Again the finer 'human' qualities of gratitude (something extremely rare at the present time), concern for the safety of his benefactor, and caring sufficiently as to swim towards him and save him from being drowned by the boisterous waves. Was there also, we wonder, some sort of feeling of affection for his friend? Otherwise, why should he have decided to save a human being who under ordinary circumstances would have provided his next meal?

The Noble Bison

This incident occurred probably in one of Africa's wild-life sanctuaries the author had viewed on television some years ago. The programme had already started when she sat down to view it. The large herd of wild bisons was thundering past at break-neck speed, as fast as their legs could carry their bulky frames. Suddenly into view came stalking four hungry lionesses with fangs bared, ready for the kill. The bisons kept forging ahead, looking neither to right nor left fully aware of the danger lurking on their right side. The hungry felines attempting to make a kill from the sides of the speeding animals, kept on failing while the herd, numbering probably more than a hundred members, kept thundering past. Eventually, the tail-end of the herd came into view and the lionesses found themselves looking at the hind-quarters of the animals. They started making frantic attempts as a team to snatch one of the beasts. It was at this precise moment that one of them, regal and majestic, in the full glory of his robust body, bursting with health, emerged from the rear end of the herd and took on single-handedly the pack of lionesses, presenting himself as a single target. It was an unbelievable sight!

One could imagine him making this bold and brave decision all by himself, for there was no time for herd consultation if, indeed, there is such a thing. Jungle life is a continuous series of emergencies, sudden attacks by predators, alive one minute, dead and eaten the next. There is hardly time for thought, the instinct being instant action or reaction. This is jungle law. In the case of our brave bison, there was enough time to think, as he was a close witness of what the predators were aiming at. His actions, presumably, were based on thought. It was obvious to the onlooker that he had made this fatal decision to engage the predators in battle, keeping them occupied while the herd thundered to safety. The young bisons had been well guarded by their elders on all sides, for they were placed in the middle of the moving herd. There was no way the lionesses could catch even a glimpse of them.

Our courageous and bold bison started butting his enemies as they attacked him from the front. He continued battling them with great vigour and confidence, inflicting injury and wounding them with his massive horns. Finding themselves on the defensive, his adversaries resorted to the strategy of taking him on from all sides. One began attacking him from the rear, others from his bulging sides and legs, while one was kept engaged in front. Under such circumstances it seemed impossible for a single animal to protect himself on all sides simultaneously. Persisting in his fight with the lioness in front of him, he bravely continued his vigorous butting-right, left and centre, non-stop, while the other predators continued to inflict severe wounds on his body. It was at this point that he suddenly ceased fighting and uttered a cry so loud, so piercing and so full of anguish that even his Creator would have been moved. Was this cry equivalent to the human cry to God for help in times of crisis? But then, animals are not supposed to have such awareness, despite the fact that they have consciousness. Who knows what goes on in the mind of a bison? With this cry of extreme anguish, his energy suddenly failed and he fell to the ground, weakened by the numerous wounds inflicted by the bites of the predators. It was an unfair battle.

Needless to say, the herd by this time was safely at a distance, their thundering hoofs no longer audible and only the tail-end could be seen in the distance. Our brave hero had accomplished his task. He lay on the ground, a helpless victim, while the predators began tearing him apart, apparently still alive to know what was happening, his only consolation, perhaps, during his death throes being the feeling of satisfaction that his precious herd had been saved. Simply the recall of that loud cry of anguish directed as it were to an indifferent Cosmos, as if beseeching help which was not forthcoming, and the thought of the supreme sacrifice made by that wonderful, brave, courageous and daring animal, would move the hardest of hearts.

Knowing fully well the laws of Nature and the fact that they were laid down from the beginning of time by a Being no less than the Creator himself, one still tends to question the creation of the food chain which entails so much violence and gory acts. To these questioning minds, Sai Baba gives the following explanation. "Lions and tigers belong to the highest form of predators. Somewhere the link of eating and being eaten must stop or else it would continue unendingly. Man would eat those predators and would in turn be eaten himself. With the predators, the process of continuously being eaten stops. That is one more reason why man should not lend himself to take part in the animal process of eating and being eaten. If even large animals, like the elephant, do not take part in it, should man degrade himself to being a blood-thirsty animal. With man, a new evolutionary process begins in which the weaker is no longer threatened by the stronger."[6] Sai Baba also stated that in the animal world, all are sacrifices for one another. But for whom should man sacrifice himself. For no one. His body does not serve to be consumed as food for other species. That is why he himself should not feed on other species.[6]

Knowing that what our brave bison did was an intrinsic part of jungle law, and as Sai Baba has said, that in the animal world all are sacrifices for one another; yet this sort of sacrifice seems to stand out by itself. One does not know if this is an everyday occurrence in the jungle. But whatever it may be, it certainly leaves a lasting impression on one's mind. Most animals run away from their predators and after being caught up, they sacrifice themselves for each other by having their bodies eaten, after losing the battle for survival and being eaten against their wishes.

The bison deliberately left the relative security of the herd and voluntarily made himself the sole target for his adversaries, probably knowing the outcome of his decision. In retrospect, it seems strange that no other member of the herd who saw when the bison dropped out of its ranks thought it necessary to join him. Surely they knew that alone he could not survive the combined onslaught of four large hungry felines. Whatever the pros and cons, he alone made the fatal decision. It was apparent to him that someone had to break rank to take on the predators. Who will it be he must have wondered. Apparently he waited to see what would happen. Since no one volunteered, he took it upon himself to do what the circumstance merited. Some time had elapsed between the appearance of the four lionesses and his decision. There was certainly enough time for him to think. This was a well thought-out decision and when he made the final move and stepped out of rank he must have been prepared both in body and mind for the consequences of his thought and subsequent action.

Sai Baba has said that even the pain of animals is his pain. How much He would have felt the suffering of that bison. His loud, piercing hollow cry of agony would certainly have reached the ears of the Avatar, for He says noting escapes His attention, and as the animal was doing his duty according to his dharma (duty), laid down by the Creator Himself, the

Avatar would not interfere. Sai Baba Himself has said, "Even the animals call me, and I respond."¹ We can take comfort, therefore, in the thought that He would have looked to the future welfare of that magnificent soul as it emerged from the dying body of that noble animal.

In the examples described above, whether it was a deer, a dog, a bison, a mongoose, or a crocodile, it seems that along with the instinctive reactions of fighting to protect themselves, or running away to preserve life, there is a common denominator running through their actions. What made Stinky wrap a human being around his little mongoose heart, so that on her return even after a brief absence of a few hours, he became frenzied and frantic and standing on his little hind legs, his loud, ecstatic, exciting and boisterous greeting was enough to arouse the entire neighbourhood; what made Bambi—hungry, thirsty, exhausted and wounded—wend his way back to the only place he knew as home, to stand silently outside the closed gates patiently waiting for something to happen or someone to appear; what motivated that faithful canine to remain for hours beside her dead pup; what instigated the bison to leave the protection of the herd or the crocodile to refrain from swallowing his benefactor. Surely, apart from instinct, finer feelings that we naturally associate with human beings were also at play—feelings of concern, caring, affection, trust, confidence, courage, bravery, loyalty, fortitude, sacrifice and above and beyond all these, how do we know that the motivating factor behind these noble acts was not the greatest force on earth—the simple four-letter word LOVE. Sai Baba has said that love will awaken the compassion of man towards all God's children, human and animal; it will fill him with wonder and amazement at the handiwork of God and he will see divinity everywhere and in everything.

In this chapter the subject of animals has been purposely dealt with at length. They will be playing an important part in the Golden Age, not as objects to satisfy man's taste for flesh or to be used for man's pleasure and whimsical desires. With the reversal of the magnetic poles sometime in the near future, all biological life on earth will undergo immense changes both in body and mind. The cells of animals will also have to increase their vibratory rate in order to survive. We can look forward not only to a more advanced race of human beings, but also to a more highly evolved animal kingdom. It is said that in this Utopia, man and animal will walk together without fear of each other and who knows, perhaps communicate with each other. It has recently been reported that dogs have evolved an unusual ability to read human gestures and cues, and manipulate and predict human behaviour. Dogs have been found to be better at a test of their ability to interpret social cues, than even our primate cousins the chimpanzee and the dog's relation, the wolf.

Love in the New Age

According to Wise, "Unconditional love means there are no conditions to diminish the constancy and quality of your love.... Unconditional love, compassion and the tolerance that comes from knowing yourself as a timeless and inviolate Being are the bridges that will elevate you above the duality of good and bad. Living with this inclusive heartfulness frees you from emotional entanglement, leaving your energy available to facilitate resolutions and unifications in yourself and in your world."[3]

Further to Sai Baba's comments on love, "Man is love embodied. He thirsts for love and finds real joy in loving and receiving love.... Love all as the embodiments of the same divine principle.... The bliss that you give, the love that you share, those alone will be your lasting possessions.... Love must see the best in others, and not the worst.... Love cannot ignore the divinity in others.... The greatest of the virtues is love.... When you know that you are but a spark of the divine,

and that all else are the same divine spark, you look upon all
with reverence and true love.... There is only one royal road for
the spiritual journey—love. Love all beings as manifestations of
the same divinity, that is the very core of yourself. Love all beings,
that is enough.[7] See God in everyone, even in persons whom
you regard as your enemies... Expansion is life. Expansion is
the essence of love..... To attain God, love is enough. Love is the
key to open the door locked by egoism and greed... Expand into
universal love.... Love, not lust, is the essence of life.[7] Krishna, in
the chapter on Devotion (Gita) quoted by Sai Baba says, 'Fill
yourself with love, and use this love to reach Me. In that way you
will develop nearness and dearness to me' ...Love is the only
bond that can unite and make us realize the one Reality behind
all the seeming diversity... How does one love? See all as but the
expression of the same God, as appearances on the same screen;
as lit by the same current, though of manifold colours and
wattage..."[7]

"Scatter the seeds of love in dreary desert hearts, then
sprouts of love will make wastelands green with joy; blossoms
of love will make the air fragrant; rivers of love will murmur
along the valleys; and every bird will beat, every child will
sing the song of love... Loving God is not a pose; it is a series
of little acts directed by an attitude of reverence for the divinity
of all beings. Watch for the lie that lurks on the tongue; the
violence that lurks behind the hand; the ego that lurks behind
the deed. Restrain them before they grow into habits and settle
down as part of your character, thereby interfering with your
destiny" says Sri Sathya Sai Baba.[7]

And finally on the same theme He says, "How can you
find God when He appears to be hidden within? You can
find Him through love. When your heart opens, you open a
door, and there the Lord is revealed in all His glory. You feel
His presence and His divine love welling up from within.
From then on, you start to vibrate with His love, and can
express that love in your own life."[1]

"God is love, and without God and His inestimable love, nothing could exist.... The universe itself is God's creation, a moment of thought, a moment of creation through the power of love.... When you talk to the flowers, the plants and the trees, you are talking to God. Let your love flow to them and they will respond. With the animals you can see how quickly and warmly they respond to your love."[1]

In the May 2005 issue of His journal He says, "It may be easy to give lectures on love; but it is difficult to understand it. Make every effort to comprehend it. If you understand the nature of your love, you will understand the love of others. Love is in you, with you and around you. Once you understand love, you will become the very embodiment of love. If you just talk about love without understanding it, then you cannot become the embodiment of love. The more you understand the principle of love and put it into practice, others will also try to emulate you."[5b]

Eight

The Fourth Dimension and How it will Change the World

The Timing of the Golden Age

The actual timing of the Golden Age, according to Sai Baba, depends on us, yet at the same time He declares, "The time is approaching when all humanity will live in harmony. That time will be sooner than one expects."[1] Sai Baba drops hints of a 'storm' that will affect the earth and its inhabitants, "After the storm there will be a new beginning and the atmosphere will be completely different. It will be like a new age, the age of love, harmony and cooperation replacing the age of war, fighting, hatred, jealousy, greed and all those negative aspects of life. Everyone should prepare for this change, for I promise you that it will come, and only those who are ready will survive."[1]

He laments, "Man has virtually destroyed the world through evil thought, selfishness, greed and jealousy. But all is not lost and all can be saved." He continues, "Man is indeed imperfect, the product of his own creation and undoing. But all that will eventually change, and when that happens man will once again live in peace and harmony. Love and peace will return to the earth and cleanse the horrors and excesses of the dark ages which today pollute the very atmosphere.... Only through love can the world be saved."[1] He assures us that suffering and misery are the inescapable acts of the Cosmic drama. God does not decree these calamities, but man invites them by way of retribution for his own evil deeds.[7]

Views of the Earth Changes

Views of the stage of development during the advent of the New Age have been expressed by several people. Wise states, "As the transformation process progresses fewer people will hold as reality the ideas and beliefs that currently govern your civilization. When new models emerge, people will feel safe, acknowledging that what they have always called reality is just one set of choices from the menu of possibilities."[3] Again commenting on the future of the new world order, Wise states, "You cannot afford to have the new invading culture—no matter how elevated or Universal—consume your old body politic, your old body of thought or your old three-dimensional bodies...not quite yet. The consciousness of the future is already functioning among you, but it has not yet been successfully formulated for societal embodiment. The future is still developing, using the resources of the current unenlightened collective body."[3] According to Wise, more than one fifth of the population is consciously attuned, in other words, they could recognize the shift and deal with it. Commenting on the attunement of the population in different parts of the world she referred to India as the classic model, where there is a "central placement of spiritual integrity" in the lives of these people and that even in the worst situations they can continue to live in an honest, enlightened and non-violent manner. She goes on to state, "I don't believe that all of us are going to get wiped off the face of the Earth because great Earth Changes are happening. Instead what is happening is that we are having a planetary change in both frequency and magnetism. We are altering our collective consciousness. And as we do that the disparity between the transformation going on inside of us and the old order still happening—is so great that it is almost as if it were different worlds.... There is a spiritual drive inside of us guiding us toward integrity and wholeness and love and devotion and creativity and joy and expression."[11]

Earth Changes—The Internet

Reports of the Shift are now available on the Internet, and as they describe in a language the layman can understand, some excerpts are reproduced below. "Earth's background basic frequency or heart beat is rising dramatically...for decades the overall measurement was 7.8 cycles per second. This was thought to be a constant; global military communication developed on this frequency. Recent reports set the rate at over 11 cycles per second and climbing. Science doesn't know why or what to make of it. While Earth's pulse-rate is rising, her magnetic field strength, on the other hand, is declining. According to Professor Bannerjee of the University of New Mexico, the field has lost up to half its intensity in the last 4000 years. And because a forerunner of magnetic polar reversals is this field strength, Professor Bannerjee believes that another reversal is due.... The possible outcome of this reversal can include some of the following changes, such as, time appearing to speed up as we approach 'Zero Point' and a 24-hour day will seem to be about 16 hours or less.... Zero Point or the 'Shift of the Ages' has been predicted by ancient peoples for thousands of years... Zero Point or a flip of the magnetic poles will probably happen soon, within the next few years.... After Zero Point the sun will rise in the west and set in the east approximately. Past occurrences of this change have been found in ancient records.... The Zero Point flip will probably introduce us to the fourth dimension. Here, everything we think or desire will instantly manifest.... Our physical body is changing as we approach Zero Point.... A new light body is being created and we are becoming more

intuitive. The Mayan Calendar predicted all the changes that
are occurring now. They say we are going beyond technology
and back to the natural cycles of nature and the universe....
All this information is not fearful. Be prepared for changes
that will bring in the New Age of light. We are going beyond
money and time where fear-based concepts are totally
dissolved."[10a]

"Although no one is sure when the pole-shift will take
place this time (but 2012 seems a bit of a sure bet,) one thing
is certain, it will happen within this generation..."[10b]

Regarding the time preceding the actual Shift, that is, before
the onset of the new paradigm or the new world order, the
following information from the Internet sums up the changes
that will take place: "As the Shift approaches, things begin
to go out of balance, and the magnetic field begins to fluctuate
significantly over a very short period of time.... What happens
then is that people start to go crazy emotionally. This breaks
down economical and social structures on the planet, because
it is only people who keep these structures together.... The
key is the magnetic field of the Earth, which is what we use to
interpret who and what we think we are and also to store
our memory.... About 5 to 6 hours before the actual shift
happens, an extraordinary visual phenomenon should take
place. The third and fourth dimensions actually begin to
interface. Third dimensional consciousness gradually
recedes away from us as we approach fourth dimensional
consciousness. As the third dimensional grid begins to break
down, synthetic objects disappear" (e.g., electric equipment,
synthetic drugs, chemicals, nuclear materials, pollutants,
etc.). "In order to survive a polar shift, objects must be made
purely out of natural materials...that are in resonance with
the earth.... As the synthetic objects begin to disappear, fourth
dimensional objects may suddenly emerge. Colours and
shapes unlike anything we have ever known will appear on
the landscape...." According to the spiritual masters we have

already reached the point where 1.5 billion people will definitely make the conscious shift...and perhaps, everyone, or almost everyone will make it into the next dimension. "Even if we are able to keep the magnetic field together up until the actual Shift, there will almost certainly be a three and a half day period when it will be completely gone.... As soon as the magnetic field collapses, the Earth may disappear for you, and you will be in the Great Void...for three and a half days.... Then life will come back in the fourth dimensional world. You will find yourself in a brand new world the likes of which you have never conceived.... You will appear just as you are now.... However, the atomic structure of your body, though it comes through, will have changed dramatically. The mass of your atoms would have been converted to energy. The individual atoms will have separated from one another at a phenomenal distance. Most of your body will be energy— a light body.... Remember, in this new world you would be creating your reality moment by moment with your thoughts. Manifestation will be instant.... This is why thoughts like peace, beauty, love etc. are so important. If you are motivated by fear in the fourth dimension, you will create and manifest your reality instantly and you will find yourself confronted by something terrifying. The quality of thoughts is totally important on the fourth dimension...hence the purity of thoughts. Love and peace and unity and being kind to your neighbours are ultimately very practical because they work reciprocally."[10b]

No Place for Fear

It is the belief of the author that those persons who survive the devastation prior to the Shift and who successfully attain the stage where the vibratory rate of their cells have got into synchrony with Earth's enhanced frequency, it can be assumed that such persons will have fulfilled all the criteria for attaining this high state. It is inconceivable, therefore, to attribute fear or other negative feelings to such persons. This appears to be a misplaced notion. Once divine love flows through the human heart, it displaces everything else and occupies the entire space. And at this time every cell in the human body will be emitting the purest frequency of energy which is love. Since love is God and God is love, according to Sai Baba, then it is God who occupies centre-stage in the heart. With the Divine firmly ensconced, no longer is there room for fear or negative thoughts. All those who survive the Shift will be at different levels of achievement, except perhaps, for those highly evolved souls, the realized beings, who would be vibrating at the highest possible level, having attained the greatest vibratory rate capable of shifting into the fourth dimension at will. The human beings populating the new world will act as a collective body. In such an enlightened society, there will be no place or need for fear.

We can assume that all the 'isms' invented by third-dimensional man such as fanaticism, casteism, factionalism, racism, sectarianism, etc., will have been swept away along with the disassociation of all the inharmonic energies of the old paradigm including the mentalities that ensured their survival.... Otherwise, how shall we have a world that will be the Utopia everyone, including Sri Sathya Sai Baba, envisages? It will be Paradise, heaven on earth, some say. This can happen only if the collective behaviour of the people eschews superiority and inferiority in their interaction with the group. As Wise says, "When both the greatness and the smallness in each person is readily recognizable, an equalizing will occur that will redefine your experience of Humanity. Judgments will be more easily replaced with compassion and support. Your understanding of reality will change as a result. You will recognize that you are all working on the same challenge in different ways and that no one is working against it."[3] With the establishment of the Golden Age, we shall be looking at an idealized society consisting of ideal men and women.

Responsibility and Instantaneous Thought Manifestation

As referred to in previous chapters, the reason for instant manifestation of thought is the removal of the time-lag between a thought and its consequence, due to the decrease in Earth's magnetic field. Dense magnetics tend to block the effect from the cause—that is, the instant materialization of the thought. It is because of magnetics that we are able to think, pursue thoughts and hold them in memory. Instant manifestation of thought confers on us a certain responsibility. The responsibility lies in cultivating and nurturing positive thinking including thoughts such as love, compassion, kindliness, thoughtfulness, caring, forgiveness, tolerance, acceptance, etc. As noted above, evil or negative thoughts will certainly not enter the minds of those who are oriented towards the Divine. There would be a continuous stream of noble, good and positive thoughts emanating from such mental states. This is the bulwark against negativity and fear, along with the fact that the inhabitants of the New Age will be of a superior breed of humans.

It is said that the physical form would look the same, but the internal structure of the body will have undergone drastic changes transforming most of the body into energy resulting in a light body. With this new body and the ability to have instant manifestation of thought we shall become superbeings—alike to the Gods.

All the changes occurring at present and those predicted for the future in and on the Earth, are the result of Earth's zero magnetism and high frequency resonance. This indicates our close connection to Mother Earth. We are inextricably linked to her in so many vital ways. Isn't this sufficient indication that we should treat her with the respect, reverence and love that she deserves and that we show to our own human parents. Instead, what have we done to her within a short span of 200 to 300 years? The Eastern countries, the

African continent and other so-called developing countries
have co-existed with Mother Earth for untold millennia,
without producing holes in the ozone layer, or causing the
glaciers of Antarctica to melt, or raising the level of the oceans,
or contaminating her soil, her waters and her air. These
nations treated the elements with the respect they deserve.
In India, particularly, the rivers are considered sacred and
India's largest river is referred to as the holy Ganges; even
fire is given a place of reverence, and Agni, the God of fire,
has been worshipped from time immemorial. But this sacred
approach to Nature and her five elements was sacrificed long
ago at the altar of development and material progress, and
today obeisance is paid to the gods of commerce, industry
and materialistic pursuits. We have eventually arrived, only
to find that there is no way out of the morass and chaos we
have created. So, it is Mother Earth herself who will have to
pull us out of the quagmire, but not before chastising us to
the extent we deserve for our omissions and commissions,
and the shabby way we have treated her for so long. The
chastisement has begun. On December 26, 2004, she gave
us her first warning signal. It is for us to take note. But have
we changed?

The Necessity for Catastrophic Events

Commenting on the Shift, Wise says, "When the paradigm
shifts, there will be a planetary energy change of frequency
and magnetism...what we hold here to be valuable doesn't
even make much sense in another dimension. As the
frequency and magnetism change on the planet, our entire
perceptual context is going to change. So it's not going to be
like giving up this for that. The very psyche, the context, is
going to change."[11] There are 55 millions (26 per cent of the
population of the U.S.A.) who can be categorized as the
transformational population or cultural creatives and
according to Wise "This study is a landmark for the world. It

gives the transformational population a powerful position in the world's marketplace from which to influence the current, dominant material reality toward integration—if these individuals bond and initiate collective action."[3] The keywords here are 'if' and 'bond'. While appreciating Wise's positive approach to this problem, we as three-dimensional beings, know only too well that this approach is fraught with danger—for no sooner a group of three-dimensional humans based on duality, decide to form a group for collective thought and action, the dormant egos become alive, raise their heads, spread their hoods and watching intently, are always ready to strike. Isn't that the experience of all of us?

In His discourse in the May, 2005 issue of *Sanathana Sarathi* Sai Baba's statement on human nature seems to support this contention. "It is said out of all living beings, human birth is the rarest. Man is the crest jewel of the entire creation. He is the main cause behind the phenomenal progress of the world. But man today is unable to realize his humanness. Because of identifying himself with his physical form, he has forgotten his humanness. Since he calls himself a human being, it is his duty to realize the greatness of humanness....

"Man, in fact, has a special status in the entire creation. But he does not try to realize his true nature. It does no credit to a human being to derive satisfaction from studying scriptures and talking about them. Real merit lies in practising the ideals of humanness in one's life and setting an example to others. Man has no authority to teach ideals to others without putting them into practice himself first. In fact, he is gifted with human birth to be an ideal in the entire creation....

"One can be called a human only when one has human quality. One should therefore understand the real meaning of the term, human quality, first. Human quality emerges from one's own Self. It cannot be acquired by reading books, listening to others or talking about it."

"Human birth will find fulfillment only when man practices human qualities."[5b]

Wise does not think that cataclysmic changes on the planet are necessary to propel mankind into making the necessary adjustments to accept drastic changes that will occur for the transition from old to new; but past experience and the present behaviour and attitude of the majority seem to indicate otherwise. Also without cataclysmic and catastrophic events it is difficult to visualize how Nature will go about cleaning up the unwholesome and widespread mess man has made of Earth. How will polluted soil, water and air be made clean and pure again? Will 'frequency filters'[2] and vibrational change alone be able to transform the elements, purify them and restore them to their pristine state? Do we really know? All previous planetary changes recorded by ancient civilizations have been brought about by calamities and cataclysmic events. Why should this one be different?

To repeat here what Sai Baba has said about the future scene. Peggy Mason, author of "Sathya Sai Baba—The Embodiment of Love", during a private interview with Sai Baba, posed the following question, "But what about the planet, Swami?" Sai Baba replied that there will be physical repercussions because of growing selfishness, minor adjustments to the planet and a certain clear-out. He also told her "Man's inhumanity to man expresses itself in the form of natural catastrophes, like earthquakes". He added, "The world is the body of God. There is a cancer in the body, and it must be removed."

The Fourth Dimension

Earth's decreasing magnetism and increasing frequency have such an effect on us that they are able to change our physical structure and transform us into beings with light bodies which will be mainly composed of energy, and with an enhanced vibratory rate of our cells can allow us to make the shift into the fourth dimension. In this state some humans will be vibrating at such a high pitch, and with a light body composed mainly of energy, may at times become invisible to others around them vibrating at a lower velocity. With this ability to step in and out as it were from one dimension into another, we may be able to interact with disembodied souls and thereby come to realize that nothing dies, and thus shall be convinced that we don't really die, that only the physical body perishes and returns to the five elements from which it originated; that the spirit which informs matter lives on. Discarnate entities may have no body made of matter, but are alive, perhaps more so than we are and may be more fully aware of themselves than we are. Having this knowledge of the world of the departed souls, we shall be able to understand what Sri Krishna said to Arjuna, that just as a person casts off worn-out clothes and puts on others that are new, so does the Self which is embodied casts off worn-out bodies and enters into new bodies.

With knowledge of the structural changes that will take place in our physical bodies and the mental and spiritual changes occurring, we can understand much better what Braden has described about these changes. He writes, "Each holographically tuned cell within our bodies is attempting to match the vibration of our new experience... Our bodies are being asked to restructure their physical and morphogenetic fields of energy, information and light, to accommodate the new codes of geometry activated by the Shift. Our restructuring and realignment results in profound effects, radical shifts of thought, feeling and emotion."[2] Again relating to the changes that will take place, "This is the Shift to a new way of expressing the human form, through the lens of higher frequency.... The changing paradigm is accomplished through a realignment of two digitally measurable, fundamental parameters—those of planetary frequency and planetary magnetics. These parameters alone have a far-reaching and profound impact upon human consciousness, human thought and perception specifically, and the behaviour of matter in general."[2] Continuing on the same theme he says, "The net effect of this environment is that those who introduce themselves into these null-magnetic fields have nearly direct access to themselves as pure information without the interference patterns of judgment, fear, ego or the buffers of lag-time between thought and the consequence of a thought. With that access comes the opportunity of cellular and core level changes directed through the will of the individual consciously toward the life parameters of choice. As the individual, the ancient initiate chose to think and feel differently, he or she was able to consciously alter the frequency of each cell of the mind, body and spirit complex.... The timing of the magnetic shift to coincide with the dimensional translation is a 'gift' that allows us direct access to ourselves to balance, heal and accomplish the dimensional shift successfully."[2]

The New Age Inhabitants

It is estimated that approximately 1.5 billion people will survive the Shift and that most of them will enter the Fourth Dimension. If this is so then the remaining five billion people will have been removed; will have made the transition or 'clear out' as Sai Baba has announced. In this manner the New Age will be composed of only those who survived the Shift. Those of us who do not survive will have only ourselves to blame. We may not have changed our ways, our life-style and our thinking, but have instead gradually put into cold storage our philosophy, religion, human values and the noble qualities that distinguish us as civilized beings, slowly deteriorating over a period of time, recklessly throwing ourselves into sensual pleasures regardless of the dangerous consequences; indulging our weakness for money, wealth, status, pomp and fame; not caring a whit for our less fortunate fellow human beings. Then how is it possible for us to suddenly turn somersault and correct our ways, right ourselves and behave like civilized human beings. It is well-nigh impossible for some of us to make the right about-turn at this late stage in the game. Many people after listening to what is expected of them to enter the new world order which they are told is due anytime now reply that the criteria for making the change are too drastic and they cannot afford such changes. When it is explained that failure to do so may be the determining factor as to their survival on the planet, they simply shrug their shoulders and retort "So be it". Can anything be done for or with such individuals? It is a sheer waste of time, and may be better spent trying to improve oneself for what lies ahead in the future.

The Events Leading to the Golden Age

From the material presented by Braden and the predictions and pronouncements of Sai Baba, with respect to the occurrence of events on Earth leading to the Golden Age, we can visualize the following sequential progression of events: As the electromagnetic changes on Earth continue, geophysical events will increase. There will be calamities of diverse kinds, severe accidents, cataclysmic and catastrophic events, such as earthquakes, volcanic eruptions, cyclones, hurricanes, tornadoes, 'harsh storms and killing winds',[4] tsunamis of increasing height and ferocity from undersea volcanic and earthquake eruptions, excessive rainfall, flooding, excessive snowfall, a rising ocean level, increased temperatures, droughts, failure of crops and famines. At the point of threshold resonance at or near 13 Hz, magnetics are approaching zero. The chaos leading up to this time has ceased. That portion of earth which is bathed in sunlight will remain in sunlight for the duration of the process—that which is in darkness for the same period of time.[2] After the reversal of Earth's magnetic fields there will be the temporary failure of electrical and magnetic technologies based upon the movement of electrons through a conductor—computers, broadcast technologies may become temporarily invalid. Technologies that depend upon a directional flow of electrons may prove invalid as the flow of electrons is reversed.[2] During the event of the Shift itself many individuals will experience the 72 hours in an unconscious and relaxed state akin to the Tibetan Bardo state—essentially a dream experience.[2]

Pari passu with the catastrophic events, millions, possibly billions of us will make the transition and those who remain will be removed by 'frequency filters',[2] that is, those of us with inharmonic traits, who will be unable to increase the vibratory rate of our cells to bring it into harmony with Earth's increased resonance, thus making it near to impossible for us to remain embodied. In this manner, Sai Baba's repeated warning about a 'clear out' will reduce the present population of approximately six and a half billions to probably 1.5 billions as predicted by some spiritual masters. This figure is also in agreement with the 20 per cent to 26 per cent Wise describes as arrived at by a survey in the U.S.A. some years ago. Thus by the dawn of the New Age, the population of the earth will have been drastically reduced. It has been said that the New Age will not countenance any individual with a polluted or a warped mentality. The Golden Age will be such only if those sort of mentalities are completely removed so that after Nature has spent her fury, there will be a small population left on the surface of the planet. Those fortunate souls will be the New Agers, a highly evolved group of *Homo sapiens* possessing body cells vibrating at a velocity perfectly in harmony with the earth's high pitch of frequency. A large proportion of their cells will have been transformed into energy, producing 'light' bodies, enabling them to gain entrance into the Fourth Dimension after the Shift. Whether or not all survivors will move into the fourth dimension is not definite. At the same time it should be recalled that free-will to make the choice will be the determining factor in these cases. As the process will affect all biological life on Earth, it is to be expected that all living cells whether of man, animal and possibly plant will undergo similar changes, that of enhanced vibratory rates. This would be what many people have been looking forward to—a Paradise on Earth! A world that Sai Baba describes thus, "It is not what anyone alive can imagine. It is not something that one can try to aspire to. It is beyond all comprehension. I can say its beauty is magnificent beyond all dreams. And as each of you perform your silent work, I will embrace you to my heart and henceforth your souls shall be lifted up and your eyes will reveal My Presence within.... This I say to all My devotees from the Lord's Mountain Top where all the Universes become one. Be about My work, My beloved devotees. Your breath will carry the scent of the Blossoms of Heaven. Your example will be that of Angels. Your joy will be My Joy."[1]

The Requirements of the New Age

Commenting on what we should do to meet the requirements of the New Age, Wise advises us to get practical; to establish systems for providing organically produced food; aesthetic and environmentally suitable and acceptable housing; all-inclusive integral health care; education based on human values. "Any practical manifestation will create positive public awareness and a popular desire to change the existing system, bit by bit."[3]

Elaborating on the ill effects of inorganically produced food she states, "Most inorganically produced food-stuffs are not of the same nature as you are. While inorganically produced or highly processed foods sustain you, they starve essential subtle dimensions of your well-being. When they go into your body, they are in you, but not of you because they are not sympathetic with your nature. This is an adversarial relationship. Who will suffer? ...As you expand into higher levels of love, consciousness, integrity and response ability, you have more need to feed yourselves at these levels.... You want your body to vibrate at the same level as the essential Universe—not the same level as the grocery store.... With undeveloped awareness you cultivate and consume food that is not sufficiently developed in its integrity to fulfil your potential for health.... Any misalignment with nature that goes beyond your organic tolerances will increase your overall vulnerability.... Your body and the Earth are two expressions of the same intricate formula of nature. They are both environments. Pollute one and the other is invariably polluted. If either is polluted beyond its tolerances, both will eventually demonstrate the misalignment as unwellness, disease or other forms of disintegration."[3]

The Consequences of Imbalance

Nature abhors imbalance. Everything in Nature remains in a state of balance if not interfered with. As soon as imbalance occurs her forces are employed to rectify the cause and to restore the balance. If however, the imbalance becomes compounded by failure to remove the cause, Nature is unable to deal with the imbalance and the situation reaches the point of no return. It is as if she surpasses her physical or physiological limit such as occurs in humans. She then sounds her danger alarm. It is at this stage that man ignores the danger signals and the forces of Nature, unable to restore the balance, get out of hand and become hostile, the consequences of which are only too familiar—earthquakes, storms, tidal waves, tsunamis, floods and other calamities.

Everything in Nature is balanced because she adheres to certain laws and does not deviate from them, unlike humans. The accuracy with which Nature conducts her various activities is seen in such daily occurrences which we take for granted: the timings of sunrise and sunset; the rotation of the earth on its axis, an accurate movement, except at the present time when the earth's rotation has started slowing down; the orbiting around the sun, so accurate that the seasons of the year can be relied on for sowing of seed and harvesting at their proper time. In short, everything moves with clock-wise accuracy, and man for millennia have depended on this accuracy for the business of living. Everything therefore is in a state of ecological balance and moves with accuracy; and whenever and wherever there is imbalance, usually man and his unnatural activities are the cause. Nature has therefore to resort to certain remedial measures in the form of natural phenomena to repair the damage and regain her balance. She has no alternative. She has to 'shake' herself to fill up the gaping holes and yawning caverns man has made into the depth of the bowels of the Earth. This she has to accomplish as early as possible so that whatever little is left undisturbed can at least be saved from the iniquitous acts of man. Thus the inhabitants of the planet will have to accept with courage and equanimity whatever means and methods Nature may adopt to achieve her ends—the restoration of the earth wherever it has undergone damage, and in doing so bring healing to the planet so that man may once again live his life on Earth in health, peace and joy as Nature intended him to do.

The Changes During the Establishment of the Golden Age

Some comments Sai Baba has made about the changes that will occur physically, mentally and spiritually during the establishment of the Golden Age:

"Let there be light. Let the light shine forth to show the way for a reawakening of the human race. The Golden Age is here now, waiting for man to experience it just as soon as he is ready. What more can a man want than God realization and ultimate bliss.... Everyone should strive to achieve peace of mind so that they can help to build a new atmosphere in the world and accelerate the arrival of the new Golden Age."[1]

Again about the establishment of the New Age He states, "The day of awakening is not so far away and when it comes there will be a revelation of the true power of God, a manifestation of the omnipresence of the Lord. This will be a signal for a great move forward, and the weeding out of those who are not ready to accept the challenge of the moment. It will be just so; mark My words. But few will listen, very few."[1]

Continuing His comments on the same theme, He says, "All of you are torch-bearers. You have been given this opportunity to carry out the work of the Lord. Do not have any fear about the outcome. My mission will succeed and My love will cleanse the earth and lead mankind to a new Golden Age. The Golden Age is here now, just waiting for man to move into it and find the peace that has deluded him all this time.... Mark My word...the time has come. The time is here now. Awaken, awaken, take up your bed and walk. Walk towards the light and realize your own divinity."[1]

Sai Baba has affirmed that the calamity which has come upon mankind will be averted; a new Golden Age will recur. He asserted that the time will come when He will have to move across the sky and use the sky as an auditorium. "Yes, that too will happen, believe Me", He said.

"Your mission has begun. Those are my words to you, My devotees. Each of you has a unique and valuable part to play in this lifetime. Only those whom I have called can serve Me."[1]

"My Mission has now reached this point in time when each one of you now has work to do. This planet has a purpose in the great galaxy in which it is held. That purpose is now unfolding before our eyes. I call upon you to radiate the Devotion within you so that its unseen power will envelop all who come into your orbit. To allow yourself to impart that purity of heart within you towards all human beings and all living creatures and do not reach for the fruits of your work.

This part of My mission is performed in absolute silence. You are my instruments from whom my love will pour. Be always aware that the moment you let your ego descend upon you My work ceases. When you have overcome your negative unmindfulness you will again become My Source."[1]

"The multiplication of my love will be felt throughout the world. I have prepared you for this work over many incarnations. I have drawn you to Me. I have made great steps in My Mission over these past Incarnations. My work is ceaseless, and so your work too is without end. Know that I am within you and without you. There is no difference. Rid yourself of petty matters forever. You are now Me and I am now thee. There is no difference. My Darshan will pour forth from Me to and through you. You may be unaware of this constant action. Be ever pure of heart and soul and mankind in your lifetime will benefit from your unique qualities.... Others too will join me in this Mission when I draw them to Me."[1]

"As children of Sai, you have this unique opportunity to become leaders of the world, leaders of humanity, and you can help to transform the world and hasten the arrival of a new Golden Age. That is my promise, that the new Golden Age is there waiting..."[1]

Ron Laing, writing in "Sathya Sai Baba—The Embodiment of Love" confesses, "...I had come to the firm conclusion that the Divine Principle had incarnated...indeed, that an avatar had come to save the world from destruction and to usher in a new Golden Age."

Nine

Geophysical Changes and Other Events as Portents of the Future

The Sumatra Tsunami

It is necessary at this stage in Earth Changes to take note of the geophysical events that are occurring and have occurred prior and subsequent to the Sumatra tsunami, the first to strike India, and to cause much damage to the Southern Indian coast, along with a dozen other countries of the Indian Ocean region with devastating results and loss of life, amounting at the latest count to almost 500,000. The wall of water raised by the tsunami reached a height of more than one hundred feet as subsequently determined by scientists who discovered that the seventh storey of a building in Indonesia had been hit. The amount of energy released by the undersea earthquake with a magnitude of 9.3 on the Richter Scale was reported to be equivalent to 30,000 pounds of TNT or 2.5 million Hiroshima bombs. This massive release of energy shifting laterally and in a northerly direction was sufficient to shake the massive Himalayan mountains, the mightiest on earth, that have stood the test of time for millennia, without being affected by geophysical occurrences—so great was this colossal amount of energy.

Post-tsunami Earth Changes

Reports currently describe the earth as wobbling on its axis since the Sumatra earthquake; also that there is somewhat of a change in her orbit around the sun. It has been reported that the days and nights are becoming longer. There is also a hint that the volcano in La Palma, one of the Spanish Canary Islands, is becoming active, with the possible danger of producing a mega tsunami which could rise to such a height as to affect several countries in the region, including the United States of America, flattening the structures along the Atlantic Seaboard, inundating New York city and the cities on the eastern coast. This erupting volcano could release a tsunami larger than any in recorded history. One explosion of this kind could send a chunk of rock the size of the Isle of Weight into the Atlantic at up to 220 miles an hour. A wall of water up to 165 feet high would crash into the Atlantic Seaboard of the U.S.A. flattening everything in its path. In the U.S. alone, tens of millions of lives will be at stake. Spain, Portugal, France, Britain, Brazil, the Caribbean and West Africa would be swamped by great waves.

Nature's First Major Warning

The Sumatra tsunami was Nature's first dose of the first medicine from her vast therapeutic armamentarium. There are more to come. We can trust Nature's resourcefulness whether the next one will be a repeated dose of the same medicine or an altogether different medication, and this will depend on her judgment of what is best suited for the earth at the time. These healing episodes will return our beloved planet to us sometime before 2012, according to the ancient predictions, healed and healthy again, a fit planet for a highly evolved race of human beings as foretold for the human species.

The Himalayan Glaciers

Reports have been coming in that the Himalayan glaciers are melting rapidly and that there would be flooding of Northern India, China and Nepal whose rivers are fed by the Himalayan snows. It is surmised that within 20 years the rivers of these countries will dry up due to lack of water at the source.

Earthquakes

As of this writing earthquakes are occurring all over the globe, varying in magnitude from 4 to 8 on the Richter Scale. Earthquakes throughout the globe are increasing in frequency and magnitude decade after decade for more than 100 years. Warning has been given about the possibility of a major earthquake striking the western coast of Sumatra as a result of the monster quake that generated the December 26 tsunami. The Indonesian City of Banda Aceh, which was already badly hit by the killer wave, could be at risk from a quake measuring up to 7.5 on the Richter Scale and there is a potential for a tsunami-making 8.5 quake offshore.

Seismologist John McCloskey at Britain's University of Ulster stated that there is no doubt. Their calculations show a very significant increase of stress on two major active faults in the Sumatra region since December 26. He stated that in so-called subduction zones, an earthquake can be swiftly followed by another one if certain geological conditions are met. There is a very well established link between these stresses and following earthquakes, he said. "Energy released by the December 26 quake has boosted stress in adjoining parts of two dangerous faults. One fault runs under-land to the east of the December 26 quake and crosses the northwestern tip of Sumatra. The other fault, known as the Sunda trench, runs under the sea to the south, parallel to the coast, where two fatal tsunamis occurred in 1833 and 1861", he stated. McCloskey's team has redrawn the geological map of one of earth's seismic hotspots after the 9.3 (Richter Scale) December 26 quake. The massive movement ruptured 250,000 square kilometres on a stretch of the Burma micro plate, a narrow tongue of the earth's crust that is jostled by the neighbouring Indian, Australian and Sunda plates. That peaked plunge, by as much as 20 metres, triggered the tsunami killing more than 273,000 people in eleven nations on the northern rim of the Indian Ocean (*The New Indian Express*, March, 2005).

Unsettling reports currently coming out of Japan by Japanese seismologists and scientists describe the four seismic plates beneath the Japanese Islands, as being subjected to pressure from increasing energy beneath the land mass and pose a great danger to the country as a whole. The plates run under almost all the islands. There is also the formation of a large trough in the earth under the sea, south-east of Osaka. With seismic activity already occurring in that region the possibility of a strong quake at the location of the trough can result in a mega tsunami which could flatten Osaka and its surroundings. There is another trough east of Tokyo, which also poses added danger. It seems at the present time at least that three areas on the globe are in the process of developing more and more seismic activity. The disaster caused by the Sumatra quake and subsequent tsunami is now common knowledge—the first to have occurred in 40 years with a recording of 9.3 on the Richter Scale. The other area concerns a volcano under the sea in La Palma in the Canaries as described above, with fatal consequences to the Atlantic Seaboard of the United State, if the volcano were to erupt producing a mega tsunami. The third area seems to becoming localized to Japan with an earthquake of 8 on the Richter Scale occurring off the coast of Osaka. These areas cover a great part of the globe and increasing seismic activity in those locations alone can endanger the planet.

Glaciers of Antarctica

Another threat is the rapid melting of the glaciers of Antarctica, something the scientists thought would not happen in a thousand years, as the ice formation of Antarctica was solid enough to withstand any geological event. Not so, it seems now. This new phenomenon would increase the sea-level which has recently been reported to have risen especially in the Bay of Bengal following the recent Sumatra tsunami. The dangers of an increase in sea level are obvious—flooding of low-lying areas and small islands. Groups of islands like the Caribbean, the Canaries, the South Sea Islands, the Maldives and the Andamans are among those threatened. The geoscientists, however, are not agreed on the cause of the rising of the ocean. Since the beginning of the 21st century, the shrinking of the glaciers of Antarctica has become greatly increased. The fact that half a century ago the glaciers were growing in length, and that within a few years, they have started shrinking rapidly is sufficient evidence that the increased temperatures in the region may be partially the cause. This melting of the glaciers could result in the increase of the sea level. They are now retreating at the rate of 50 metres per annum faster than a half century ago. They are losing more ice annually than they can gain through falling snow.

El Nino

As if adding insult to injury, reports have recently come in that El Nino may return. This weather pattern had caused 96 billion dollars of crop and property damage in 1997 and 1998. An unexpected warming of the Pacific Ocean in February 2005 reduced air pressure from Tahiti to Australia to a 22-year low. Similar changes eight years ago developed into an intense El Nino that caused droughts in Asia, floods in South America and tornadoes in the U.S.A. The chances of an El Nino pattern developing by mid-2005 are about 50 per cent compared with 20 per cent normally, according to an associate professor of climatology at the University of Southern Queensland in Australia. The return of El Nino emerges first in Australia and takes months to develop. El Nino which means 'little boy' in Spanish got its name from Peruvian fishermen who noticed that warmer sea temperatures reduced their catch around

Christmas. El Nino occurs about two to three times in a decade and can last 18 months (*The Hindu Business Line*, April, 2005).

The Pacific Ring of Fire

Reports from Indonesia state that massive quakes have activated two huge volcanoes and sent shock-waves reverberating along a vast and volatile region known as the 'Pacific Ring of Fire'. Both on land or underwater the volatile edges of the north Pacific, bounded by the east Asia rim and the west coast of the Americas are alive with near constant seismic activity; one of the most dramatic natural disasters of recent history has happened within the Ring's arc which stretches from Chile, north to Alaska and then west to encompass Japan, Southeast Asia and the Pacific Islands. From the explosion of Krakatoa volcano off Indonesia in 1883 to the eruption of Mount St. Helens in the U.S. in 1980, the Ring's power is legendary (*The Hindu*, April, 2005). Referring to an incident in New Zealand as a 'wake-up call', a news item in *The Hindu Business Line*, April 2005, quoting Reuter, reports a geo-thermal eruption which created a 50-metre crater about 26 km south of Auckland. The eruption uprooted trees, tossed rocks into a nearby field and blanketed the once thick pine forest with pale grey mist.

Volcanoes

From *The Weekly Volcanic Activity Report*—a cooperative project between the *Smithsonian Global Volcanism Programme* and the *U.S. Geological Survey's Volcanic Hazards*. The Report contains data on volcanic activity worldwide during the months of April 2004 to April 2005. During this period of approximately one year, the number of volcanic eruptions reported exceeded eighty, occurring in more than fifty countries. All the major countries and continents of the world have been affected, except Canada, India and China. In Japan alone, eight eruptions, varying in intensity have been recorded; in

Indonesia fifteen; in Russia eight, all in the year 2005; in Papua New Guinea, six eruptions, four of which took place this year; in the U.S.A. at least five, three occurring in 2005; in Central America, seven eruptions and in South America six such. In Europe, Mount Etna in Sicily (Italy) erupted this year in February; in Mexico two occurred this year including Popocatepetle; notably Mount St. Helens in the U.S. erupted this year, the only eruption during the one year period; in the Congo two and Ethiopia one all in 2004: one in Iceland last year, one in the Canary Islands in 2004 and one in New Zealand in November 2004.

The eruption in the Canaries is noteworthy, because on La Palma Island an undersea volcano has become active and geophysicists have sounded the warning of a mega tsunami following its eruption which could spell disaster to the Atlantic Seaboard of the U.S. The New Zealand eruption is also important because (April in 2005) a geothermal eruption took place not far from Auckland, in the midst of a pine forest, only five months following the volcanic eruption. Note has to be taken of Mount St. Helens eruption in the U.S.A. in April this year, as another eruption occurred in 1960. Apart from the above, eruptions have taken place in the West Indies, Reunion Island, the Philippines and Tristan da Cunha.

The data recorded above is evidence enough to indicate that something has gone wrong somewhere to cause the earth to erupt in so many places within a relatively short period of one year. While it is necessary and wise to keep track of these geophysical events as recorded by satellite and personal observation, the authorities should proceed one step further and try to make some sort of investigation into the causes producing these events. Recording of detailed data is not enough. The earth appears to be undergoing rapid changes, causing her to exude 'fear, pain, tremors and spasms.'⁴ With impending disaster only a few years away according to the prophets of doom, perhaps it is too late to start thinking about causes; nevertheless, there is nothing wrong in starting to think. The question is, are we really interested in thinking?

The Ozone Layer

The Hindu, April, 2005, reproducing material from *Guardian Newspapers Limited,* 2005, reports that research by Cambridge University has dashed hopes that the ozone layer is on the mend, and that this layer over the Arctic has thinned this year to the lowest levels since records began when scientists were beginning to believe that it had begun to heal. The increased loss of ozone allows more harmful ultraviolet light to reach the earth's surface, making children and sportspersons such as skiers more vulnerable to skin cancer. The scientists have shown that it is not increased pollution but a side-effect of climate change that is making ozone depletion worse. At high altitudes, 50 per cent of the protective layer had been destroyed. Scientists believe that it could take another 50 years before the problem is solved. Stratospheric clouds in the winter 15 miles above the earth are responsible for causing further loss of ozone. These clouds in the middle of the ozone layer provide a platform which makes it easier for rapid chemical reactions to take place which destroy ozone. For three months from the end of November (2004) there were more clouds for longer periods than ever previously recorded.

The scientists found the lowest levels of ozone recorded since measurements began 40 years ago. Pollution levels have levelled off, but changes in the atmosphere have made it easier for the reactions to take place that allow pollutants to destroy ozone. With these changes likely to continue and get worse, as global warming increases, then ozone will be further depleted even if the level of pollution is going down. Over all about 30 per cent of the ozone layer was destroyed. The stratosphere above the earth is getting colder, consequently ice clouds form between 14 and 26 kilometres above the earth, exactly in the region where the protective ozone is found.

Another instance of Earth Changes relate to 'Global warming'. Dr. Rajendra Pachauri*, Head of the official U.S. intergovernmental Panel on climate changes, said he now believes the world has "already reached the level of dangerous concentrations of carbon dioxide in the atmosphere". Pachauri's statements included a call for immediate "very deep cuts in pollution as necessary for humanity's survival."

Under-reporting of Official Information

Unofficial reports state that melting north and south poles of the earth, melting glaciers and rising seas are occurring, and these as far as the media is concerned are under-reported for reasons best known to those who are responsible for monitoring geo-physical events. Only when the cities along the coast lines are inundated by several feet of water will the public at large come to know the actual situation. It has been reported that the U.S. authorities knew about the Sumatra earthquake and under-reported it as 8.1, then 8.5, then 9.0 and finally were forced to reveal the correct magnitude as 9.3. Apparently, the *modus operandi* is that where the results of seismic and related events are minimal, these are made public. The more damaging events are underplayed.

Upon further review, NASA announced that the Sumatra quake shifted Earth's north pole by about 2.5 centimetres. The mass displacement caused by the seismic event also changed the planet's shape, making it more evenly round by one part in 10 billion (NASA Estimating Quake's Effect January, 2005). One explanation for the displacement of the Indo-Australian plate is a torque effect, the North Pole moving in the opposite direction of rotation with the South Pole being held back. It is the opinion of some people that there is a rigid network in the U.S. Government, the military and even in

* <http://www.earthlink.net-lifespirit23/solar.htm>

industry to ignore rather than explore the current Earth Changes. The earth moved, the water remained, and the USS San Francisco, a submarine, was in strange terrain, and thus ran aground some 350 miles from Guam while it was conducting submerged operation, by being smashed into an undersea mountain that was not on its charts. It is therefore unfortunate that seven innocent U.S. marines were accused of neglect in carrying out their duties and were disciplined. One questions the ethical approach of this action. If it is a fact that the U.S. authorities were aware of the Earth Changes, as they should be with their sophisticated hi-tech monitoring technology, then was it fair to accuse a group of innocent marines who were doing their duty, sincerely and conscientiously, completely unaware that the earth heaved and moved under the sea, displacing a mountain of which the submarine crew was totally unaware, since the presence of such a structure was not shown on their charts. During the earth wobble, the earth moves under the atmosphere as well as under the oceans. This was the case when Intelsat IS-804 went out of alignment on January 14, 2005 and was then lost on January 15, 2005. In this case the Earth moved under the atmosphere producing unstable conditions in which the satellite was unable to function.

Reports* are also available that the Mediterranean Sea level was unseasonably low in Venice during the flood season, off the coast of Barcelona to the west thus affecting the entire Mediterranean which shares a water level with the Atlantic Ocean and to the East in Croatia, where the beaches were so low that the people cannot remember such a time.

It has even been postulated that the above ground and under-ground detonations of the atomic bombs have shifted the core relative to the mantle position of the Earth. It also caused a wobble of the Earth's axis.

* <http://www.zetatalk.com/index/lou0128.htm>

Summary of Earth Changes

If we are to accept the above non-official material as factual information, the logical conclusion is either we are mis-informed or inadequately informed about the actual conditions relating to Earth Changes. It surpasses one's comprehension as to why the concerned authorities are reluctant to release information vital to us as inhabitants of an endangered planet. Are we so paranoid or hysterical as to lose our mental balance if we know the truth? From whom are they concealing the facts? If they are capable of accepting with equanimity Earth Changes, why should they assume our incapacity to do the same?

Whatever may be the reason, of one thing we are certain. Both official and non-official reports agree that drastic changes are occurring throughout the globe and apparently there is little any one can do about them. The earth is being rapidly destroyed and if this is allowed to continue, we shall end up living on a planet incapable of supporting and sustaining protoplasmic life one-celled or multi-celled. Tiwari has given us three-hundred years to annihilate ourselves. This seems to be a very generous offer. At the rate humankind is destroying the limited resources of the planet and interfering with natural forces, the amount of time left for survival of the species is anyone's guess.

At the time of writing reports continue to come in about earthquakes almost simultaneously occurring in widespread areas of the globe—Indonesia, Mumbai and in Northern California where an undersea earthquake of 7 on the Richter Scale caused sufficient concern for the authorities to consider evacuation of the inhabitants, fearing an after-quake tsunami. Apart from earthquakes, we all are aware that the Earth is wobbling on its axis after the Sumatra quake; there is a change in its orbit around the sun; the nights and days are becoming longer; volcanoes are threatening to erupt and within the period of a single year 80 volcanoes have erupted on every part of the globe with a few exceptions; the Himalayan glaciers are melting: the Japanese Islands are under threat of the plates beneath the Islands rupturing resulting in widespread damage; the glaciers of Antarctica are melting for the first time in recorded history; sea-levels are rising: the geophysical signs are pointing directly to another El Nino; the Pacific 'Ring of Fire' is showing signs of activity; the ozone layer instead of being on the mend as scientists thought is thinning; as for global warming, carbon dioxide has reached a level of concentration as to endanger humanity's survival; mutation of the Asia flu virus which could affect human beings resulting in a pandemic etc.

The Hindu, July 2005, reports that France is running out of water; there is imposition of rationing and in several regions rivers have been reduced to a trickle, with fish dying. France is facing its worst water shortage since 1976; in some regions water levels are at their lowest for 54 years with 60 per cent less rainfall than normal. Crops are at risk and farmers are ignoring the ban on irrigation in spite of fines (*Guardian Newspaper Ltd.,* 2005).

The Mumbai Flood

During the last week in July 2005, Mumbai (Bombay) has experienced the worst flood in almost a century, a record of more than 944mm. the highest ever recorded in India in a single day. Life was brought to a standstill in the metropolitan and suburban areas; transport by road, rail and air ceased and people were stranded in their work-places, children in their schools and many commuters had to remain where they were as suburban trains were affected. In some places the water was chest-high and people had to wade through this to get home.

From rivers becoming a trickle to incessant rain for almost twenty-four hours flooding a large city, to recent reports of several earthquakes occurring in California, U.S.A. within one week, the news of the current Earth Changes could not be more unsettling. Mother Nature seems to be going ahead with the process of balancing her chaotic Earth. The silver lining in the dark clouds of the Mumbai calamity is the spontaneous and immediate assistance offered by all sections of Mumbai's residents to those who were in difficult situations and in danger of losing their lives. Even at the risk of their own lives, human hands were physically extended to assist their fellow beings who were in hazardous situations. These are the individuals forming part of the transformational population, the 20 per cent of the cultural creatives who it is said will survive the 'Shift'. This is an example *par excellence* of service without 'reaching for the fruit' in Sai Baba's words.

The Havoc caused by Hurricane Katrina

The latest event relating to Earth Changes occurred at the end of August, 2005 when hurricane Katrina lashed New Orleans in the Southern U.S.A. leaving 80 per cent of the city submerged, a city already six feet below sea level. The flood waters described as a 'witch's brew' were contaminated with heavy metals, chemicals, fuel, pesticides and raw sewerage flowing through New Orleans and heading for other U.S. coastal states. The refugees clamoured for food, water and attention for four whole days, while surrounded by dead bodies (*The Hindu,* August, 2005/*New York Times*). It is stated that prior to the hurricane one million residents had evacuated the city.

The majority of people caught in the flood were blacks as seen on TV. Official orders were given to shoot at sight. On busy streets where bodies were rotting, gunmen opened fire on troops and rescue workers. The final death toll could reach thousands. This is considered the biggest domestic relief and security effort in U.S. history. In flooded hospitals with no electricity, patients were dying for lack of oxygen, insulin and other emergency drugs. Even there gunmen opened fire on doctors and soldiers who had to stop evacuation. The shelters were without food and water and families slept near corpses and piles of human wastes for days. Even after four days the situation was still not under control, and there is fear of outbreak of diseases. The U.S. Government has appealed to Europe for food and to Canada for materials like beds, etc. (*The New Indian Express/Reuter,* August 2005).

The inordinate delay in rushing troops, food, water and other necessities and for not paying attention to their plight has evoked much anger among the people against the Bush Administration.

An article headlined "American Nightmare: The Chaos of New Orleans was the Worst Advertisement for Western Civilization", by Swapan Das Gupta appeared in *The New Sunday Express,* September, 2005.

Among other things it stated that most striking was the widespread demonstration of criminality...not just crime, but the descent of a big city into complete anarchy; organized armed gangs looting empty houses and ransacking shops. There was the widespread instances of rape and the desertion of one-third of the police force. There was little organized philantrophy in the first six days after Katrina struck and, more significantly was the irrelevance of church bodies. "The evangelists who litter the landscape of the Deep South...are cash-rich and have an amazing knack of turning up at odd places in India...promising deliverance. How come we didn't hear of them providing solace to their flock and engaging in Christian charity at New Orleans." There were reports that the few charity workers who turned up beat a hasty retreat after being threatened. "What does this reveal about the supposed importance of Christian values in the civic life of America, and to imagine the U.S. evangelists have the gumption to preach to Indians."

What was equally striking was the horrific lack of compassion for both human and animals—a Baptist hospital turning away homeless survivors at gunpoint and a distraught boy being forcibly separated from his pet dog by National Guards. "...we have been taught that human life is cheap in our part of the world and that there is more human dignity in the West. We saw a very different story emerging from the soggy remains of one corner of Louisiana.... The next time some insolent Senate Committee presumes to make some disparaging comment about what we are not doing right in India, one should force them to sit through TV footage of post-Katrina New Orleans. In the past week we have witnessed the deflation of American sanctimoniousness."

Certainly it is not necessary to chronicle further details of Earth Changes, as those that have occurred and are occurring are sufficiently alarming to increase the awareness we need to face the global events threatening us.

The Threat of Asian Flu Mutating

A leading scientist, Professor Osterhaus, at the Erasmus Medical Centre in Rotterdam, one of the world's leading research laboratories, has issued a warning that the Asian flu virus is on the point of mutating into a pandemic disease and could cause 7.5 million deaths according to current estimates. Yet there are not sufficient vaccines manufactured to meet the demands for a pandemic which could affect the global economy.

So far 90 human infections have occurred in South-east Asia from which 54 persons have died. Culling and vaccination of poultry have slowed the outbreak in Thailand and other parts of South-east Asia, but Vietnam has shown an increase of human infections—a precondition for a pandemic. China has reported 178 deaths of migratory geese from H5N1 at a wildfowl reserve. The geese's death could be another indication that the virus is mutating and becoming more virulent. China and Vietnam are not providing animal and human health officials with enough data, leaving scientists in the dark. If a pandemic occurs 130 million people would need hospitalization within a few months, of which 25 per cent would be expected to die. It is estimated by Prof. Osterhaus that a pandemic could infect 20 per cent of the world's population and cause 7.5 million deaths. The Spanish flu pandemic in 1918 took 40 million lives worldwide; while the 1957 Asian flu pandemic and 1968 Hong Kong flu claimed less than one million lives, each. WHO and international efforts have been criticized by experts to develop vaccines against H5N1 (*The Hindu*, May, 2005 from *Guardian Newspapers Limited*, 2005).

Two months following the above report, a second warning has been issued from London confirming the findings of H5N1 avian influenza virus in migratory geese in China. The danger here is the spread of the disease across the world as tens of thousands of birds that could be carrying the virus are due to leave the reserve in September 2005, heading for warmer climates across the Himalayas to India and Bangladesh and south towards Australia and New Zealand. Experts have called for urgent action to prevent the disease from escaping its stronghold in south-east Asia. Eighty-four people have been killed already.

This is the first time the virus common among chickens has spread among wild birds. Genetic analysis of the virus extracted from dead birds has shown its close relation to the strain that has jumped to humans in Thailand and Vietnam. The virus does not yet have the ability to spread easily from person to person, but it could be just a matter of time. The Chinese have taken almost no action to control the outbreak and should have asked for international support. These birds will go to India and Bangladesh and there they will meet birds that will come from Europe according to a virologist from the University of Hong Kong (*The Hindu*, July, 2005).

Planetary Temperatures

It is possible that planetary temperatures could rise by as much as 5.6⁰ C in the next century with sea level rises of a metre. Since 1993, the world's oceans have risen at the rate of 3.2 cm per decade (*The Hindu*, April, 2005). Recent reports have stated that spring has arrived earlier than expected. Blossoms have already appeared on trees

Unusual Human Behaviour

A report by the *Guardian Newspaper Ltd.*, 2005 headlined "Happy Slappers on the Prowl" stated that the attacks have become more menacing and a phenomenon across the United Kingdom. The *modus operandi* is described thus—a youth approaches a woman at a bus stop and punches her in the face; in another attack labeled "Knockout Punch" a group of boys wearing uniforms lead another boy across a school playground and floor him with a single blow to the head. These youths are termed the "Happy Slappers", a youth craze in which groups of teenagers armed with camera–phones slap or mug unsuspecting children or passers–by, while capturing the attacks on camera. The attacks which started in London in 2004 are now a nationwide phenomenon. The attacks have become more menacing with increasing numbers of violent assaults and adult victims. As the police have become more vigilant, the gangs have become more sophisticated, seeking victims in parks or public areas where their crimes are unlikely to be spotted. These youngsters can be prosecuted for committing assault and also for harassment if they upload the images onto the internet or a phone system. A recent case in April, 2005 involves a 34–year–old journalist who was attacked by three teenagers—while one youth blocked his path, another hit him with a rolled–up magazine, and another who had been hiding behind a scaffolding, leapt out and hit him hard on the head.

The above appalling episodes demonstrate how far behind our progress and advances in science and technology is our moral teaching, relating specially to human values. When philosophy fails to keep abreast with science, human behaviour goes berserk, and since the human mind controls the five senses, in the absence of philosophical or spiritual guidelines, the mind becomes uncontrolled, leading the senses to indulge in animalistic behaviour. This only goes to illustrate the importance of moral and spiritual teachings, especially to the young. However, in the 21st century, such teachings are considered out of date or old fashioned, thus giving young people the liberty or rather license to do just as they please. This, however, is only one reason for the erratic behaviour of the British teenagers.

The other factor involved here is the effect on the human body-mind-spirit complex by the geophysical changes occurring at present on Earth. It is stated that Earth Changes can affect this complex in many ways. Apart from the effect on thought patterns, level of consciousness, human values, ideals and the vibratory rate of human cells, the latter being the basis for many or, perhaps, all of these changes, which would be positive and acceptable changes, there is the possibility of some humans, who being unable to cope with earth's enhanced vibration, which it is currently undergoing, would exibit bizarre behaviour. Since we are so closely linked to Mother Earth in many ways, this important factor has to be taken into consideration. These hapless and helpless individuals may go berserk, losing control over their thoughts and subsequent actions and may be considered crazy or mad by society. While the above incidents may be just a stray happening on the part of a certain section of society, in this case teenagers, we cannot dismiss this erratic and abnormal behaviour as just another prank of an unruly bunch of untrained, indisciplined youth. Moreover, psychologists and others may attribute the exponential spread of this behaviour pattern to the tendency of young people to follow the crowd and to imitate their actions; and the activity of one group in a certain part of the country can rapidly influence similar groups throughout the land due mainly to the widespread availability of information today through various electronic means. Since the imitative tendency is strong in young people, it is just possible that they acted as 'copy cats'. This is certainly one aspect that has to be taken into consideration. However, this should not blind us to the fact that current earth changes can and do have a definite effect on human attitudes and behaviour patterns as is being reported by many people, the effects involving the entire body/mind/spirit matrix.

Signs of Hope

Apart from the calamitous events predicted to occur in the near future, there is abundant evidence to prove that *pari passu* with these, there is an increase of precociousness and idealism in the generation who will inhabit the new world. Children are becoming more and more intelligent, way ahead of their counterparts of yesterday. They are also becoming more conscious of the environment and the ecological factors that are so important for the maintenance and integrity of the Earth. Here is a poem by a 13–year-old school boy, expressing his thoughts concerning the ecology of the planet. There is hope and a gleam of light shining through the chinks as Sai Baba has stated:

> We remember the earth in our prayers,
> To bring to life again this land,
> restore fresh air,
> renew the forests,
> protect the clean waters,
> preserve the forests,
> rejoice in the sunlight
> enjoy the morning streak of golden rays,

enjoy the evening sunset,
promote justice and peace,
care for plants and animals
make other fellow beings happy.

Dinesh Kumar
(*The New Indian Express*, 2005)

Our hope is that other 13-year-old children would think along these lines and hasten the onset of the New Age. If the calamities recorded above which are occurring at present and the predictions both of scientists and people attuned to higher spiritual values are not sufficient reasons to shock us out of our present feelings of complacency and make us aware that earth changes are taking place which will revolutionize our thoughts, attitudes and actions as well as change our three-dimensional world into a four-dimensional one, then nothing else on earth will.

The Aftermath

The Shift of the Ages is now a thing of the past. Buried deep within the womb of Mother Earth lie all the pollutants of the 20th century—the nuclear wastes, nuclear weapons, nuclear power plants all reduced to the five elements by the process of disassociation. Along with them are the pesticides and other poisonous chemicals used to pollute the food we ate, the water we drank, the air we breathed, all buried deep within the bowels of Mother Nature.

This is the picture within the Earth. On her surface is fresh, clean, fragrant, rich soil, brought up from her body by the earthquakes, volcanoes, storms and floods to provide a rich medium for man's welfare; organic food for everyone, pure, healthy, invigorating food, nutritious, rich, vital and balanced. Gone for a thousand years the effluents from industrial wastes, the poisonous gases from the polluting chimneys of industry, and the contaminants poured into the soil. The

Shift of the ages had served to purify the Earth, to heal her of the numerous wounds inflicted by the avariciousness of 20th century man, gone along with his poisonous products, the outcome of his perverted thinking that served only to further his vested interests at the expense of suffering humanity and Nature.

The mantle of the Earth and her core are once again rotating in synchrony, and all seismic, volcanic and other geophysical activity are at rest, probably for millennia to come. Mother Nature is at long last at peace with herself, her soil disrupted only by the plough of the farmer. Her fossil fuels on land and undersea remain undisturbed serving Nature's needs; other methods of producing power from such natural sources as sun, air and water are providing all the energy the people of the Golden Age need for daily living. Only recently, a motorbike has been developed by a group of young engineers using hydrogen as fuel. We can surmise that more of this is already available, awaiting recognition.

The atmosphere is clear and sparkling with golden sunshine—no smog, fog, gloomy surroundings and pollution. No raucous sounds of the clash and clang of giant metallic machines rent the air. The stress is now on the land and not on industry. The creatures of the air, land and sea are back in strength and the earth is full of bird-song. Zoological gardens, animals in enclosed areas, wild-life sanctuaries and parks are nowhere visible. Man and wild animals walk the earth in trustful and loving companionship; no longer is the animal relegated to the role of an inferior being on the earth which is his rightful place as much as man's. His dignity has been restored as a being created by the One who created All. Vegetarianism reigns supreme on Earth. Man no longer takes a life to preserve his own as he once erroneously did. The forests and the jungles are back, clothing the hills, mountains and plains in lushness and greenery. Even the weather is kind—be it on plain or mountain as no longer does man tamper or interfere with Nature's secrets. Mother Earth is no longer burdened with the weight of hundred-storied structures in which human beings were housed like rabbits in their hutches, buildings that stood like packing cases, cutting the sky into ribbon-like strips, with the sun, moon and stars becoming as alien as extraterrestrial beings, illusive and at times altogether invisible—a heartless deprivation of young and old from the natural glories and beauty of the Universe. A study some decades ago revealed traumatic psychological effects on children living on floors above the third storey. These children were obviously out of touch with the Earth and Nature and this factor has to be considered as a possible cause. At long last Earth is healed and has regained her pristine vigour and health.

We have been participants in the cosmic dance drama since the beginning of creation. We have had to learn painfully over aeons the different steps in order to progress spiritually. Sai Baba says He alone knows the agony of teaching us the next step in the dance; that everything we experience is part of this cosmic drama, and not the acts of God, as the Divine does not cause the afflictions that beleaguer mankind. These are the consequences or retributions accumulated by our own actions as determined by the inexorable law of Karma—the universal law of cause and effect. We have only ourselves to blame for whatever befalls us in life, be it good or bad. If we become aware of these experiences as being the result of our own actions, we may be able to accept them and do something about them, rather than apportion the blame for our miseries to Divine intervention.

Indeed, we have only ourselves to blame for the present situation as an irresponsible collective body and we shall have to face the hardships and suffering of the future as an enlightened collective body if we are to survive. All this will happen before the 'collective initiation' of Braden, that is, before the reversal of the magnetic poles of the Earth, and the exact timing of this shift to usher in the Golden or New Age, says Sai Baba depends on us. Were we to change our present materialistic life-style to one centered on the human values of truth, righteousness, love, peace and non-violence, the New Age will be here sooner than we expect it. If however we resist the called-for change and are determined to maintain the status quo, turning a deaf ear to the predictions both of ancient and modern prophets, the agony will be prolonged, and calamities, catastrophic and other disasters that are already occurring on Earth will continue. The Sumatra tsunami, the U.S. hurricanes, the Mumbai flooding, the droughts, floods and forest fires in Europe, some occurring for the first time in recorded history will not only continue, but will increase in severity and frequency causing great hardship and loss of life. The recent devastation in late September, 2005 in New Orleans is only a taste of what to expect, according to those who know. The choice is solely ours and we are endowed by the Creator with free-will to use it judiciously to make the right choice. Let us not put the blame on God. As "Earth Changes we change as well"[2], and also we have to remember that as we change and as heart and mind become separate from each other, Earth will also change, for the worse.

We have been progressing slowly, ever so slowly through the evolutionary process to arrive at our present stage of *Homo sapiens*—with a highly developed brain, an expansive mind and an immortal spirit. We have been in the learning process for aeons, but it appears that as we learn new lessons we tend to forget the old time-tested ones. At this point in time, we have forgotten the presence of the Divine Spark that informs matter—our body and mind—the physical part of us, since we have become obsessed by the body and its manifold demands. This was the fall from grace in the Garden of Eden, and the price we are paying for it continues to this day. The time may be long past when we could have made amends for the mistakes committed. Perhaps it is too late to change as the Earth and its current activities do not seem to allow us the time necessary to effect this change. Even at this late stage some political leaders of the world are still baying for the blood of those they consider their adversaries, an attitude somewhat akin to the big predators of the jungle. They are talking in terms of aggression, of attacks on Iran for supposedly stockpiling nuclear bombs. They invaded Iraq and reduced it to chaos—politically, economically and materially for supposedly possessing weapons of mass destruction (WMD). But these WMD have been as illusive as the Scarlet Pimpernel. To this day no such weapons have surfaced and they seem to exist only in the minds of the aggressors. But in the process of their traumatic searches they ruined an ancient civilization, destroyed historic structures, smashed valuable artifacts and reduced the people to poverty. The process continues. It is 'aggression at will' according to A. Chaudhuri and is Iran next on the hit list—or is it Venezuela or...? And so—Armageddon awaits us all—we have only ourselves to blame!

According to some prophets of doom, the entire animal including human and the plant kingdoms will be completely wiped off the face of the earth during the coming cataclysmic events leaving only the mineral kingdom on the planet. This seems to be a far-fetched idea, and a prediction not rationally acceptable, especially when Sri Sathya Sai Baba's statements contradict it. Why should the Creator have allowed us to evolve phylogenetically, albeit, slowly and painfully, from the one-celled to the multi-celled stage and to have progressed from the lowest level of consciousness to attain the level we have today, if only to consign us to oblivion at this stage of our development. This cock-eyed prediction reminds one of Newton and Descartes by conveniently ignoring the Creator, who so far as we have seen from past planetary history, does not indulge in exercises in futility. Lemuria (Mu) and Atlantis, two of the greatest civilizations that were supposed to have existed on Earth, broke up and disappeared beneath the waves of the Pacific and the Atlantic Oceans respectively, when the inhabitants allowed their philosophy to be overtaken by technological advances, which exceeded all norms for making it possible for biological life to remain on their continents. But this did not result in the extermination of all biological life on Earth. Human, animal and plant life continued in the remaining areas on the planet and resulted in the development of great civilizations in different parts of the globe.

Sai Baba has repeatedly stated that the present age will be replaced by a new world—inconceivable, unimaginable and beautiful beyond all dreams—presenting to us a completely different picture than that visualized by these modern prophets of doom. According to recent U.S. research mentioned earlier 20 per cent of the people on earth can be described as the transformational population who are aware of the Earth Changes sufficiently to do something about them, by changing their lives to become in harmony with what is happening to the earth. Why should this relatively enlightened group be dumped along with the remaining 80 per cent who are yet to become awakened to the ground realities. This does not seem to be compatible with the past history of the planet, otherwise how can our present existence in all three kingdoms be explained.

Some Precautionary Measures

Although we may be at the mercy of Mother Nature and may not be able to do much to escape her wrath, yet there are certain precautionary measures that can be taken at least to mitigate the suffering and hardships that the spiritual masters and others say we may have to undergo during the coming years.

Those living along the coastal areas should move inland 100 miles or more, as geophysicists state this is more or less the limit mega-tsunamis can travel inland, and preferably take refuge on higher areas, on hills and mountains, elevated regions, plateaus, etc. wherever available. Those inhabiting known seismic regions should move to areas relatively free of severe seismic activity. People living on plains or flat lands, along river banks liable to periodic floods should preferably move to higher areas, low hills and other more elevated land where the flood waters cannot reach. High-rise structures should be avoided as they would be the target of violent storms, hurricanes and cyclones which are becoming more and more violently destructive, worse than those that occurred along the Atlantic Seaboard of the United States in 2004. Needless to say, new houses should be built to withstand strong raging storms, violent hurricanes, fierce winds, etc.

Having said this we must remember that in spite of all precautions, nothing is fool-proof. Some people are considering taking refuge inside the earth itself, building structures, bunkers, etc. which they hope will resist the destructive forces of Nature. It has been said and we all know it, nothing we can do by our own efforts to face the coming predicted calamities will suffice to save us from serious injuries or even death itself. We have to strive to protect not only our physical bodies, but more so our minds and emotions from succumbing to the cataclysms awaiting us. Fear for one's life and for that of those near and dear to us is the most important factor in this situation. We have to overcome this fear of what is going to happen, remembering that it is a relentless law that whatever is born must die and it would be well for us to keep this foremost in mind when we stand facing the wrath of Nature in her uncontrolled fury.

From the Internet, Simon Hunt* reports "In an unprecedented and totally unexpected way, Hopi Elders for the first time in history have openly shared their sacred and heretofore secret

---

* <http://www.groups.yahoo.com/group/circle2012dreams/>

prophecies with the world.... Hopi prophecies of the coming earth changes are among the most ancient and accurate available. The Elders have come forth at this time because they believe that we have passed the point of no return and major changes are imminent, beginning within the next few months (September—October, 2005). It is their hope 'to soften' the effects by appealing to all to return to a simple, more spiritual way of life". Also modern day prophets have confirmed that 'The Great Shift' has already begun and that it is happening now.

"So the Earth is changing? The Great Shift is upon us? What is one to do?" He offers the following in reply: "Get over denial and open your eye, take a look around and question about the weather and you may find that it's a little different than it's ever been for your locality. Try to find out what's really going on—tornadoes have been spotted for the first time in history that are spinning the wrong way; in Mexico the ground temperature is heating up in excess of 200 degrees; during a seven–day period there were 172 earthquakes recorded in the California Nevada border. There is also the possibility of a volcanic eruption there; all over North America, migratory birds have stopped returning to their nesting grounds; salmon are no longer returning to their spawning grounds.

"Accept that change is happening and let go of fear. Realize that it is a time of change and not necessarily a time of fear. The earth changing will not kill you, but fear, denial and not open to your Inner Self and your intuition may". He suggested that one should keep abreast of the news through the Internet, radio, videos, taped radio programmes, magazines, books— not the television. Advice offered by the Hopi Elders to the world on National radio (June 2005) says "If you change now, and change your life around, it will help in the alleviation of much of the terrible outcome from the cataclysms. There is a lot in store for all of us. And the intensity of this will be a lot less if we can all settle down and behave, and not be in the actions that we are right now.... They also said it makes no difference whether your spirituality falls in tune with an organized philosophy or religion or if it is something that you have come up with and practise on your own.... Practise your spirituality, whatever it may be like you have never practised it before—and realize that your consciousness affects the outcome. Your consciousness affects everything. Realize that your thoughts, words and actions of today contribute to what the world will be like tomorrow.

The four steps to be taken are summarized thus: Keep your eyes open; let go of fear; learn all you can; live your spirituality and concludes thus, "Only love prevails".

It is indeed heartening to see that the Internet has repeated what Sai Baba has been reiterating for so many decades, and with only a few listening. Will anyone listen to the Hopi Elders? This remains to be seen. If more and more people can accept these suggestions and more importantly, put them into practice, Mother Earth may change her approach and decrease the fury of the catastrophies that threaten all of us. Since she has consciousness just as we have, it is rational for us to accept her ability to do so. Furthermore we, as both earth and man, are inextricably linked; what affects one can affect the other.

Vinod Kumar*, a Yoga/Reiki teacher in Coonoor, Nilgiri Hills, offers Yoga as one of the ways to meet the impending disasters. He says, "Sai Baba has exhorted us to let the Lotus of the heart bloom by practising yoga and mastering the mind. He also warned us not to waste time and that only the Lord's name can remove the man-made pollution of Earth and can protect us."

"Japa or Mantra Yoga—the repetition of God's name—is considered to be the best of practices for the present age to alleviate the suffering of mankind. This *Mantra Sadhana*

---

* www.saiyoga.com

(discipline) is best for gaining happiness in this and other dimensions (Shiva Samhita, 5:188). Even at the time of death, by mistakenly uttering the Divine name one's sins are forgiven and the person attains heaven. This *Sadhana* is available to all and can be done at any time anywhere, even by the elderly and disabled. *Mantra yoga* is based on Purity and Faith, and is not meant to be practised in a mechanical way.

"Yoga is the ancient inner technology of attaining an easeful body, a peaceful mind and a joyful soul, to realize the purity of Divine Love and Light and to share the joy of this enlightenment with others. Practising yoga and observing its values in day to day life provide us an opportunity for transformation, empowerment of the Self and for service to society as a harbinger of the Golden Age."

The calamities occurring at present and the dim and not so distant future awaiting all of mankind as seen by geophysicists and non-scientists with respect to the Earth Changes and their effects on humans, leave us with only one way out, since we as ordinary human beings are completely helpless in the face of Nature's fury and can do nothing really to save ourselves. And that way out is to increase our faith and belief in a Higher Force, a Divine Source, call it what you will—God, the Absolute, the Totality, the Creator—which is the only succour in times of danger and impending disaster. Moreover, we also should remember that the safest and most secure place is within ourselves, where at the core of our being is the Higher Self, as Cosmic Consciousness. It is this fact as well as faith in and love for the Creator of All that should enable us to face whatever lies ahead without losing our mental and emotional balance. With this balance achieved, we can then reach out and be of help and support to others.

Ten

Ecology in the Golden Age

Back to the Land

The clarion call of the Golden Age will be 'Back to the Land', and the new society will live according to natural and universal laws. Apart from individual homesteads the emphasis will be on community living. The Vedic statement, *Vasudhaiva kutumbakom*—the world is one family—will materialize and there would be camaraderie among all peoples. This is not to be dismissed as wishful thinking but is the natural and rational outcome of the changes that will occur after the 'Shift'. The collective experiences of the survivors of the 'Shift' will be the cementing factor in bringing together everyone in close and loving fellowship and companionship. Since the hallmark of the New Age will be LOVE, and its accompanying values of compassion, empathy and service to one's fellow beings, the natural consequence will be a feeling of togetherness, of wanting to be of service to others, not from the pre–Shift sense of duty but out of a feeling of love for its own sake. Segregation, separateness, isolationism and other factors leading to alienation that dominated the old order, will be relegated to the pages of history. Pure love, akin to divine love, will be the essence of life and Sri Sathya Sai Baba affirms this.

The Future Scenario

Against these changes, the probability of certain customs, habits and attitudes reminiscent of the old paradigm will be conspicuous by their absence as they will be out of place and alien to the new world order. For example, the close bonds existing among the members in the home and community will be so strong that the desire to leave the family for companionship and fraternizing outside the closely knit unit will never arise. It is the feeling of isolation among the family members that drives them to look elsewhere for fulfillment and so-called pleasures as is the situation in today's society. Hence breaking up of the family unit, the dissolution of home life and the attendant ills consequent on the straying away of members from the security and moral discipline of the home, leading to alienation.

In the New Age the urge to ignore the dinner table and to patronize public eating places, such as restaurants, canteens, pizza huts, hotels, dining halls, etc. will not hold the same lure or temptation as in the old world order. The dominant feeling will be to stay together, whether at home or as a member of the community and to eschew the thought of entertainment or recreation outside, as the domestic atmosphere will be sufficiently fulfilling and conducive to satisfy and gratify such desires. Thus the New Age life-style will be something akin to that which obtained a century or so ago, when home was 'home, sweet home', the bulwark against all odds and a secure haven for one and all; where love pervaded the atmosphere and compassion and understanding the cementing factors holding the family together as an inseparable unit, the nucleus around which all activities orbited.

Ecological Changes in the New Society

If this is the future scenario and there is no reason to think otherwise, then many of the existing establishments, business places, etc. that characterize present day society, catering to man's myriad desires, such as public eating places, clubs, gambling dens, bars for serving alcoholic drinks, places offering varieties of games and sports based on money making, red light districts, etc. will automatically cease to exist, the simple reason being lack of patronage. It will be a brand new world, nothing akin to what we have come to consider acceptable as the social norms. The motto of this new world order will be 'high thinking and simple living'. It was Sai Baba who said that the present craze for higher and higher standards of living has wrought havoc in the society.

The ostentation, sophistication, superciliousness, keeping up with the Joneses, sporting of expensive clothes, jewellery and other personal adornments, palatial homes and the hedonistic propensities of present day's *glitterati* and *chatterati*, of the 'jet set' and the 'glam set' will have completely disappeared, to be replaced by a vibrant, cultured and highly civilized race of human beings, with bodies vibrating at such a high pitch as probably never before experienced in all of its planetary existence.

Atrocities of the Past

Gone will be the days when man's inhumanity to man was openly accepted by so-called civilized nations; when entire families were removed forcibly and unceremoniously by men with warped mentalities, from their native hearths and homes and transported to distant alien lands, auctioned by their slave-dealers like dead fish to prospective slave owners, men with equally warped mentalities, this process resulting in complete and permanent disruption and separation of families, producing pain, sorrow and anguish. And this form of barbarism was inflicted on members of the same species, not gorillas or orangutans, but men and women possessing the same divine core as their slave owners; and adding insult to injury, super-imposing on their ancient, native beliefs that had sustained them for untold millennia, an alien religion, the tenets of which were practiced more in the breach than the observance by the very masters who owned them. These were the atrocities inflicted upon the continent of Africa. In the sub-continent of India, by the use of such fraudulent methods as deceit, chicanery, false enticements and other ignoble acts of mentally degenerate men, young and able-bodied men, some of them having been kidnapped, were taken to the British colonies, from an India impoverished by the insatiable greed of its British colonizers to sustain the sugar-cane fields, a source of great wealth for the British, when Negro and Chinese labourers refused to work for them. In these foreign lands the indentured labourers, many of whom were from well-to-do families, were made to work for a mere pittance while the owners lived like royalty.

The New Era

Fast forward to the new millennium. Is the picture any different? Yes and no. While the distorted mentality remains the same, the roles in the drama have become reversed. At the beginning of the 21st century, this is the opinion of the writer and economist Arindam Chaudhuri, in the column "India: Today and Tomorrow" of the *Economic Times*, May, 2005. He visualizes the coming together of three important countries of Asia—Russia, India and China—as the main balancing force in this unipolar world of "aggression at will". He has termed the three countries the unique C 3: the Civilizing Three. He sees these three countries as having a civilizing effect on the "greed driven, constantly warring empty heads—with Russia representing the military might, China the economic might and India the power which flows out of the civilizing ideology of non-violence." He says that if the Russians are to bring back their lost pride through any alliance, India, its long standing ally, is its first hope. A permanent seat in the Security Council, backed up by a determined Russia lobby, could be a final seal of acceptance of India's unquestionable arrival as a global power to reckon with. "Militarily, India is not at par" with others, "but by virtue of its economic future and present growing global stature is the next best thing, India certainly is not a country that can be ignored or isolated any more. On its own today India stands tall. Its culture and history are its biggest strengths, Gandhi its biggest social brand, signifying the most civilized and futuristic ideology of non-violence in an otherwise constantly warring world, and the Non-Aligned Movement its leading global initiative. It shows all potentiality to be an equal future partner in a joint front...."

The Approaching Economical Shift

The above approach may be termed the political cum economic cum cultural ecology of the new world order. In choosing these three countries, each outstanding in its own sphere, we can perhaps look forward to a hastening of the Golden Age. Chaudhuri continues, "In the new world order peace, civilized co-existence and fair play can be assured only if the balancing opponents of the U.S. have a combined economic might that is strong enough to rival that of the U.S." The present economic situation seems to be moving in this direction. Many informed persons are seeing the beginning of the end of the U.S. as a dominating factor in the new paradigm of nations which will lead the New Age. Some are talking of a multipolar world, of a changed economic system and of no one country holding the sword of Damocles over the heads of other nations. Chaudhuri explains, "...leading thinkers across the world are also becoming more conclusive about the need for a balancing power in the world politics today, to counter the complete one-sided domination of the smoke'em out variety being carried out by the U.S. under the cowboy regime of George Bush. However, having seen the danger of one nation dominating all others, this balancing equation that many in the civilized world are in search of can no more (and should no more) be provided by an individual nation in what can be called a new world economic and military order."

Economists are more and more veering towards the view that the U.S. economy is in a state of near collapse and is holding together only because of the support of the central banks of some Asian countries, that in the face of the weakening of the U.S. dollar, may be withdrawn if the dollar continues to lose value. The U.S. economy continues to exist on borrowed funds from foreign central banks. How long can any country, in fact, any individual, exist on borrowed money?

Future Leaders of the New Era

Chaudhuri visualizes the coming together of "three of the mightiest countries in the world with each of them holding the key to future global markets; the more humane and socialistic orientation of all the three nations binding them together ideologically and the fact that they are neighbours binding them emotionally. Three nations with a common orientation towards peace and protecting it with no past record of compulsive global aggression. Unlike the U.S., all the three countries are also great civilizations with strong historical and cultural forces giving them distinct identities.... They make the unique C 3: the Civilizing Three." This scenario presents an entirely different state of affairs that existed only one and a half to two centuries ago.

A Return to Nature

As one visualizes the future of the Golden Age peopled by a superior race of humans, one can conceive of such people wishing to return to simpler more natural ways of living. And what could be simpler than to return to the land, to Mother Nature—now completely healed of the many wounds inflicted on her by pre–Shift man. Her soil, water and air are once again clean, fresh, fragrant and invigorating, like a tonic to the inhabitants.

The New Age people will look exactly like we do now, but entirely different as far as their internal structures are concerned. They will be new beings mentally, intellectually and spiritually, some of the most advanced among them functioning in a fourth dimensional world. It is necessary to remember that in this new society the dominating theme will be Love and Compassion akin to the divine state. Such negative features as competition, avarice, selfishness, duality, accompanied by the six demons of lust, anger, greed, attachment, pride and jealousy will have vanished along with those who possessed such traits. The obsession for possession of things material will find no place in the mind-set of these evolved souls. Simple living and high thinking will be the main features of their fourth dimensional life-style, having simple needs, no desire for material gadgets, using articles not for show or luxury, but for their daily needs.

What then about the mechanistic world of the old age, churning out useless goods simply to promote, cater to and titillate man's taste for possessiveness, and in the process minting money. Obviously, there would be no need for such industries. The new age industry will be geared solely to man's needs, satisfying to both his physical as well as aesthetic tastes. Most articles will be hand-crafted by a race of people with finely tuned artistic and aesthetic tendencies—articles for human use crafted with love and care, and not for commercial purposes. One may conceive a society functioning on the barter system without the use of money. It is common knowledge that money is the root of all evil, and once human needs depend on its use, there will be the desire for possessing more and more, based on greed rather than need. This commodity will be out of place in the future society. With a variety of talents available among the enlightened group of humans, the society will be provided with all their physical, intellectual and spiritual needs, and as it will be composed of outstanding individuals of a high calibre, the needs will be justifiable and utilitarian.

Articles made by hand or by simple machines will be crafted of good quality, designed to last several generations, so that consumer durables of all kinds will be handed down to posterity in good condition. In this manner there will be minimal and judicious utilization of raw materials, Nature's gifts to man. With the over-all concern of the members of the new society, there should be no wanton destruction of forests. No longer the cry of "Oh woodman, spare that tree". All of society will be personally concerned about conservation; all of society will spare the tree, none would deliberately destroy Nature in any of her manifold aspects. This attitude, of course, will be governed by the strong feeling of the Oneness of all— be it man, animal, plant or even mineral, for the simple reason that these people will have the awareness of consciousness existing in every aspect of Creation.

Work is Worship

Sai Baba has said that the secret of happiness lies not in doing what one likes but in learning to like what one has to do, and we can safely assume that this would be the prevailing attitude of the new society. The Golden Age will automatically put into practice Sai Baba's important axiom 'Work is Worship' and one can conclude that no kind of work, however demeaning, will be shirked by anyone. Since this is the atmosphere currently existing in Sai Baba's centres wherever they exist, there should be no doubt in our minds that this practice will continue. A society devoid of class consciousness and bred on the guiding principles of Sai Baba's famous pronouncement:

There is only one caste, the caste of humanity.
There is only one law, the law of duty.
There is only one language, the language of the heart.
There is only one religion, the religion of love.
There is only one God, and He is omnipresent.

This will be the guiding philosophy of the New Age and as the inhabitants will be already aware of these lofty principles, being advanced souls, they will not need to be taught. There will be community living and community farming. Old and time-tested methods for enriching the soil, using biological materials and perhaps newer methods to be evolved will replace pesticides, fungicides and the chemical poisons of the old order. Mechanistic methods will be replaced by human hands. Why use a machine to extract milk from a cow when the human hand can do the same job perfectly, except for the time factor involved.

However, in the New Age, the life-style will be based on the principles of serenity, leisure and equanimity where time will be of little consequence. It will be a life of gracefulness, elegance, dignity, modesty, decency unlike today's rough and ready life-style, like riding a tiger's back; everyone rushing, jostling their way ahead regardless of others, as long as they get there even though it means trampling over another fellow human being, elbowing one's way into any and every situation, the main incentive being to get there first—the maddening rat-race of the 20th century. What has happened to gracefulness, elegance, dignity, modesty, decency, finesse and all the other values we were brought up to admire and urged to emulate? The present situation presents a woeful scene—all the opposite traits are so glaringly evident that a sordidness has crept into modern human society. People have forgotten how to walk gracefully with dignity and modesty— instead, they have developed a sort of half-trot in their eagerness to keep up with the mad rush of today's society. In the new society, man will once again have the time to walk, with grace and elegance characterizing his gait, wearing clothes in keeping with his ideas of modesty and decency. In short, finesse and artfulness, discriminative tastes and a refined life-style will be the distinctive features of the inhabitants of the new era.

No longer will cattle be reared for human consumption but for milk and its products and for manure, even its urine for medicinal purposes. The ranches of the American West and the cowboy will be relegated to the pages of history. Domestic fowl will return to the jungle to live as they were meant to. No poultry farms, no egg incubators, no Kentucky fried chicken. The population will undoubtedly be vegetarian. The exploitation of animals will be out of sync in the new society. No taking of animal life for food, articles of fashion or for manufacturing cosmetics, etc. Some modern prophets have gone so far as to state that animals will have become so evolved that they will choose their masters, instead of the other way round. Relating to the consumption of animal flesh as food, a newspaper item runs thus, "Peruvian officials saved at least 4000 endangered frogs from being whipped into cocktails for their supposed aphrodisiac qualities. They were found hidden in an abattoir" (*The Hindu*, April, 2005). What a sad commentary on 21st century man! In a short news item, the uncultured and uncivilized behaviour and attitude of *Homo sapiens* stands revealed in all its naked ugliness. How long we may ask are such inanities to continue on the part of human beings?

Besides the elimination of heavy industry along with its pollution, it is possible that all fossil fuels will be taboo. Newer techniques from sun, wind and water will have become available. Actually, as some have reported, some of these are already available but are not allowed to surface because of vested interests, the same fate meted out to Tesla. Even bore-wells will be considered damaging to water sources. Since man will not be interfering with the Earth nor contaminating her soil, water and air, the forces of Nature will resume their normal course and soil, wind and water will regain their natural characteristics. No more 'harsh storms and killing winds'[4] no more will the earth exude 'fear, pain, tremor and spasms.'[4] Under these conditions the weather will be favourable, the seasons will return to normal as Nature intended them to be. The ozone layer will be repaired, the earth's temperatures will be adjusted, ocean levels will subside and the melting of snows and ice will cease. With these geophysical changes there will be no shortage of food and water, no hunger, no famine. It will indeed be a Paradise on earth—free from man's interference and greed.

Wise has outlined some of the practical ways that could be adopted to meet the exigencies of the future, "You need working transformative models. Get practical. Provide enlightening options for providing satisfying primary needs. Transcending your current economic model, establish systems for providing yourselves with food that is biodynamically or organically produced; aesthetic and environmentally responsible cooperative and collective housing; all inclusive integral health care; experiential value–oriented education; and numerous forums for the transformative dialogue. Any practical manifestation will create positive public awareness and a popular desire to change the existing system bit by bit."[3] And again Wise explains, "You know what needs to be done. Create new systems for sustaining your lives, founding these systems on integralism, fairness, honesty, artfulness, compassion and dedication to Universal values. Develop highly functional sources and systems for securing clean, healthy, biodynamically produced food. Develop resources for educating children and all people to the knowledge within them, facilitating the unification of their being and their behaviour. Replace dogma with discovery. Raise your infants with personal attention and without grooming them for societal dysfunctions of competition and the manipulation of nature. Spend more time and have more pleasure with the ones you love, at the same time being independent from them in your thinking, action and exploration. Cultivate multidimensional resources for healing yourselves, so that you can proceed with personal health and well–being."[3]

In the field of education apart from the 3R's and the usual academic subjects taught in schools and colleges, there would be the inculcation of human values as taught today in all the educational institutions established by Sri Sathya Sai Baba and which are functioning perfectly according to His plans. He has given the blue-print; it is now only a matter of carrying out His ideas in the educational institutions of the future. In a discourse in the May, 2005 issue of *Sanatana Sarathi*, Sai Baba explains His views, "Education is not meant to merely eke out a livelihood. You have to share your knowledge with others, give joy to one and all and thereby rise to the level of divinity...equal-mindedness is the hallmark of a true human being. ...Despite our high education and intelligence, there is a great scope for learning valuable lessons which Nature teaches us. We can learn even from small creatures, like ants, birds and animals. These lessons of life cannot be taught in the classroom. Even teachers are not making efforts to understand the principle of divinity within."[5b] Continuing on the theme of education, He says "...sacred texts will bring out the hidden treasures of divinity from within. That is why I have introduced educare programmes in the educational institutions. • Education is related to worldly knowledge. It can be acquired by going through books, whereas educare is meant to manifest the latent divinity in man. Education has temporary benefits, whereas educare bestows everlasting happiness. One cannot become great by mere acquisition of education. One should practice educare and manifest one's latent qualities. ...Educare is the need of the hour. Only through educare can you realize divinity which is present in every atom and every cell of your body. In fact you are seeing divinity every moment but are unable to recognize this truth. You can call yourself educated only when you recognize divinity which is all pervasive.... What is required is transformation and it is possible only through educare. Acquisition of information which cannot lead to transformation is a mere waste of time. But man has developed a taste for such information. Man's intelligence, knowledge and power are all the gifts of God. They have to be nourished and made proper use of through educare."[5b] More details about Sai Baba's educare programme involving children from the primary school stage to the post-graduate stage are given in the Epilogue of the book.

With respect to housing, Sai Baba has also set the example of housing for the less privileged. The system He has established there can be extended to include all other sections of humanity. His supply of clean drinking water by means of pipes, pumps, reservoirs, overhead-tanks etc, are now a well-known project to everyone in this country. His recent supply of clean water to the thirsty citizens of Chennai (Madras City) for which He spent millions of rupees from His Trust Fund, has quenched the thirst of millions in the City, for which the people have expressed their gratitude. But has the media, either the electronic or print, bothered to allot some of their 'valuable' space to this laudable and humane activity of Sai Baba? Not at all. Their space is too precious to waste on such activities by so-called 'holy men'. Such is the situation in the present-day world.

Health care which He is providing free of cost to all sections of humanity needs no introduction as many have cognizance of these activities. Sathya Sai Baba has established the blue-prints for all areas pertaining to humanity's welfare and it is only a matter of extending these amenities and establishing them when and where the need arises. The problem of starting from scratch does not arise as these institutions are functioning in a highly efficient manner for several decades, with honesty, integrity and transparency, so that all may examine, inquire and learn. None can therefore claim ignorance. The principles and practice have been laid down by none other than the Avatar Himself, setting the ideal example for all others to follow.

The Future Planetary Inhabitants

If we accept the prediction that only one and a half billion survivors will be left to inhabit the planet, then we can assume that the remaining 5 billion will have made the transition— will have cast off their bodies and entered the realm of spirit. This, of course, is based on the population of the planet as being approximately 6.5 billion, the current figure. There will be much over-crowding on the other side with so many billion souls heading in the same direction. Those in charge at the other end will have their hands full, but didn't the Nazarene say that in His Father's house there are many mansions? Sufficient, perhaps, to accommodate the vast crowd.

However, this is not the end of the story. Some among us who have failed to make it to the Golden Age and who are destined to become discarnate entities, may harbour the wish for rebirth. These souls would have made the exit from their bodies presumably by violent means through cataclysmic and catastrophic events that in most cases would have been a sudden, unexpected and violent end. It is understandable, therefore, that they would wish to return to Earth in a human body to continue and complete the unfinished business of their former lives. They would have made their exit with half-fulfilled desires, with thwarted ambitions brought to a sudden end, with the hopes and fears of an unfulfilled life. And herein lies the problem. Because of the circumstances prevailing then among the inhabitants of the planet, the question of rebirth would be problematic. In the present age of *Kali yuga*, the Age of Evil, human birth is taken for granted. Over population is the buzz word in many developing countries, especially China and India, and human birth is looked upon more as a liability that an asset. Hence the increase in foeticides, infanticides, killing of the female new-born—throwing them into garbage cans and open drains like dead rats. It is stated by a witness that in one country, the female new-born is immersed in boiling water as soon as she emerges from the birth canal in the obstetric departments of some hospitals. Such is the cheapness of life in this Satanic Age. In brief, there are too many of us, and some means, be they fair or foul, have to be adopted to cut us to size.

The situation will be reversed in the New Age. The population will be sparse, one and a half billion souls scattered throughout a planet, undoubtedly much reduced in size. Tsunamis will have transformed much of the coastal areas of several countries converting them into continental shelves. Seismic and volcanic eruptions would have devastated mountainous areas and other places and converted them into rubble that presumably would take years to be made habitable for humans once again. The highly evolved survivors of the Golden Age, although apparently unchanged physically, looking like normal human beings, will be actually a different variety of *Homo sapiens* with internal bodies completely transmuted. This process, as explained earlier, will have been effected by the conversion of most of their atomic structure into pure energy, the atoms spreading themselves far apart from each other thus leaving large spaces in the body, transmuting it into a 'light' body. Such transmuted beings will not act and behave as we do. These evolved souls will lack body consciousness, the characteristic of the age in which we now live. Their sensual desires will be subdued and their interest in progeny of secondary importance. As such, families will be small, and children few in number. Since the population will be greatly reduced, there will be too few wombs available for rebirth making the return to earth almost impossible. Finally, apart from the two foregoing reasons, whenever the desire for progeny will occur, the soul that will be attracted to such evolved potential parents will be themselves the most highly evolved, the only ones to qualify for rebirth. Also individuals wanting progeny will naturally wish and pray for souls of a high calibre. A situation somewhat analogous to the stiff entrance examination for admission to the portals of a prestigious university. Only few will qualify, very few, perhaps. The others will have to accept disembodied existence and hope and pray that sometime in the future they may obtain rebirth. This may take thousands of years to be realized.

A Sobering Thought

If this be the future of those who do not qualify for the Golden Age it is indeed a sobering thought and should jolt us into the awareness of what we should do to avoid this doom. We may recall what Sri Sathya Sai Baba has repeatedly said about changing our present life-style and turning towards the spiritual life. He has told us that birth in a human body is a very precious thing, that even the gods long for and are unable to obtain. We took birth and became embodied beings with the sole purpose of learning how not to be born again, He affirmed. In other words, the purpose of human birth is not to traverse the beaten path leading from 'womb to tomb and tomb to womb' He says; not to fall into the trap of materialism, the hedonistic way of life or to become a prey to carefree and useless living. The body of man was meant not to be used for indulging in sensual activities but as the vehicle of the Atma or soul and was gifted by the Creator to enable man to realize the full potential of his divine nature, to become aware of the Higher Self as an integral part of the Absolute, to realize that he originated from the Absolute, that he subsists in the Absolute and that his destiny is to return to the Absolute. Sai Baba explains that if we so desire, by the use of our free-will to choose the divine life, and to put into practice the tenets of truth, righteousness, love and peace, with faith in God and love for Him, then it is possible to break the bonds of the seemingly endless circle of birth and death and to attain liberation in this very lifetime; becoming one with the Absolute, our individual stream of consciousness merging with the stream of Cosmic consciousness from which we came and to which we are destined to return, the origin and the goal being one and the same. This seems to be the only way out for those of us who wish to become participants in the Golden Age.

More on the New Age Inhabitants

The present day mechanistic society as we know it will have been swept away by mega tsunamis as are predicted by geophysicists. One of these tsunamis travelling at the speed of a jet plane will have demolished the entire Atlantic Seaboard of the United States. The behemoth of multinationalism will have become buried under waves and sand as likewise the remnants of imperialism.

It is questionable if the highly evolved souls of the New Age will wish their enlightened offspring to be exposed to the history of the dark ages of the 20th and early part of the 21st centuries, the pages of which are so lavishly embroidered with personal bias that there would be no desire of these individuals to waste precious moments of the new life on things of the past, dead and gone into oblivion. The new generation looking exactly like *Homo sapiens* physically, will have undergone a 'sea change'.

All the ills of *Kali yuga*—the Iron Age—will have been buried for all time beneath water and sand and whatever was preserved of it in the pages of history, provided the books survived Zero Point, will remain unread, an absence of curiosity on the part of the new age inhabitants. The changes at 'null-point' will have removed the third dimensional world which will be replaced by the fourth dimensional realm of existence—both humankind and the planet having been transformed into something 'rich and strange'. Seventy-two hours at Zero Point when Earth remained apparently still—no rotation, no apparent movement, lulled like her inhabitants into 'the Bardo state',[2] the strangest transformation will have taken place. On awakening from the hypnotic state of seeming sleep the survivors of the 'Shift' will see a new and strange landscape, a new world, that of the fourth dimension—something that it could not have conceived of as Sri Sathya Sai Baba has described to us on more than one occasion—inconceivable, unimaginable, beautiful, devoid of the demons of lust, greed, anger, attachment, ego and jealousy, as well as the other ignoble traits of the old world of humans. It would be difficult for the new inhabitants to conceive of such an unenlightened race of human beings as those who lived during the past century.

And the leaders of the New Age? The cultured countries of Asia will have come into their own again. The ancient civilizations of India, China and Russia will take charge and bring peace and goodwill towards all men—the spiritual guru of the world, India, the economic giant of the new age, China and the military might of Russia, never to be used in the Golden Age where wars among men will be heard of no more. The keynote of the new world order will be universal love, compassion, peace, service to others, faith in and love for the Creator of all, the strong feeling of Oneness of all living beings—man, animal, plant and even mineral, as all of His Creation possess consciousness at one level or the other—attitudes alien to the old body politic of the three-dimensional world, whose vision was limited by duality.

Led by Chaudhuri's C 3, the three civilized nations of India, China and Russia, and with the accent on love, peace and goodwill to all men where 'aggression at will' will be an alien concept, there will be a paradise on Earth, the actualization of the long felt dream of men of vision of the old world order now past and gone forever. It is conceivable that the out-worn old-fashioned, mechanistic methods of world-wide communication will have gone into limbo. Anything mechanistic will no longer form part of the new age. The hardware that made communication possible world-wide will have most probably become disassociated and reduced to the elements that constituted their structure as the 'blue-prints' under which they had been produced no longer existed, hence their automatic disassociation. The new communication system? Surely, with such evolved inhabitants living in harmony with earth's enhanced resonance, and with 'light' bodies, will be able to communicate with each other by methods now inconceivable to us. To people existing in a fourth dimensional realm the things necessary for their existence in the new dimension should be capable of being created and in simple ways, in keeping with the laws of the new paradigm—so different from the now defunct mechanistic age. They probably would be able to communicate with each other by mere thought, somewhat in the manner Sai Baba communicates with some devotees. If it will be possible for them to merely think and materialize the thought instantly, then what is there to obstruct communicating with each other. Time and space, the dimensions as we know them, will no longer be a limitation in the fourth dimensional world. These new inhabitants will be multi-dimensional beings, having the ability to move freely from one dimension to another; and with some thinkers talking about the fifth dimension, likely to be attained by those of the fourth dimension, then the sky will be the limit of the new era.

A recent incident concerning an octogenarian illustrates some of the characteristics which presumably will dominate the society of the New Age. It concerns the decision of this individual who gave up all his occupations to look after his wife, the victim of a massive stroke in 2001 and another stroke in 2004, leaving her right hand paralyzed, with difficulty in speaking and unsteadiness of gait. He undertook full responsibility to look after her, knowing that it was going to be a twenty-four hours job. He gave up everything—his church duties, his piano business, workshop undertakings, all meetings, conferences, etc. so that he had no other commitments except to look after her twenty-four hours a day. "It worked out beautifully. I was under no stress whatever.... I do all of the cooking and she enjoys my meals better than the restaurants', so all is working well for the present. Her speech is slowly coming back, but we still have a long way to go". It should be stated that this 80-year-old person has had four by-pass operations during the course of the past thirty years. He says that he is in the pink of health and moving around, working, driving, attending to household chores, like any 55-year-old person. Indeed, an achievement for cardiac surgery one might say.

Sai Baba said, "Duty is good/Duty without love is intolerable/Duty with love is desirable/Love without duty is divine". This octogenarian seems to fit the category described in the last line quoted above. Doing duty as he is doing it cannot be described in the terms he has used, unless such selfless action amounting to sacrifice has love as its basis— the love Sai Baba describes as akin to the divine, pure love that is, not based on emotion like worldly love. It is likely that there are many more instances of such people making similar sacrifices for loved ones. There may be hundreds of them scattered throughout the globe and if this, indeed, is the case, one need have no fear for the future of humanity. Recently, this octogenarian had a stent operation to dilate a serious blockage in the main artery to his heart, and after the operation he says he felt as if he was 45 years of age again.

In another incident having no connection with the one documented above, this person described his experience when violent hurricanes struck Orangeburg, his home town in South Carolina. His description follows: He said that Nature longs to move upwards...but she is tied to us and has to rise and fall alongside of us.... In his own words, "With this in mind, I have become convinced that like us, Nature possesses a Cosmic Intelligence or mind, and as long as a mind is present one can communicate with it. And this is how I became involved with this great cosmic mind. I started first by thinking of it as being very real; then I began to send messages to it and finally began to talk to it as one person to another. I became very sympathetic to Nature in that when she displays her functions, she gets only curses and derogatory descriptions from our media and general conversations. Words like devastating, destructive, horrible, awful, terrible, are used to describe them. All of her manifestations have purpose and functions.... I find myself communicating with her cosmic mind and apologizing for the treatment she gets at the hands of mankind". He said he believes it is our evil ways—the sins of mankind—that cause disturbances in nature and he felt personally responsible that this evil committed by people including himself had triggered the succession of extremely severe hurricanes that began to occur along the eastern U.S. Seaboard last year.

So when hurricane Hugo threatened to overrun South Carolina, eight to ten years ago, he communicated with the hurricane and apologized to it for all the sins that people had committed. He said, "I spoke to her and said: 'If one person on earth expresses respect for you and appreciation for your function, will you spare that person by avoiding him' and I got the assurance that she would. When the hurricane hit Orangeburg that night the first thing to go was the electricity.... I went out on the front verandah only to be greeted by 90 miles per hour winds swaying the trees all around the house but not a breath of wind on my verandah". He then called to his wife to come out on the front porch and they sat down and enjoyed the little breeze that occasionally blew through the verandah. An empty juice can that was lying on its long side and not making a single roll was proof. "Another hurricane two years ago was heading straight for South Carolina when I decided to talk to it reminding it of my respect etc. That hurricane came to the south border of South Carolina, veered heavily to the left, crawled up the west coast then veered back to the right in the north boundary. We had little or no winds above 40 miles per hour."

"Communicating with nature is essentially communicating with God...." He said that to him "the hurricanes are very personal, they have their minds, they can make decisions, change their course to spare this area or that." He concluded by saying that there was no one in South Carolina he knew to whom he could describe this experience for they would not understand and would think he was crazy.

The above anecdote is true. The author can vouch for its authenticity, as the octogenarian who related it is the youngest of her siblings. This incident illustrates what the foregoing chapters of this book have been attempting to explain. It also highlights the considered opinion of many spiritual masters who affirm that even if a single human being brings himself into contact with the Higher Forces, he can produce a miracle and can avert the most dangerous situation, even change the course of a war. This is the sort of future we can look forward to where the inhabitants of the Golden Age will be at one with nature, at one with the plant and animal kingdoms and at one with their Higher Self or Cosmic Consciousness—the Divine within us.

If a single individual can by concentrating on the Higher Intelligences or Forces avert serious danger to mankind, how much more can the spiritual giants who have been coming into earthly existence since countless ages. Three recent examples are described to illustrate this. During the Second World War when the Allied forces were being pounded by Hitler's army on the battlefields of France and the situation seemed to be going out of hand on the part of the Allied forces, Sri Aurobindo, the Sage of Pondicherry in South India, used his yogic power and intervened to stop the successful onslaught of the Germans. This he said he did, because it was patently obvious that if at that particular stage in the conflict positive action of some kind had not been taken,

Hitler would have emerged victorious. And what would have been the fate of Europe, not to mention the world. There was no alternative to immediate intervention, and he did just that.

Another incident relates to the invasion of India in 1962 by the Chinese army. Prime Minister Nehru had been completely overcome by the Chinese affirmation of friendship and the thought of a Chinese invasion was least on his mind. Our armed forces were completely unprepared for war, and instead of guns and bullets, ordnance factories were manufacturing coffee percolators. Our soldiers were easily pushed back when hordes of Chinese soldiers crossed the border and started their onward march, heading for the city of Calcutta (Kolkata) in the state of West Bengal in Eastern India. The Government of India was caught napping and there was nothing it could do to stop the foreign invasion. It was around midnight if the author's memory serves her correctly that they heard the fateful news. The Indian nation seemed to be preparing itself to accept another foreign master, after only fifteen years of independence. Within a short time they heard the news again, this time announcing that the Chinese soldiers had turned back and were heading for the Chinese border. No one up to this day has offered any plausible explanation for this strange action on the part of the Chinese Government. It was years later during one of Sai Baba's discourses, He revealed that He had held the Chinese soldiers by the scruff of their necks and hurled them back over the border. Not many may know about this incident.

The third incident was related to the author by a member of the Indian Air Force. It was during the 1971 war between India and Pakistan when India intervened to assist the Government of East Bengal against the Pakistan invasion. The conflict ended in the establishment of Bangladesh as an independent country. The writer was told that a Pakistan Jet fighter plane had escaped Indian vigilance and was heading for the Parliament building and the President's

House. At that moment the Pakistani fighter pilot spotted a large portrait of a very beautiful woman that was suspended in the sky. No sooner he saw this phenomenon, without a moment's delay, he turned his plane around and headed back for the Pakistan border. The portrait was none other than that of Anandamayi Ma, the famous female saint of Bengal.

What is more powerful than spiritual Force? It has been said that it can move mountains. A single human being by the mere force of his yogic powers breaking up the ranks of the German army, perhaps the most disciplined army in the world at that time; another single human being stopping the Chinese soldiers by physically throwing them back into Chinese territory. Unbelievable? We have to remember here that the Divine is also omnipresent as well as omnipotent and omniscient. Sri Krishna multiplied himself and danced with the Gopis 5000 years ago, and Sai Baba probably did the same in order to hurl so many soldiers over the border; and lastly, a single woman through her spiritual powers instilled fright into the mind of a fighter pilot, preventing him from reducing Parliament House and the residence of the President of India to rubble and throwing India into a state of turmoil and utter chaos.

Guidelines for the Future

Some of the sayings of Sai Baba which can be used as guidelines for the future:

- "Concentrate your mind on God and His inestimable love which is the very basis of the universe and all creation. That is the way ahead, the only way out of the bottomless pit at times of deep depression. Come out into the sunshine and bask in the warmth of God's love. He is always waiting for you, even calling you, but you have remained deaf and aloof for so long."[1]

- "Listen to the inner voice, the call of God, and realize that the Lord Himself resides in your heart. He is always there to help and guide you, and He is always ready for your call."[1]
- "Life itself is eternity and there is no death, as you understand it. Life is one long journey back to the source, that source itself is eternity, the eternal God, Lord of the Universe...dedicate your lives to the service of mankind. Go out and help those in need and in distress. Learn to love them as the Lord loves all of you."[1]
- "...out of His divine love God incarnated in human form to draw man back from the brink. He has come for one purpose only, to save the world and all mankind, including those who have attached themselves to the earth and who are caught up in the endless cycle of birth and death. It is the attachment and all the desires associated with it that bind man to the earth. Reincarnation is inevitable, so long as these desires remain unfulfilled."[1]
- "Each one can play his own part, knowing that it is all part of the divine plan and that the Lord Himself is watching, not from afar, but from within."[1]

A Brief Review

The chapters of the book document Sri Sathya Sai Baba's enunciations on the changes that will occur during the Golden Age, both on the Earth as well as within the human beings living at that time. He has described the Golden Age as something inconceivable, unimaginable, something one cannot aspire for and beautiful beyond dreams. He said the human being will come to a realization of who he is and his place in the scheme of things, as well as to reveal the true purpose of existence. Braden's explanations as to how these changes will be brought about and the mechanics operating behind the changes help to throw light on Sai Baba's statements. He describes in detail the two basic factors involved in bringing about the changes in the Earth and in humankind. These are two digitally measurable parameters namely, Earth's magnetic field that is rapidly decreasing at present to reach Zero Point sometime in the near future, probably around the year 2012, as predicted by ancient prophecies. The other parameter is Earth's frequency or pulse rate, which is rapidly increasing and rising to attain a maximum of 13 cycles per second, possibly at the same time as the magnetic field reaches Zero Point.

Currently, these two parameters are causing changes in the Earth as well as in its inhabitants, as they are intimately linked to the Earth and its changes. But many human beings are not aware of these changes, some of them relatively drastic. For example, magnetics produce a block between thought and its consequence, causing a time lag between them so that we are not even aware that there is any connection between what we think and the consequence. This is the present condition and has been for countless years. However, with the decrease of magnetics, and removal of this block between a thought and its result, the time lag is removed or almost so, and a thought may have near instant materialization of that thought. In this way for the first time in our experience, we shall be able to actually realize the importance of our thoughts, which we have always taken for granted.

As for the effect of Earth's increased frequency, Earth's vibratory rate or her heart beat will vibrate at a high pitch causing each cell of every human being living on the planet at that time to increase its vibratory rate to bring it into resonance with Earth's increased harmonics. This is absolutely essential if humankind is to remain in a human body. Those whose cells will not be able to resonate in tune with Earth's increased resonance will make their transition to the spirit realm. The acme of achievement of this enhanced frequency will be the change over from our three-dimensional world to the realm of the fourth dimension, accompanied by extreme changes both in the earth and in the body–mind–spirit complex of the human being. This will be a collective experience that Braden describes as 'the collective initiation', something not experienced at any time before in man's conscious history. This experience was limited to those highly evolved spiritual souls—the liberated ones—of ages past. These changes will be brought about by transmutation of most of the atoms in the body to energy with the atoms becoming widely separated from one another, so that the human body will be transformed into a light body, capable of moving into the fourth dimension. Some of these humans will be vibrating at such a high rate that they will become invisible to those around them and preferably should not be touched. Although they will remain in the same place, they will not be seen. After achieving the fourth dimensional state, some of these human beings will be able to reach the fifth-dimensional realm, according to some authorities.

We can assume that human beings existing at such high levels of spiritual development, will possess all the human values Sai Baba speaks about and will be akin to the Divine in many respects. What more can we mortals ask for—a renewed planet, healed and cleansed by the events of catastrophic changes and 'frequency filters';[2] a new race of planetary inhabitants transmuted beyond the wildest dreams of the inhabitants of the three-dimensional world just gone into oblivion; a new race of fourth-dimensional beings, who look like us physically, but who will have surpassed us in every other respect. A new era where men and women think, speak and act as super–humans. A new age, gifted to us by Mother Earth herself, through the slow and steady process of decreasing magnetics and increasing heart beat (basal resonant frequency), so that her magnetic poles became reversed and presented to us a brand new home, a renewed, purified, healed planet for a new race of fourth-dimensional humans.

This is the Utopia we have all been longing for; and if there is to be a Paradise on Earth—this will be it—that even the Avatar has found words inadequate to describe its marvels. Sai Baba says, "The time is approaching when all humanity will live in harmony. That time will be here sooner than one expects. Before it arrives be prepared for whatever is needed to reveal to every living being the true purpose of existence. It is not what anyone alive can imagine. It is beyond all comprehension. I can say its beauty is magnificent beyond all dreams."[12] If this be the future, then what more do we want? This Paradise is worth making any sacrifice for—by completely changing our lives to bring us into harmony with the Golden Age.

The Creator through the forces and resources of Nature has forged a futuristic Age which we can only glimpse through the lens of the cognitive and perceptive processes. But we can become legitimate occupants of this Promised Land only if we accept with grace, willingness and equanimity whatever the precursors to this Age hold in store for us—that is, the calamities, cataclysmic changes and catastrophic events that will precede the Golden Age. The New Age cannot occur suddenly. It will be a very gradual process, allowing time for three-dimensional humans to make the changes necessary for transition to the fourth-dimensional state. This of course, will take its own time. It is not as if the old paradigm will disappear overnight and the next morning we wake up as fourth-dimensional beings. This will happen only after the 'Shift'.

By the use of our free will to make the right choices we shall be assisted on the inward journey towards the Divinity within—the secret passage to the core of the Higher Self or Cosmic Consciousness which is the Spark of the Divine within each and every living human being on earth.

In the final analysis, the Avatar, the scientist cum mystic and the multidimensional author all agree on almost all points. Can all three be wrong? Sai Baba speaks from His mountain-top of omniscience and if we third-dimensional beings find it difficult to put into practice His suggestions for change in order to save ourselves, how can we begin to question Him who is beyond dimensions.

Sri Sathya Sai Baba

Epilogue

Sri Sathya Sai Baba—A Brief Life Sketch

His Early Years

Sri Sathya Sai Baba was born at dawn on November 23, 1926, in the small remote village of Puttaparthi (Putta means anthill, Parthi—multiplier) in the state of Andhra Pradesh in South India. Easwaramma, Sai Baba's mother, prayed to Lord Sathyanarayana for the birth of a son. Preceding the birth of the child, music was heard at midnight issuing from musical instruments in the house as if played by human hands, apparently heralding the auspicious birth. On being questioned about the nature of His birth and whether it was the normal conception as is common for all human beings, or from Divine intervention, Sai Baba asked His mother Easwaramma to describe the incident she experienced at the well. She stated that while at the well drawing water a large blue ball of light came rolling towards her and she felt as if it entered into her, causing her to faint. Sometime after His birth the women who were in the room noticed a peculiar to and fro movement of the baby as He was lying on the bed. On searching, they found a cobra under the bedding, another auspicious sign.

The name Sathyanarayana was given to the baby after the Lord Sathyanarayana Easwaramma worshipped. Sai Baba became known thereafter as Sathya. His father was Pedda Venkapa Raju and his paternal grandfather, Kondama Raju. The Raju family was devoted to God and had lived a life of piety for generations. Sathya's grandfather was a gifted person, a musician and actor, and his illustrious grandson showed all the signs at an early age of having these gifts. Sathya was a precocious child and showed talent for singing, acting, dancing, composing songs and poetry. At school he was a clever student, knowing all the answers without having to study and also helped his fellow students to cope even with the examination questions.

He revealed His divine powers at an early age by materializing small objects for his schoolmates such as pencils, pens, sweets, etc. Even as a school boy, He demonstrated his feelings of tolerance and compassion. When bullied by his peers who would abandon him with his clothes torn, he showed no anger nor did He retaliate, but would pluck a thorn from the bushes and pin the torn shirt, continuing on His way to school. At the sight of the naked and hungry, He would remove clothing and food from His house and clothed and fed them, bringing down upon Himself His mother's wrath. From the beginning, young Sathya was averse to meat eating, although all around Him were non-vegetarians. He has to this day been a strict vegetarian. Because of his precociousness, vast knowledge at His young age and other unusual abilities as well as the advice of the parents of His schoolmates to learn from Him, He was given the name "guru". Needless to say, He was also against the misuse of animals for cheap entertainment in the villages.

Sathya grew up showing ever increasing signs of His divinity, both in His ability to perform miracles and in His vast knowledge of the scriptures and other subjects. The people around continued to look on Him as someone special. Following the incident of a supposedly scorpion sting at the age of fourteen years when He shrieked and became unconscious which lasted throughout the night, He emerged from this experience with a strange and different personality, causing great anxiety to the parents. They consulted several doctors, witch doctors, black magicians, etc., the last of whom subjected Him to unheard of torture which the young Sathya bore without a trace of emotion; once more proving to those around His divine nature. After recovery, He started materializing sweets, flowers and other items of food and distributed them to those around Him, which so incensed His father Venkapa Raju when he heard of his son's strange behaviour and suspecting foul play and fraud on Sathya's part, Venkapa Raju threatened to beat Him. He shouted "Are you a God or a ghost or a madman?" Sathya without the slightest hesitation said, "I am Sai Baba". Only after He flung a bunch of jasmine flowers on the floor which formed into the name of "Sai Baba" in Telugu that those around began taking Him seriously. Thus Sai Baba revealed His true identity and His spiritual lineage.

It was while He was staying at His elder brother, Seshama Raju's house for the purpose of higher education that He returned home one day in 1940 and announced to His sister-in-law who was in the house, "I am no longer your Sathya. I am Sai." Casting away his school books, "*Maya* (illusion) has left. I am going. My work is waiting." She was shocked at seeing the great halo around His head. Following this incident, Shesama Raju sent for his parents at Puttaparthi who travelled to Uravakonda where he lived to take Sathya back with them. At this time Sathya had moved over to a neighbour's garden. There He started His bhajan singing and teachings. On her arrival, His mother coaxed, persuaded and finally got Him to agree to return to Puttaparthi, on the condition that He should be left alone to carry out His work. He chose to stay in the house of the village accountant and Subbamma, his wife, took care of Sathya like a loving mother.

The Birth of Prasanthi Nilayam

During the ensuing days, Sai Baba performed many miracles for the people around Him, getting to where the tamarind tree was without apparently climbing the rocks, producing whatever fruits the devotees wanted on the tree and numerous other miraculous acts. He even ate poisoned food and proved to all that not even poison can affect Him, by vomiting the entire stuff. He also started healing people, curing wounds and making the dumb speak, treating diseases, etc. Even operations were performed by the young Sathya during these days, materializing the surgical instruments and curing the patients. As time passed the buildings He worked in became too small for the ever increasing crowds, in spite of additional quarters, extensions, etc., until eventually the devotees decided that a proper place was necessary to accommodate the vast crowds that became increasingly larger day by day. Thus Prasanthi Nilayam—the Abode of Peace—came into existence and is situated in the same place up to the present. Twenty-five to thirty years ago, the journey to Puttaparthi was fraught with physical inconvenience s testing the endurance of those who were determined to visit Sai Baba's Ashram and have His *darshan*. The bus journey in rickety vehicles bumped along ill-maintained roads that took several tedious hours to get to its destination. On arriving at Parthi, one had to resort to bullock cart transport to cross the Chitravathi river that had to be negotiated to reach the Ashram. But the devotees continued to flock to Puttaparthi and nothing deterred them. Within the span of thirty years or so, the changes made are unbelievable. Today, there is rail connection with trains terminating at Puttaparthi itself. Also there is a direct flight from Bangalore to Puttaparthi several times a week landing and taking off from the Sri Sathya Sai Airport. Roads have become modernized and by car only a short enjoyable drive directly to the Ashram. The village has become transformed beyond recognition.

Anyone knowing and seeing the village of Puttaparthi twenty-five to thirty years ago will certainly experience a shock on seeing the modern, thriving, large, beautifully designed modern village of Puttaparthi, spreading over acres and acres, interspersed with greenery, beautiful lawns and most impressive of all, the buildings that stand out from many cities in India, some of which were designed and supervised by Sai Baba Himself. The village boasts of a Super-speciality hospital, of which there are only a few scattered throughout the land; a planetarium, a Music School, a beautifully designed Books and Publications Trust Building, several schools ranging from the primary, secondary and higher secondary to colleges, all fully equipped to take the child from the earliest stage of learning through high school and college to the postgraduate stage in several disciplines. Information Technology has not been sidelined and there are well-equipped modern departments teaching computer science. And, believe it or not, something unheard of in these days of rank commercialism in education and medical services everything is offered free to both rich and poor in all the disciplines. Priority is given to urgent medical cases and a high academic standard is expected of students who wish to gain admission to the portals of this unique centre of learning. No less a person than the Avatar Himself, Sri Sathya Sai Baba, is the Chancellor of the University who also holds complete control of financial matters; as the sole Trustee, He is authorized to sign cheques. No one, therefore, can ever question the use of the funds that keep pouring into the coffers of Prashanthi Nilayam by donations from millions of devotees, millionaires and others from many countries worldwide, as well as the common man, making the Sri Sathya Sai Central Trust one of the richest trusts of its kind in India if not in the world.

The Achievements of a Single Person

To think of the colossal achievements of a single person, establishing a gigantic project of this kind that could compete, probably even surpass global standards in some ways, and founded in a place which an American author described as "ten minutes past the stone-age" more than twenty-five years ago, simply boggles the imagination. It has been said that Sai Baba is the first single spiritual person to have done so much for humanity and on such a vast scale. Apart from the academic, health and spiritual programmes being carried on daily in the sprawling campus and in the *Mandir* (temple) at Prasanthi Nilayam, Sai Baba has provided drinking water for villages catering to thousands of people in Anantapur District in the State of Andhra Pradesh; and the entire cost of this gigantic project was met from the Sri Sathya Sai Central Trust. Recently, He also supplied thirsty Chennai (Madras City) in the State of Tamil Nadu with badly needed water by rebuilding a derelict canal and transporting the water several kilometres away from the source of supply in one state to another, again fully funded by the Trust.

Has the media taken note of these philanthropic acts by Sai Baba? Not in the least. The media, quick to sensationalize the slightest incident taking place in the Ashram at Puttaparthi, if perchance it smacked of some sort of notoriety, such as the murders that occurred in the Ashram some years ago, printing and publishing reports by questionable correspondents who as everyone knows are interested only in sensationalizing news that can increase the sale of their newspapers, regardless of the authenticity of information gathered. Negative occurrences which any gigantic organization such as Sai Baba's cannot escape are highlighted by the media, both print and electronic, making every attempt to denigrate and besmirch the name of Sai Baba. Aitken has stated in his book 'Sri Sathya Sai Baba', "...just one murder in the Ashram will bring hordes of press persons keen to revive the mood of the ancient blood sport of throwing Christians to the lions."[14] And again on the press as he should know from his own dealings with the media, "Newspapers are not printed for the welfare of our soul but to make money for their owners. Since their proprietors have their own gurus, it is not surprising to find on occasion scurrilous reports on rival spiritual leaders."[14]

As far as positive activities are concerned the silence on the part of the press is deafening, turning the Nelsonian eye on them and, completely ignoring the unique and gigantic humane acts of Sri Sathya Sai Baba and His Central Trust. Again, quoting Aitken, "Sathya Sai Baba has brought life to over a thousand thirsty villages in Rayalseema, but no journalist will think it worth his while to spread the word about the historic dimensions of this unique act of charity."[14] The media was denounced by Marie Corelli more than a century ago, as being interested mainly in sensational news—crime, murder, violence, rape, the antics of politicians—both honourable and dishonourable—and all the other questionable incidents occurring in the society both at home and abroad.

In a recent article in the column entitled "India: Today and Tomorrow" (*The Hindu Business Line*, April, 2005), the writer and economist Arindam Chaudhuri in discussing a huge scam that took place in the country involving "very important persons" stated, "...no newspaper or TV channel picked up this huge scam. The apparent reason was that the Indian media does not encourage peeping into the private lives of individuals (primarily politicians). The reality of course is that the Indian media acts in connivance with the politicians in such matters, partially because they are scared of political dictates and partially due to the fact that at top positions in the media itself there are people with multiple skeletons in their own cupboards". He concluded, "Sad that the market forces don't allow them to mess up with the rich (the advertisers) and the politicians (who can mess up their basic existence)." The boldness and courage of such writers in exposing the media by stating facts without mincing matters deserve our gratitude and appreciation. May their tribe increase. A sad commentary indeed on the state of the media in the country today. This, of course, does not exclude the media in other countries, some of which are much worse than the Indian—as they all seem to be birds of the same feather. How fortunate for us that this particular newspaper published this article.

Sai Educational Activities

Sai Baba's unique educational system has now become known the world over and has actually been put into practice in some countries as well as in some parts of India. The curriculum apart from offering all the main academic subjects taught in schools all over the world, includes important sections on human values, so that students graduating from the Sai schools and colleges at any level will have been exposed at one stage or the other to moral teaching based on Human Values or educare as Sai Baba describes it. Some of these graduates stand out from the society for the sterling qualities they exhibit. Sai Baba has said that the end of education is character and His students testify to this. In this connection it is interesting to note how Ron Laing in his book "Sathya Sai Baba:The Embodiment of Love" describes Sai Baba's college students. Since Laing himself was a graduate of Eton and Cambridge University, he should know what he is talking about. He writes, "I have seen a sample of the Brindavan students (Bangalore Ashram) and I have never seen a finer cadre of young men in my life. They were tidy, well mannered, respectful, happy and integrated—brisk and intelligent, devout and inspired—indeed the elite of the elite. And yet they were not the sons of the rich—more than half came from the rural areas."

The multifarious activities of Sai Baba can fill the pages of many books, and his achievements in the field of education are unique as His approach to the discipline is based on the inculcation of human values into the entire student body of His educational institutions. These values are the hallmark of His teachings and He has demonstrated this in the type of individuals who graduate from His colleges every year. His boys and girls stand out from the crowd and His graduates are employed in a variety of professions and activities with laudable achievements. Sai Baba has been quoted as saying that the students who are emerging from His colleges will be the ones who will perpetuate the new race of human beings to populate the Golden Age.

Some details of His educational programme are given below.

- Education from 1st standard to post-graduation is free of cost and admission is by an entrance examination.

- Education in Human Values (EHV) programme has become a worldwide movement operating in many countries throughout the globe. Devoted to the younger section of society, the EHV programme seeks to train children and young people in social, moral and spiritual values thus producing a future generation of enlightened, upright, spiritually oriented and a morally disciplined society.

- Inculcation of Sai Baba's human values of righteousness, truth, love, peace and non-violence are the leavening agents leading to integration of the human being who then can take his place in society and contribute to its uplift, advancement and enlightenment resulting in a better world. These human values Sai Baba has affirmed must become an integral part of the educational process. He bemoans the divorce of human values from secular education, hence His emphasis on these values.

- The Sri Sathya Sai Institute of Higher Learning in Puttaparthi has been accredited by the National Assessment and Accredition Council (NAAC) of India at A++ level. This Institute is the brain child of Sri Sathya Sai Baba who has Himself designed it and is also the chancellor of the Institute. It admits men and women from all over India and it offers free education to all. The NAAC gave the highest grade to the Institute among all

the universities in the country. Only one other institution shares this honour. The NAAC in its report stated:
"The Peer Team feels that this Institute stands out as a crest jewel among the University Education System in the country and this model is worthy of emulation by the institutions of Higher Leaning in the country and elsewhere, so that those benefits would be reaped fast and on the widest possible scale.

The Peer Team puts on record its appreciation for NAAC to provide the members of the team the opportunity to spend time with the Institute faculty and the students so as to develop a thorough insight into the higher education process of the Sri Sathya Sai Institute of Higher Learning, particularly the integral higher education interwoven in the blueprint and design of higher education products.

This made us realize that there is a way to correct our already degrading university education system in India, if we decide to do so."

Three campuses function under the Institute of Higher Learning:

1. The Anantapur Campus (for women) offering undergraduate courses of 3 years, in history and Indian culture, economics, philosophy, political science, English and Telugu; and postgraduate courses of 2 years and one year duration.

2. The Brindavan Campus (Whitefield) for men offering undergraduate courses of 3 years duration in mathematics, physics, chemistry, biosciences and commerce.

3. The Prasanthi Nilayam campus for men offering undergraduate courses in economics, mathematics, physics, chemistry and biosciences as well as postgraduate courses of 2 years duration in pure mathematics, applied mathematics, computer science,

functional analysis and applications and decision theory, physics with specialization in photonics, nuclear and particle physics and electronics, chemistry and biosciences.

The professional courses offered include M.B.A. and M.Tech. and the research programme offers M.Phil. and Ph.D. The Institute also has a College of Music for boys offering vocal (Carnatic, Hindustani) and instrumental courses.

The Sri Sathya Sai Institute for Higher Medical Sciences are two in number, one in Prasanthigram and the other in Whitefield, Bangalore. The services are free and some beds are reserved for the economically weaker sections of the community. The services offered include cardiology, cardio-thoracic and vascular surgery, urology, plastic surgery and ophthalmology. The institutes possess state of the art equipment and cater to all sections of the society regardless of caste, creed, race or religion. The Whitefield Institute has a 308 bed charitable hospital, and services are provided completely free to all patients without discrimination.

Apart from the above educational facilities, there are also 10 Bal Vikas (primary education in human values). There are Bal Vikas schools in other countries as well. Full-time schools for children in their early teens offer a curriculum which includes *sadhana* (spiritual discipline), yoga, social service, meditation and singing. The stress here in these schools, which Sai Baba has also established in different parts of India, is on character building and service.

Added to the above, Summer Courses are held every year during the college vacation. They are well attended and even university professors and educationists from all over the world attend these. Again the emphasis of the course is on values: A broadbased approach to religion and again to inculcate human values leading to the making of a better human being with a noble character whose example others may wish to follow.

Sai Baba has said that the only way to transform society

is to transform the individual through love, to a realization of the Atma (soul) in all mankind and in all the kingdoms of nature. And by this method He has promised that a new Golden Age will recur.

Other Activities of Sri Sathya Sai Baba

Sai Baba has provided drinking water by the setting up of a system of pipelines, tanks, pumps, etc. The pipelines alone were 2500 km in length. The system also consisted of hundreds of reservoirs and tanks. This project serves the people in 731 villages in Anantapur District in Andhra Pradesh. The total cost of the project met solely by Baba's Central Trust amounted to more than 250 crores of rupees, approximately fifty million dollars.

He also initiated a project whereby water was transported all the way from one state, Andhra Pradesh, to another state, Tamil Nadu, to supply water to thirsty Chennai (Madras) all at the cost of the Sri Sathya Sai Central Trust.

He also holds regular feeding sessions for the poor and His students and volunteers often visit the villages in and around Puttaparthi to distribute food items, clothes, and other daily necessities. This sort of service is also carried out by the numerous Sathya Sai centres in over 150 countries of the world. "Service to man is service to God" says Sai Baba and also that hands that serve are holier than lips that pray. Service is one thing that Sai Baba stresses in every facet of His activities. To feed the hungry, clothe the naked, relieve the downtrodden, console the bereaved, these are the pathways to union with God—Service to humanity. Again about service, He says, "Always think that whatever service activities you are undertaking are for your own upliftment. These service activities must be undertaken to develop self-confidence, which will lead to self–satisfaction, self–sacrifice and ultimately to self–realization. Thus, service is meant to realize your true self. It should never be considered as help for others."[5b]

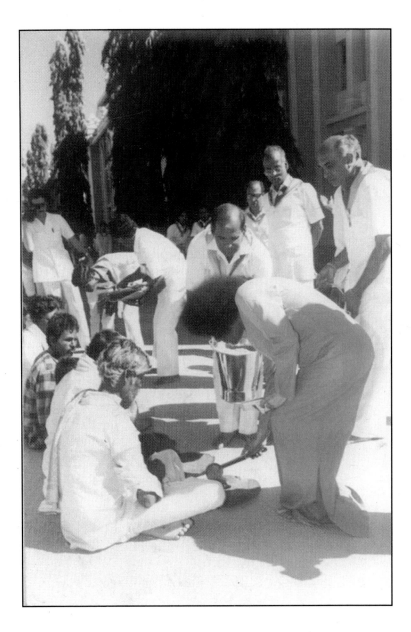

Performing *Narayan Seva—feeding of the poor*

Distributing clothes to needy women

Distributing clothes to needy men

And again on service He says, "...you are yourself the beneficiary of all your service activities and not others.... You can depend upon your own innate strength and energy. The power of your Self will help you in all your endeavours...; you do not need the protection of anybody else from outside."[5b]

Sri Sathya Sai Baba's Account of Shirdi Sai Baba's Parentage and Birth

Even at the present time there is still a raging controversy among many people—both Shirdi Sai Baba's and Sri Sathya Sai Baba's devotees—mainly about the events surrounding the birth and parentage of Shirdi Sai Baba. The following information was given to the author by one of the sons of the Maharastrian family she knew who lived opposite the Whitefield Ashram. Their son was one of the students at the First Summer Course and spent fifteen days with a group of boys as Baba's guests in Brindavan, living and eating with Sai Baba. This was in the year 1979.

The account as told to her by the student:

One evening the students asked Baba the question, 'How do you know you are Sai Baba?' 'I know everything, not only about Shirdi Baba. Certain information is not known', Baba said, and He proceeded to disclose it. The following account is given as Baba told it to the boys:

"Shirdi was a small village. Parthi is also near there—a village. A Brahmin family, Ganga Pawah (Writer's spelling), worshippers of Shiva and Parvati, learned in the Vedas, especially the wife. They considered everything as a form of God. If a dog would come they would consider it as God.

The husband left home one day and remained away for a few days. That night his wife heard a knock on the door and wondering who could be knocking at that time, she opened it to find an old man asking for shelter and food which she gave. He was told to sleep in the verandah. Then some hours later she heard another knock on the door and again, wondering

what it could be, she opened it and the old man said his
legs were not feeling good, and he wished her to massage
them. At this time the poor woman went inside and tried to
find a maid servant to do the job as it was not her custom to
massage a man's body. But no maid-servant could be found.
So she appealed to Shiva and Parvati asking them not to test
her so much, and help her. Immediately a maid-servant
appeared saying she heard the mistress was looking for her.
So Mrs. Ganga Pawah put her to massage the old man's
legs, and she went back to sleep. Some hours later another
knock was heard on the door and the woman now
wondering what could be wrong, opened it to find Shiva
and Parvati waiting outside. She fell down and worshipped
them and they asked her what she wanted. She said she
had no children and would like to have children. They told
her that after two children, they, Shiva and Parvati would be
born as the third child.

On the husband's return the incident was related but he
scoffed at her saying how could Shiva and Parvati appear to
her and dismissed it as hallucination. Some months later the
first child was born, some years later the second and the third
pregnancy was on the way, but the husband decided to leave
the world and head for the forest. But the wife wished to follow
him and asked him to wait for a while so that the third child
could be born. After some time he set out for the forest and
she started to follow him. A little way on she developed labour
pains and a baby boy was born.

Shortly thereafter, a Mr. and Mrs. (name confused),
Muslims, were passing that way and the woman decided to
sit down and rest when she heard the cry of a baby. Search
revealed the newly born infant and she took him up and
claimed him for she had no children. He was brought up as a
Muslim. Baba then continued by saying that as Shirdi Baba
he was very naughty, so He used to go to the Hindu temple
and quote the Muslim scriptures and to the mosque and recite

the Hindu scriptures. As this caused a lot of trouble his foster parents decided to send him away to an Ashram.

Once, Baba said that Shirdi Sai Baba being slapped by a woman whose deity he had swallowed having won it in a game of marbles, and refusing to yield it on request, opened His mouth and revealed to her the universe. On seeing this, she fell down and worshipped Him and became His devotee."

This was the tale told by Sai Baba which the Summer Course student wrote down as Sai Baba spoke. He dictated the account which the author in turn wrote down verbatim. This account is as authentic as could be found anywhere and as told by Sri Sathya Sai Baba Himself. The student showed great excitement when he told her about the incident and while describing it. Sai Baba had said at the outset of the talk that certain information was not known; we can therefore conclude that this is the first time details about Shirdi Sai Baba's parentage and birth had been disclosed to anyone, and it was this aspect that excited the student. It is hoped that this authentic account will stop the controversy regarding the parentage and early life of Shirdi Sai Baba that has caused so much confusion and has been written about by so many.

The Perfect Model

Devotees who have seen, met and spoken to Sai Baba, and have seen at first hand the simple state he lives in, can easily look on Him as the model on whom they can base their lives. His simple habits, so much at odds with present day social norms, His frugal meals, His unostentatious life–style, His sparsely furnished room where He has lived for most of His life, until recently in His eightieth year a house has been built for Him by devotees. His meals for the greater part of His life have been provided by members of the family so that He does not add to the burden of the Trust He established, as some devotees have disclosed. Yet what Sai Baba eats, according to those close to Him and the amount He consumes daily can hardly sustain anyone who engages in activities from dawn to dusk as He does. Sai Baba devotes His entire day to the service of others not sparing Himself physically or mentally even when medical doctors advise rest. During the healing of His several fractures He even defied medical advice and walked. His devotees come first and He dislikes denying them the *darshan* they crave. In the language of the day, Sai Baba would be described as a workaholic.

Sai Baba has said that there will be three Sais—Shirdi Sai was the first, Sathya Sai is the second and the third will be Prema Sai who will be born in the Mandya District of Kanataka, one year after Sai Baba leaves his body. Sai Baba has hinted that the mother of Prema Sai has already taken birth.

We may be able to copy His life-style as this is at the material and physical levels. On the spiritual plane, however, we shall have to make an all-out effort to put into practice some of His teachings. However, Sai Baba Himself has said that He is God; that we are also God. The difference is that He knows He is, but we don't. This should inspire us with hope and propel us to do what is necessary to discover our divinity. We can no longer hide under the guise of ignorance since He has spelt out in simple language a thousand times what we are expected to do to advance along the spiritual path. In the book "Sai Baba:The Embodiment of Love" by Peggy Mason and Ron Laing, the latter writes that Sai Baba has said of Himself that His power is immeasurable. His truth inexplicable, unfathomable, and that He is beyond the most intensive enquiry and the most meticulous measurement. He stated that there is nothing He does not see, no where He does not know the way, and that His sufficiency is unconditional. He affirmed that He is the Totality, all of it, and only those who have recognized His love and experienced that love can assert they have glimpsed His reality.

Appendix

Some Experiences with Sri Sathya Sai Baba

The author came into contact with Sri Sathya Sai Baba in 1979. During the time she spent at His Ashrams in Puttaparthi in the state of Andhra Pradesh and at Whitefield, Bangalore, India, over the subsequent seven years, Baba gave her several glimpses of His omniscience, omnipresence and omnipotence. Documented below are some of these experiences she was privileged to have had through His Grace and Compassion, and through which many valuable lessons were learnt.

The Anguished Cry for Help

Episode I

This incident took place before the author came to know about Sai Baba. It was the latter part of the monsoon season in West Bengal, India, and the Teesta River had been in spate, followed by a flash-flood, causing widespread havoc in the town of Jalpaiguri in North Bengal. She, her husband, Dr. K.C. Chaudhuri and her 9-year-old son, Ananda, left for Jalpaiguri without knowledge of the catastrophe. While flying over the devastated area prior to landing, they were dismayed to see the widespread damage. Railway lines had been broken, lifted up, bent and were pointing upwards like sticks.

After checking into the hotel, her husband suggested they drive down to the river to have a close look at the damage. They approached the edge of the embankment very cautiously to see the river forty to fifty feet below flowing innocently through the gorge as if nothing had happened. The embankment was a dangerous place to stand on as there was only rubble—stones and sand loosened by the flood waters. She and her son returned to a safer area some distance away from the dangerous edge. Dr. Chaudhuri, however, took out his camera and while endeavouring to have a good view for a good shot, he slipped on the rubble and fell down. By Divine grace he fell in the prone position and ended up hanging over the gorge, half his body on the embankment. Her young son told her later that her scream was so loud and high that he was sure she had hit high C on the piano à la Maria Callas, a famous opera singer at that time. The ability to scream is not one of the author's accomplishments and the fact that she did scream indicated the severity of the trauma she had experienced. She threw herself flat on the ground, crawled to her husband's feet and grabbed with the right hand the hem of his right pant leg, steadying herself with the other.

At this point a digression is called for. Twelve years previously, her second sister who was studying at the University of London, developed breast cancer. She had a radical mastectomy, prolonged periods of radiation and all the appropriate drugs for cancer available in the therapeutic armamentarium of allopathy at that time. Nothing worked. Her condition continued to deteriorate and she died after much pain and suffering within three years. After her death, the author rejected God and everything spiritual. She had been told by her sister's mathematics tutor at the University that he had never before met a female student with such a brain for mathematics. She could not forgive the Divine for taking her sister away so early. Little had she realized then that in rejecting the Divine she was rejecting her Self and separating herself spiritually from her Self. It was learnt much later that this attitude was fraught with danger to both the physical as well as emotional health of aspirants on the spiritual path. She was not aware then that God does not inflict pain and suffering on us, and that we of our own accord invite these hardships by our own actions and thus have to suffer the consequences. She had conveniently forgotten about the law of Karma. However, in retrospect, she can honestly say that she had not lost confidence in herself, and Sai Baba has affirmed that without self-confidence we cannot proceed on the spiritual path. So all was not lost, perhaps.

To return to the story. While holding on to the hem of the pants with all her might, she looked around for human help. On her left were standing in a row about half a dozen Nepali men wearing khaki shirts and short pants, probably soldiers from the armed forces. She shouted to them to give her a hand. She said she could not hold on for ever and could one or two of them please pick up her husband and bring him away to safety. Regardless of repeated pleas for help, in Bengali, the language they all understood, not a single man moved, their features remaining immobile with no trace of emotion. She knew she was asking them to risk their lives.

Several minutes passed, while pleading with the men for help, simultaneously warning her son not to approach the bank. She was at her wit's end, not knowing what to do next. Her mind went blank and it was at this point she heard herself shout, "Oh God, help me!" in a voice full of anguish. No sooner were the words out of her mouth, a short man with a head of thick tousled hair, wearing the same outfit as the Nepalese immediately appeared, standing astride the prone figure hanging over the gorge. The stranger lifted him up with ease and put him to sit down at a safe distance from the dangerous edge. She was so relieved that ignoring her benefactor she went to her husband, and seeing that he had sustained a fracture of his right wrist, made an emergency bandage with a large handkerchief, gave him an Aspirin for pain, and asking her son to keep a watch on his father, went in search of their saviour. The Nepalese denied picking him up, neither did they see who picked him up. She questioned the taxi driver who denied seeing anyone enter the grounds at that time. Failing in her efforts to find the man, they returned to the taxi and headed for the nearest hospital.

It was many years later, after Dr. Chaudhuri's death, that her mother who was visiting at the time, explained that his life was saved by none other than Sri Sathya Sai Baba. She asked her mother who was Sai Baba. Her mother was shocked beyond words that even though the author had been resident in India for nineteen years she had never heard of nor seen Sai Baba. Little did her mother know that apart from being wholly occupied with pediatric and human cytogenetic research for all those years, she had also renounced the Divine in 1956, after her sister's death; it was kinder not to enlighten her mother she felt. Shortly afterwards her mother visited Sai Baba at Puttaparthi and had a very fruitful two-week experience with Him—an interview, the curing of a chronic shoulder condition that allopathy failed to relieve and materialization of her favourite milk sweet in her hands from which Sai Baba fed all the California devotees who were present in the room. On her return from the Ashram, in spite of all her experiences, the author was not yet ready for Sai Baba. It was four years later that a friend, Mrs. K.K. Chanana, insisted that she should read books on Sai Baba which she kindly loaned her. This was the turning point and she made her first visit to Sai Baba's Ashram one year later.

She never had the opportunity to confirm this experience with Sai Baba Himself, but her mother was certain that it was He. "Who else could it have been?" she said. She also said that Sai Baba did not always reveal His identity when He answered a call for help. He usually assumed a disguise of some sort. Years later in retrospect, after the author had made her peace with God, she realized that though we may reject Him, He is always ready to answer our call for help and Sai Baba Himself has said that He is within us and can answer the call immediately. This incident revealed Sai Baba's omniscience, omnipresence and omnipotence. The fact that He appeared standing astride the fallen human being is an indication of His omniscience, for the author had not revealed what the cry was for; and since He answered the call for help instantaneously, an indication He was already residing within, otherwise how could He have heard the call, proving His omnipresence—being present everywhere, at the same time, all the time; finally, single-handedly lifting up a well-built male adult with the greatest of ease from the prone to the upright position with half of his body hanging over a forty to fifty feet gorge, while standing on dangerous terrain, revealed His omnipotence.

We may well ask ourselves whether any normal human being could have performed the dangerous act Sai Baba did while standing on dangerous ground which could have become displaced with the slightest pressure, something the Nepalese men realized fully. Sai Baba has said, "I will never abandon you, even if you turn away from Me for I am the totality."[1] And also relevant to the above episode, "It is better to turn to God when in despair. Help is always there for I am never far away. I come instantly when I am called, here, there and everywhere."[1] After the experience described above no one should doubt that God does answer our call for help even though we may have rejected Him.

The Voice of the Avatar

Episode II

The author had already planned her trip to Puttaparthi to have her first *darshan* (viewing) of Sai Baba, when the latest book on Sai Baba arrived in the mail. The book was entitled "Sai Baba, Lord of the Air" by Tal Brooke. She immediately sat down to read the book which took several hours to complete, skipping some pages which she considered could hold for another time. The contents of the book devastated her and left her in a bewildered state of mind, so much so that she broke down completely. The accusation, denigration and wholesale blackmail was so extreme that it was obvious the author was hell-bent on destroying Sai Baba for all time, which seemed to him a strong possibility.

Since she was looking forward to seeing Sai Baba who had by this time meant to her the end of the search in spirituality, she felt as if the ground beneath her suddenly caved in and that she was falling freely through empty space. It was at that moment she heard a voice, a soft voice she had never heard before, and this is what it said, "Why do you feel pain when others deride me? Why do you shed tears when they criticize Me? Don't you know that no one can do any harm to Sai Baba? They are afraid that I would make inroads into their religious communities and weaken them; so they are trying to break up my organization. Isn't it obvious to you that this author has been bought by my denigrators to malign Me through the written word? Millions of rupees have been paid to him to carry out this dirty job. You should not allow something like this to upset you so much. Remember that no one can cause any harm to Sai Baba".

This is what she heard; whether the voice came from inside her or was coming from somewhere in the room in which she sat, she is unable to say. Relating to Tal Brooke's publication, Aitken says, "When an American devotee-turned-critic published a book...in an attempt to smear Sai Baba's reputation and call him the anti-Christ, Dr. V.K. Gokak (a well known writer and poet) took up the gauntlet to set the record straight. His 'In Defence of Jesus Christ and other Avatars' exposes the doctrine of hate that inspires and funds such books." Again Aitken says, "One of the alarming aspects of the inner path is that it tends to attract the unstable character.... Certain rival missions feel threatened by Sai Baba's popularity and are envious of the exponential spread of his message. Once favourite disciples whose egos are deflated by being relegated to the back row can become prime targets for these missions, ready to fan any smouldering resentment into fire."[14] Continuing with Aitken, "Throughout history every religious leader worth the name has been the target of some avenging group and the easiest way to cast doubt on a holy person's character is insinuate deviant sexual conduct." Of Tal Brooke and David Bailey, two of Sai Baba's denigrators, Aitken says, both "plead that their innocent belief had been abused by Sai Baba. By closing their eyes to the reality that every new disciple is fussed over and thereafter conspicuously dumped.... they have only themselves to blame.... Sai Baba never invited either to Puttaparthi, nor did He ask them to become his disciples.... They came of their own free-will. When he gave them importance they called him God. When he transferred that importance to others they called him Satan."[14] Pertaining to the adverse criticism in the foreign press about Sai Baba, Aitken continues, "There is a clue here as to why Sathya Sai's success has earned a bad press abroad. In all the adverse reports the common thread is phobia, a fear that Sai Baba's supernormal powers prove he is a bogey man. To aggravate these often racist feelings of the international press is the economic reality that in the West, where church funds are declining, the newcomer Sai's mission is attracting high-profile donors. Envy at such spiritual success is another reason behind the critics' wanton downplaying of Sathya Sai's true spiritual status."[14]

Following the advice given by the voice, the author became greatly relieved and a few days later arrived in Puttaparthi. She described in detail the entire incident to a devotee from

Malaysia on the night of her arrival who was very impressed with the story. The next day she went directly to the Ashram's office and reported to the person then in charge the scurrilous information contained in Tal Brooke's book about Sai Baba. She told them that such denigrating publications will be a deterrent to new comers wishing to visit Sai Baba's Ashram. They then said that apparently this did not deter her, and that only those whom Sai Baba calls can visit the Ashram. About her report, they informed her that the Central Trust was seized of the matter; there had been a meeting of the trustees who had discussed the subject threadbare and their conclusion was there would be no rebuttal, retaliation or clarification, and Tal Brooke would eventually fall on his own weight; the matter had been finalized and nothing more will be done about it. Although the writer was told that the decision to leave things alone was that of the Central Trust, she entertained a sneaking feeling that the decision could have originated from no one else than Sri Sathya Sai Baba Himself. It revealed His tolerance towards and compassion for even someone who indulged in such heinous and wicked denunciation of Him with the intention to besmirch His name. This attitude on Sai Baba's part is nothing new. Even as a school boy He tolerated whatever His young peers inflicted on Him without complaint or retaliation. Even the traumatic beating His elder brother gave Him on His palms for what he considered young Sathya's dereliction of duty, He tried to hide from His parents giving a concocted version to explain His bruised and swollen hands so as to protect his brother's action.

Today on the Internet there are dozens of Tal Brookes accusing Sai Baba of the same perverted sexual activities. Yet the Sai movement grows apace, becoming larger and larger and extending to more and more countries across the globe. In this connection, Aitken spares no one in his comments on those writing anti-Sai books and indulging in denigrating Sai Baba on the Internet, "Writing books against Sai Baba or seeking to tarnish his reputation on the Internet might merit an audience if the authors of these grievances possessed some *locus standi* in the world of philanthropy. If they had done a thousandth part of what Sathya Sai has accomplished in furthering the welfare of humanity we would be justified in taking their complaints seriously and consider investigating whether pure water can flow from a polluted spring. The critics belong to the category of intellectuals who cannot face the reality of the spirit and desperately want to explain it away. They are haunted by the truth Sathya Sai embodies and wish to negate a presence that millions of ordinary people regard as the most beautiful evidence they have of life's ultimate meaning."[14]

Sai Baba's life is an open book, and anyone can find what goes on behind the scenes. His students are now graduates scattered throughout the land and abroad. Thousands of His male students are studying at His schools and colleges and anyone wishing to have information can approach them and obtain it. Many people have talked to these students, yet not a single word of criticism has been uttered by them. Instead they have all been consistent in their praise of Sai Baba. If no one knows about the twenty-four-hour activities of Sai Baba, these boys do. Throughout the ages outstanding spiritual masters have been severely criticized by those unable to understand them or recognize their spiritual greatness—whether it was Rama, Krishna or Jesus. They ended up by crucifying Jesus; Sri Sathya Sai Baba, however, enjoys the unique distinction of being repeatedly nailed to the cross. Sai Baba Himself has said that the barren tree is left untouched and only the fruit laden tree is pelted with stones.

The night following the author's arrival Sai Baba gave His usual discourse. He was standing in front on the platform. She was sitting only a few rows from the front of the hall. They were directly facing each other only a few feet away. To her utter surprise and bewilderment Sai Baba began His discourse by repeating the entire talk she had heard in her room in the Himalayas a few thousand kilometres away. She was astounded. He did this while looking her directly in the eyes. Her Malaysian friend was too excited to keep quiet, poking her in the ribs and repeating that it was exactly what the author had disclosed to her the previous night. How did Baba know all this she wondered. She was flabbergasted! The author failed to keep her quiet; she knew that no one should speak while Sai Baba was giving His discourses. She immediately realized that Baba was demonstrating His omniscience to them and she felt very happy and relieved to know it was really He Himself whose voice she had heard for the first time thousands of kilometres away which also revealed His omnipresence. He says that He is here, there, everywhere; how true.

The question as to how He knew what the author was reading and what her reactions were persisted in her mind. The answer He Himself has given us. He says He is the resident in the human heart and knows what we think even before we give voice to our thoughts or even before the thought is created! What more proof do we need to accept Sai Baba's omniscience and omnipresence.

The Blinding Flash of Light

Episode III

The day after her first visit to Puttaparthi, the author was sitting in the line for *darshan* and as luck would have it, was in the front row when Sai Baba emerged from His interview room and stood on the steps of the verandah of the temple. She said to herself while looking at Him, "How can you be God as you say you are?" A few seconds later she saw a thick brilliant white light, about ten inches in width, a blinding light which started from the top of His head and flashing down the entire left side of His body, disappearing as quickly as it appeared. She was so taken aback by this instantaneous reply to her question doubting His divinity, that she heard herself repeating silently, "Yes, Baba you are indeed God." Again, an example of His omniscience. In this connection it should be stated that Baba has repeatedly told us we have not heard Him correctly: What He actually said was, "Yes, I am God; you are also God. The difference is I know I am, but you don't." However, the author heard this only after the experience.

Two Blue Moons

Episode IV

It was Christmas time, 1979, and a drama was being enacted by Baba's college boys depicting the last days of Jesus before the Crucifixion. The author sat enthralled while the boys performed their act, thinking all the while that here in this out of the way village of Puttaparthi, "ten minutes past the stone age" as Arnold Schulman described it in his book "Baba", a first class drama was in progress, rivalling any Broadway show with appropriate stage props, background scenes, beautiful costumes, perfect make-up and above all first class acting, as if by professionals. How was this possible, she kept asking herself, repeating silently, "Baba, this is simply wonderful, fantastic, first class acting and everything so perfect, in this remote village?"

She then made a sudden decision to see how Baba Himself was reacting to the play, which she learned afterwards had been written, produced and directed by Him. He was sitting just across the aisle, in the same row as she was, not far from the front of the hall. Only two women separated her from Him. No sooner she turned her head to take a look at Him, He turned and looked at her. The lights in the hall were out, but in the reflected glow of the foot-lights she saw what she had never seen before. Instead of two ordinary human eyes, she saw

two round, bright, large, blue objects looking at her out of
Baba's eyes, like two miniature full moons, which held her
astonished gaze for what seemed some minutes—yet it could
have been seconds. She was stunned by what she saw and
didn't know what to make of it. Then He turned His head away
and resumed His viewing of the drama.

Again, Baba was acquainted with all the thoughts that raced
through her mind and so they turned to look at each other
simultaneously. Another example of His omniscience. Not a
single person saw what she saw for she had made a mental
note that all eyes were focused on the stage. Only the two of
them were looking at each other in the half-light of the
auditorium. And the two blue moons like little saucers that
were His eyes? They were the same blue eyes they saw when
He was born. In this case, presumably, Baba apparently
dilated His pupils fully to show the effulgence of the
Atmajyothi—the light of the Atma (soul). At other times one
can get only a glimpse of the blue due to normally contracted
pupils. In some photographs of Baba taken by devotees and
others, a blue glow can be seen in His pupils. And once
more, an example of His Divinity, His omnipotence and
omniscience.

Zones of Vibration

Episode V

The writer was again sitting in the front of the *darshan* line
waiting with thousands of devotees for Baba's arrival. He
appeared on the verandah, walked briskly down to where she
was sitting, came within a few feet of her and then turned His
back towards her. She kept wondering what He was up to
this time. He motioned to Mrs. Rattan Lal to come to where
He was standing. She is like a mother to Him, and He engaged
her in conversation while pointing to the temple as if
discussing its architecture. All the while the author was

looking intently at His back and lo and behold!—a broad band of vibration about six to eight inches wide, grayish-black in colour, surrounded His entire body forming an oval shape from head to foot. This was quickly followed by another zone of vibration exactly conforming to the first in shape and colour and surrounding the first zone of vibration. In a short while another zone of vibration appeared surrounding the first two zones. So there was Baba, completely surrounded by three thick concentric zones of energy, vibrating so rapidly that the energy from the zones made her feel as if she was going to faint. She tried hard not to allow herself to faint; somehow she couldn't take her eyes away from the strange scene being enacted only a few feet away. Just as she felt she was going to fall on the sand on which she was sitting in the lotus posture, Baba abruptly dismissed Mrs. Rattan Lal and quickly walked away. At this point the sound of *Aum* issued from the temple, the signal for the *bhajans* (hymns) to begin and she immediately fell forward, stopping herself from hitting the ground by her outstretched palms. The feeling of faintness disappeared due probably to the position she assumed, allowing greater flow of blood to the brain.

Baba knew exactly what was happening to her, hence His walking off before she actually fainted, having given her the required dosage of energy she needed according to His assessment. To interpret such actions as these is difficult. But since we are aware that Sai Baba never does anything without a good reason, there must have been the necessity on her part for this strange and bewildering experience. It is possible by these means He takes us along the spiritual pathway, testing us repeatedly with increasingly more difficult tests, making us stronger and stronger for more tests in the future, one of which is described in Episode VII.

In Front of Krishna's Statue

Episode VI

The author was, as luck would have it, or perhaps, as Sai Baba willed it, again sitting in the front of the *darshan* lines, awaiting, like everyone else, Baba's arrival. Within a few minutes He appeared walking briskly towards the Sai Ram shed, where we were all eagerly awaiting His *darshan*. He walked past the men's section and approached the women's section. He continued walking down the line in which she was sitting, came near to her and stood in front of the Krishna statue, facing her, He kept looking at her with piercing eyes, until she began to feel as if her body was being lifted up and approaching Him. However, since she was in full control of her senses, and was fully conscious and aware of what was happening, neither hypnotized nor mesmerized, she realized that her body was still seated on the ground in the lotus posture, and that it was presumably the subtle body that had taken leave and was approaching Sai Baba. The subtle body continued steadily on its way until it came to within two or three inches of Sai Baba's body, when a feeling of fear entered her mind and she kept thinking, "Oh, what will happen to Mamma? Who will look after her if anything happens to me?" No sooner this thought entered her mind, she saw the look on Sai Baba's face change from a pleasant one to one that seemed to her a look of disappointment with a tinge of disgust. He then quickly turned and walked briskly away, leaving her to deal with the subtle body. She does not know what actually happened at this juncture. All she can recall is that Baba left her with a splitting headache, the likes of which she had never experienced in all her life. Her head felt as if it was actually going to split. She became helpless, unable to stand or walk. By Baba's grace the *darshan* session ended shortly after and she was hoisted to her feet by devotees holding her up on both sides. They conducted her to the canteen some few hundred feet away; gave her a double coffee, took her to her room and dosed her with a strong pain killer. Nothing worked—coffee, medicine, bed rest, nothing. The headache continued unabated until dawn, after which it left so that she could attend the Ashram programme on that day.

It took her quite some years to understand what Sai Baba was trying to get her to do. It was just possible He had hoped the subtle body would enter His body and thereby gain whatever experience He wished it to have. But that was not to be. Why? After giving much thought to the matter, it occurred to her that she developed FEAR.and was worried about her mother's future, as she thought something drastic was going to happen to her, and her mother would be alone, old and ailing. Why did Baba turn away in obvious disgust? He saw immediately that this individual lacked complete FAITH in Him; she did not realize He was in full control of the situation and He would arrange everything including her mother's care. What was there to fear? It was said before, wasn't it, "O ye, of little faith". Jesus knew that the disciples lacked it. Sri Sathya Sai Baba realized with disappointment perhaps, that this particular person was not yet ready for advanced spiritual experiences. Fear plus lack of faith proved to be her undoing. Truly He has said, "Only I know the agony of teaching you the next step in the dance". Since Sai Baba has stated that faith comes first before love for God can develop, it was natural for Him to conclude that this devotee had no faith in Him, not to speak of love. Even though we may fail the tests He sets for us, there is always another chance. He says we were born again because we failed some of the tests in our previous lives. What a lost opportunity! It has been said that there are some things that come not back—the sped arrow, the spoken word and the lost opportunity. According to Vedanta, the spiritual path is as hard and sharp as the razor's edge.

Matter *versus* Energy

Episode VII

For three or more years Sai Baba had ignored the author's presence in the *darshan* line. If she was sitting in the front row, He would approach the person next to her, smile, speak sweetly and without so much as a glance at her, turn and walk away, taking great care to see that He kept at a safe distance. Needless to say, she felt like an outcast. Here was she, visiting Puttaparthi and Whitefield, His two ashrams, regularly and staying on for weeks, sometimes months, without even a glance or recognition of her presence. She was at a complete loss to understand what she had done to deserve this treatment. But try as much as she could nothing emerged to explain Baba's sudden rejection and to continue this for more than three years! She accepted it with a feeling of calm resignation, realizing that Baba alone knew the reason for putting her into cold storage. Perhaps she was now in His repair shop for badly needed repairs. Since He knows all our thoughts, He is the only one qualified to administer the required remedy best suited for whatever abnormality existed. With these thoughts she had a feeling of being orphaned. She has since learnt that this is a regular feature of Sai Baba's method of teaching us "the next step in the dance". It seems to be an integral part of the spiritual training programme He has devised and the demon He exercises by this method is called the Ego. She must confess that those three years in His repair shop effected the greatest transformation in her life. So it works and He knows it. She visited Brindavan, His Whitefield Ashram again in 1982. She was sitting in the front row as usual waiting for Baba's arrival one December morning. She felt a tap on her shoulder and a small girl informed her that Dr. Rajeshwari, the Medical Director of the Sri Sathya Sai Hospital, not far from the Ashram wished to speak to her. She met Rajeshwari outside the Sai

Ram shed who informed the author that Baba's instructions were that she should go into His residence every morning for private *darshan* and every evening for the college boys' *bhajans* (hymns) as long as she was in Bangalore. She couldn't believe what Rajeshwari was saying, recalling quite vividly that Baba had kept her in the repair shop for three full years. She felt she didn't dare accept the invitation and thus resolved not to go. But Rajeshwari who left her body many years ago, was a very determined person and told the author to meet her the following morning to be escorted into Baba's residence, that she could not take her in that morning as she had to perform an emergency operation.

The author returned to her place in the *darshan* line in a state of utter confusion, resulting almost to dismay. Was Rajeshwari sure about what Baba said. She didn't give the author's name or identity. She had said to Baba that there was a friend outside and Baba interrupted her to say, "Yes, ask her to come inside for private *darshan* and evening *bhajans* until she leaves Bangalore". Impossible, she thought. There must be a mistake somewhere. Baba hardly looked at her for the past three years and now this! No, she couldn't possibly accept this unless she was quite sure. Suppose she went inside and they turned her out. Her thoughts ran helter skelter until the usual hum followed by the hush announced Baba's emergence through the front gate of His residence. Resplendent in red with a beaming face, He approached the crowd of devotees. Rapidly moving along the men's section He came and stood at the end of her line, looking at her and smiling. She hesitantly returned the smile as she was not quite sure for whom it was meant. He then swiftly walked along the line and stood before her, bending down with a smiling face and bright beaming eyes full of love and tenderness and in the sweetest voice said to her as one would to a three-year-old tot, "Did Rajeshwari tell you I told you to come inside for morning *darshan* and evening *bhajans?*" Her tongue was tied, her lips sealed. All she could say was, "Baba, Rajeshwari..." and stopped. Three times He repeated this question in the same sweet voice and with such patience and three times she uttered the same two words. The author is one of those humans who is never at a loss for words and can always find the right answer or repartee in any situation. But in the presence of Sri Sathya Sai Baba something happens to this inborn ability.

Then, as He continued to stand before her silently, she heard herself say, "Thank you Baba, I am very happy. Very, very happy. Thank you so much". He kept standing and she kept looking up at Him when her neighbour nudged her and whispered, "Do *padanamaskar*" (reverential touching of the feet); but before she could get her hands to His feet, a woman behind her threw her baby on to the feet and He immediately walked away. For the life of her the author could never remember to touch Baba's feet every time He stood before her as she was always fully engaged in looking at His face or into His eyes.

The following morning found her outside Baba's front gate requesting entrance which the gate-keeper denied her as she had no means of proving her identity. She went to the gate inside the Ashram leading directly to Baba's residence and the volunteer on duty also barred her way, saying that she could not proceed. Realizing that though God Himself may call you, He does not strew roses along the pathway leading to Him. Instead He plants obstacles, perhaps to test the degree of our patience, persistence, perseverance and tenacity. She argued with the volunteer, saying that Baba Himself gave her a personal invitation to enter His residence that morning. But of no avail—how could he know who she was? What was her identification for gaining entrance? Just at that moment of utter helplessness, not knowing what to do to keep the appointment, Dr. Rajeshwari's son, Sreenivas, at that time the warden of the college boys' hostel at Brindavan, was seen jauntily striding down the path from Baba's residence. Her heart leapt to see Sreenivas, and after explaining her plight, he instructed the volunteer that she should be allowed to enter the grounds. But this was only the beginning of her travails. On approaching the back-door leading to the women's quarters, she was stopped by some women who were on guard. They categorically refused her entrance. Even though she explained clearly that Baba Himself had invited her, they didn't budge an inch. Good old faithful guards, she thought. Then with somewhat ruffled feathers she decided to assert her rights; she said in a stern, firm voice but without rancour, "If you do not believe what I am saying, please go inside and ask Dr. Rajeshwari and if she has not yet arrived, then ask Baba Himself. My name is Dr. Amala". On seeing their hesitation and signs of weakening, she pushed her point, "Go", she insisted. "Hurry up and enquire about the matter. I have to keep my promise to Baba". They relented, apparently the attitude of firmness made them change their approach. They opened the door and let her in. She thanked them silently, appreciating their firmness in carrying out their duties.

She took her place among the women devotees and Rajeshwari, showing relief on seeing her, assigned her a place in the front line near to where she was sitting. Rajeshwari placed a string of flowers in her hands which she insisted should be placed at Baba's feet. The author remonstrated with her; Baba did not accept flowers as He Himself has announced; but of no avail. So there she was, waiting for Baba, both hands imprisoned by the string of flowers, when He was seen descending the stair-case and walking directly towards her. At this moment Rajeshwari pointed the author out to Baba by indicating her with a turn of the head in her direction, but Baba was already heading towards where she was sitting. Rajeshwari, of course, was completely unaware of His meeting with the writer the previous day. He came to where she was sitting and with a beaming face said to her,

"Didn't I tell you what I told Rajeshwari?" He kept repeating this sentence, smiling and looking at her directly in the eye, while making brief glances in Rajeshwari's direction, as if to indicate to her that He knew she had been referring to this person the previous day even though she had not given her name nor any kind of identification. It seemed to the author that Baba was making sure that Rajeshwari became aware of His omniscience. This conjecture was borne out by Rajeshwari's attitude later on. To Baba's repeated question she was again tongue–tied. All she could say was, "Baba, Rajeshwari..." again she just couldn't utter a proper sentence.

She was looking up at Him all the time when she observed that His face and neck seemed to disappear to be replaced by a mass of energy. Baba also appeared to be reduced in size. Then the right side of her face began to twitch. It is interesting to note here that even though the author was exposed to a mass of vibrating energy and not only to three concentric zones of vibration as in Episode V, yet the only reaction experienced was twitching of the right facial muscles, and not a feeling of wanting to faint. It seemed that the experience of Episode V had somewhat increased her resistance. Was this what Baba wanted to achieve in having her undergo the experience of Episode V?

As both hands were occupied she could not reach up to steady the facial muscles. The twitching was so severe, she was certain others around her could see it. She then became aware that Baba had taken hold of one end of the string of flowers and began pulling it upwards out of her hands, while she found her hands moving upwards to facilitate the process. With the facial muscles still misbehaving, and Baba as good as having disappeared from sight into a mass of rapidly vibrating energy she placed her right hand over the facial muscles in an attempt to stop the twitching, but of no avail. She was aware only of Baba as a mass of energy; she saw nothing else. But this was not what others in the room saw during this period of time. What happened then was described to her later. Baba took both ends of the string of flowers in one hand between thumb and fingers and with a rolling motion between the fingers, he fused both ends without making a knot. At this stage, apparently the writer returned to her normal level of consciousness and the twitching ceased, revealing a normal Sai Baba standing before her with the string of flowers transformed into a garland. With both hands inside the garland, He pulled against it three times, while looking at her with one of His penetrating looks. She realized that He was trying to show her how strong the garland was; but she couldn't understand why. Then a normal human reaction came into force. She wanted the garland. Looking at Him and silently requesting nay, beseeching Him to give her the garland, He kept looking at her with what she thought was a mischievous look in His eyes. While still pulling at the garland He turned and walked away disappearing into a side-room.

The aftermath of this drama was the effect on Rajeshwari. The author heard her narrating the details of the incident that occurred in the *darshan* hall to those who were not present and had missed it. Rajeshwari became very excited saying that Sai Baba knew immediately who Amala was, even though she had not said a word about her nor had she given the slightest indication of her identity. She told her audience that all she said to Baba was "There is a friend in the Sai Ram shed...." When He interrupted her to say, "Yes, ask her to come in etc...." By creating this little drama and enacting it Himself, Baba demonstrated in the most beautiful way Dr. Rajeshwari's acceptance of His omniscience. What *leelas* (sports) does He perform to enlighten us and nudge us onwards along the spiritual path. He had ensured that His knowledge of who the writer was did not escape Dr. Rajeshwari's attention.

What happened later was a pleasant surprise. From the following morning onwards and continuing for one to two days the author discovered with great relief and joy that the chronic fungal skin disease covering parts of her arms and legs which had stubbornly defied all forms of medical therapy from early childhood had almost disappeared. By the time she arrived home three days later, she was completely cured! She realized then that He had deliberately staged this drama to accomplish what He willed. Baba never does anything without a purpose. Not only the physical cure, but once again, as so often in the past, He reminded her of His omniscience and omnipotence. I suppose we all do need reminders, since it is human to accept Grace and promptly forget about it.

In retrospect, it is conceivable that Baba Himself had placed the obstacles at the three sites leading to the entrance of His residence. How do we know that he was not watching and waiting to see how the individual would cope with the problem—testing her patience, perseverance and ingenuity in facing the dilemma. Is it possible that He was also instrumental in sending Sreenivas down the pathway at the crucial time? Did He also make the women volunteers at the back-door relent to let her in? We would never know. However, Baba Himself has said that He does not interfere in anyone's free will and the making of choices. He allows the person to do whatever he thinks best under the circumstances and if the problem is not a serious one. He says, "Man has free-will...making plans and working them out belong to a person's free-will."[6] He leaves it up to a person to make his own decision and only when things threaten to go totally wrong and only if there are no other possibilities of solving them does He interfere.[6]

By transforming Himself into a mass of energy, vibrating at such a rapid rate that it caused the twitching of the writer's facial muscles, is it possible that Baba created the situation to give her a glimpse of what the fourth-dimensional realm holds in store for us? It is said that some of those who survive the Shift of the magnetic poles of Earth and qualify to enter the Fourth Dimension will have such high cellular vibrational rates that they would disappear from sight and be totally invisible to others around them, although they would still be in the same place as they were before disappearing. It is not necessary to emphasize that attempts should not be made to touch such persons. An incident comes to mind when Sai Baba on being asked by some of His students to reveal His true form, told them to make ready their polaroid camera to take a picture. As the picture was about to be taken Mrs. Rattan Lal stepped forward to rearrange the hem of Baba's gown when Baba shouted "Don't touch!" It is obvious that He had increased His vibrational rate to such a high pitch that possibly she could have been electrocuted. Ordinarily, anyone can touch with impunity Sai Baba's feet, as millions of devotees have done throughout the past sixty years or more. Apparently, He can change His vibrational rate at will as those of the Golden Age will be able to do, as has been predicted.

This episode is another example of Sai Baba's miraculous screening of His actions from the crowd and allowing only a particular individual to witness what He is doing. No one else saw Him transform His body into a mass of rapidly vibrating energy. While the writer was looking on at His energy form and twitching, simultaneously the others were seeing how He rolled the ends of the string of flowers into a garland. When the writer later attempted to explain to them that Baba had disappeared into energy, they looked at her with such disbelief, she abruptly stopped her narration realizing they would not understand. Who could explain the actions of the Divine? How was Baba able to prevent the other women seated around her, about fifty or so in number, from seeing His energy form? Was it possible that Baba increased her level of consciousness or changed her dimensionality or perhaps, partially opened her Third Eye, so she was able to see what the others couldn't? We would never know, perhaps. Baba Himself has said that we would not be able to understand the actions of the Divine. Neither with our senses, mind or intellect shall we be able to solve the miraculous acts that He performs as a matter of routine. Perhaps, when we arrive at a stage approaching Baba's, we shall no longer question these everyday acts of His. We shall then know THAT by knowing which everything is known. In Episodes I, III, IV, V and VII, the same miraculous act was observed, by Baba performing various kinds of miracles but with only one individual witnessing what He was doing, while all the others around did not see what He did, or saw something else. In Episode I no one saw Him rescuing the fallen man, except the author; in Episode III, not even the person sitting beside her saw the blinding flash of light. Unbelievable! How could anyone have failed to see such a bright light? Once again Baba's omnipotence.

The author was at a loss to interpret the changing of the string of flowers into a garland and the strange manner in which He removed it from her hands. But some devotees cleverly explained its significance—one end of the string was *jivamatma* (the individual soul), the other end the *Paramatma* (the universal soul); the fusion—the union of both; pulling at the garland—demonstrating the strength of the union; and taking it away in spite of a request—an indication that it belonged entirely to Him.

References

The writer acknowledges with gratitude the kind consent of the following authors and publishers to quote from their publications

1. Ralli, Lucas : Sai Messages for You and Me, Volumes I, II, III, IV and V, 1990, 1993, 1998. E-16,Pushpanjali, P.O. Nijwashan, New Delhi 110001.

2. Braden, Gregg : Awakening to Zero Point—The Collective Initiation. Pub. Radio Bookstore Press, Bellevue, Washington, U.S.A. 1993.

3. Wise, Elia : Letter to Earth. By Gateway, an imprint of Gill and Macmillan Ltd, Hume Avenue, Park West, Dublin, 2000.

4. Tiwari, Maya : Ayurveda. A Life of Balance,1995. Inner Traditions, India Home Office, One Park Street, Rochester, Vermont, 05767, U.S.A. Maya Tiwari, now known as Swamini Mayatitanandaji, lives at Wise Earth School of Ayurveda, Post Box 160, Candler. North Carolina 28715, U.S.A.

5. Sri Sathya Sai Baba : Sanatana Sarathi. April 2005 (a); May 2005 (b). Sri Sathya Books and Publications Trust, Prasanthi Nilayam, Puttaparthi 515134, Anantapur District (A.P.).

6. Lunshof, Geesje : Inner Dialogue with Sai Baba. B.R. Publishing Corporation, A Division of BRPC (India) Ltd., Delhi 110035, 1999.

7. Krishna Murty Tumuluru: Digest I (Collection of Sri Sathya Sai Baba's Sayings). Published for Fondazione Sathya Sai Seva, 6535 Roveredo, GR CH (Switzerland) by Dr. T. Gowri, Tumuluru & Co., Computer Services Division, Hyderabad 500007, India.

8. Skolimowski, Henryk: Dancing Siva in the Ecological Age. Published by Clarion Books, C-36 Connaught Place, New Delhi 110001, 1991.

9. Swami Nikilananda: The Bhagavad Gita. An English Translation. Published by the Ramakrishna Vivekananda Centre of New York, U.S.A., 1944.

10. The internet: <http:// www.earthchangestv. com>.(a) Crawford 2000. <http:// www.crawford 2000.co.uk/ mag.htm>(b).

11. The Internet: An Emerging Planetary Civilization. An Interview with Elia Wise by Carol Bedrosian <http://www.ofspirit.com/ carolbedrosian18.htm>

12. Penn, Charles: My Beloved. 1981. Published by Sri Sathya Sai Books and Publications Trust. Prasanthi Nilayam, Puttaparthi 515134, Anantapur District (A.P.).

13. Gandhi, Kishoo: Social Philosophy of Sri Aurobindo and the New Age. Sri Aurobindo Ashram Trust. Published by Sri Aurobindo Ashram Publications Department, Pondicherry.

14. Aitken, Bill: Sri Sathya Sai Baba. A Life. Published by Penguin Books India Pvt. Ltd., 11 Community Centre, Pansheel Park New Delhi 110017, 2004.

Index

BOOKS OF RELATED INTEREST FROM NAB

HIS HOLINESS MAHARISHI MAHESH YOGI
A Living Saint for the New Millennium
—*Helena & Roland Olson*

Helena and Roland Olson, describe in charming and intimate detail those early days as this holy man from India became a part of the daily life of a typical American family and how he began to teach his simple technique of Transcendental Meditation (TM) to friends and family in their own living room.

ISBN: 978-81-7822-217-2

MOTHER OF ALL
A revelation of the Motherhood of God in the life and teachings of the Jillelamudi Mother
—*Richard Schiffman*

Mother of All is the compelling story of one of the great mystics of our time. Mother Anasuya Devi of Jillellamudi was revered by millions in southern India of her home-spun wisdom, motherly love, and extraordinary spiritual powers.

ISBN: 978-81-7822-114-4

SILENCE SPEAKS
The Wordings from the Chalkboard of a Monk
—*Baba Hari Dass*

Baba Hari Dass is a monk who does not speak. The practice of keeping silence is called *mauna,* in Sanskrit. Its aim is less about silencing the voice and more about silencing the mind which, as we know, tends to be filled with worries, desires, and clinging.

ISBN: 978-81-7822-172-4

CAN YOU LISTEN TO A WOMAN
A Man's Journey to the Heart
—*David Forsee*

In the book, David Forsee interweaves his life with Swami Radha's and invites you to be present in their most intimate moments of joy, support and challenge. His stories will touch you with their honesty and inspire you to seek meaning in your own life. This book offers hope to both men and women.

ISBN: 978-81-7822-112-0

MOTHER TERESA
AN EAST-WEST MYSTICISM
Her Thought Compared to Hinduism and Gandhi
—*Gloria Germani*

The present work studies the person of Mother Teresa (who has been proclaimed 'blessed' in October 2003) for the first time not from the point of view of her works, but from the perspective of her thought.

ISBN: 978-81-7822-167-0

A LAMENT
Was partition Inescapable?
—*V. N. Sekhri*

The author has penned down in the book his memories of the lost culture, the pain and agony caused by partition, his movement from the other side of the shadow line i.e., Pakistan to India, his post-partition struggles and his tussle with life.

ISBN: 978-81-7822-206-6

THE PATH OF THE MOTHER
—*Savitri L. Bess*

The Path of the Mother introduces us to a divinity more whole than any we have yet encountered—her arms open to men and women of any persuasion or practice. .

ISBN: 978-81-7822-136-6

THE YOGI
Portraits of Swami Vishnu-devananda
—*Gopala Krishna*

This is a documentary compilation of primary autobiographical sources and reminiscences by disciples and friends from the life of the late "Flying-Swami," Swami Vishnudevananda (1927-1993) of India and Canada, Hindu monk and pilot.

ISBN: 978-81-7822-038-3

MOHANDAS GANDHI
Essential Writings
—*John Dear*

Gandhi's philosophy was rooted in a deep spirituality. For him the stuggle for peace and social justice was ultimately related to the search for God. These writings reveal the heart and soul of a man whose life and message bear special relevance to all spiritual seekers today.

ISBN: 978-81-7822-223-3